What others are saying about
Beyond the Edge

My conclusion after reading *Beyond The Edge* is that mission-ary service is not for the faint-hearted or self-centered. Nor is it for super-heroes. These unembellished real-life accounts of very ordinary people from fifty different nationalities serving God in all corners of the earth over a period of a hundred years are a genuine testimony of the power and faithfulness of God. Arrests, martyrdom, expulsions, falling war-time bombs, serious illness, witchcraft, loneliness, danger, financial lack, wayward children—all that and more is included in this honest, remarkable volume of human commitment and divine enablement. My heart was stirred to a deeper level of commitment to my Savior, a deeper level of trust in my heavenly Father, and a deeper understanding of the Holy Spirit's power as I read this book.

Dr. George W. Murray, Chancellor
Columbia International University

This collection of stories makes you sit up and take notice! It de-picts God's everlasting faithfulness to His calling on our lives and the way He answers prayer—not always in the way we might think—and is worth the read. This is a valuable book for anyone who has a heart for the world and is considering missionary work.

Ruth Finley, Board Member for
Paraclete, Horizon Missions Group, and Japan Partners Council

These true, faith-fueling stories helped me see afresh that God can be trusted no matter what! He is still the God of the impossible! Reading these pages motivates me to take bigger risks and have greater vision for obeying Him. He is an awesome God!

Bob Fetherlin, Vice-President for International Ministries
The Christian and Missionary Alliance

Beyond the Edge
100 Stories of Trusting God

Evan Davies, General Editor

PUBLICATIONS

Beyond the Edge: 100 Stories of Trusting God
Published by CLC Publications, U.S.A.
P.O. Box 1449, Fort Washington, PA 19034

Printed in the United States of America
First printing 2012

ISBN-10 (trade paper): 1-936143-94-1
ISBN-13 (trade paper): 978-1-936143-94-8

Unless otherwise noted, Scripture quotations are from the Holy Bible, New International Version, copyright © 1973, 1978, 1984 by International Bible Society. Used by permission of Zondervan Bible Publishers.

Italics in Scripture quotations are the emphasis of the authors.

Cover design: Jorg Ehlerding and David Montgomery

Contents

Foreword

$\mathcal{S}$ tories are about life. Expressive stories describe life. Vulnerable stories reveal life. Inspiring stories rekindle life. We need stories—especially true stories that inflame our passion and move us *beyond the edge* of our present understanding and motivation. Maybe that's why Jesus was such a constant and masterful storyteller. Maybe that's why a book of stories like this one can stir us powerfully in deep places. Maybe that's why these stories need to be told.

One story that's a hundred years old is still being told. It's the story of God's amazing work through weak human beings. It's the story of God's love and faithfulness to the people He has called to serve through WEC International since its founding a century ago. This book of one hundred stories celebrates the centennial anniversary of WEC, but these stories themselves celebrate the Master Story Creator, Jesus Christ Himself. And the life-changing power of these stories will be valid long after the anniversary celebrations are finished.

Reading expressive, vulnerable and inspiring stories like these rekindles passion. They fan the flames of our awareness of Christ's incredible love for us and His everyday power to work in us and in our circumstances. So we tell stories about

Him and we read stories about Him. He is sometimes visible and sometimes invisible, but He is always the Master behind the scenes. Sometimes He delivers in miraculous ways. Sometimes His miracle is the incredible courage and grace He gives in the midst of suffering. Some stories produce smiles at the small act of God that was perfect for the moment. Some stories make us shake our heads in amazement, the end result being almost too good to be true. But they are all authentic and true stories of a God who has been faithful throughout these one hundred years.

In one sense these are also stories about storytellers. Those called to serve God through WEC have given their lives to telling God's story of Christ's redemption to people who have never heard and have no way to hear, the unreached peoples of the world. Their passionate hope is that these people will be changed by this Story and drawn into relationship with the Redeemer Himself, Jesus Christ, and into multiplying communities of faith. These stories remind us that spreading this story is also God's passion, and they underline the privilege it is to be part of that purpose.

Don't be surprised if something happens deep within as you read these stories. Some will make you laugh, and others may stir you to tears. Some will inspire and others simply entertain. We hope reading these stories will renew your own passion to reach those who have not heard God's story and encourage you to trust God in the challenges you face in life. There is probably at least one story in this book that you need to hear the very day you read it; a story that will be life-giving for you on that day, rekindling your love for and trust in a God who is still working in amazing ways through ordinary people.

Louis Sutton
International Director
WEC International

Acknowledgments

Thank you to all who have contributed stories. Our difficulty was choosing the ones to leave out! Thanks also to my co-editors, Judy Raymo, Scott Sutton and Jenny Carter, who gave many hours editing, sharing their wisdom and providing freshness and balance to a delightful but weighty task. There were others who translated from German, Korean, Indonesian, Portuguese, Japanese and French and also wrote themselves.

Some stories have a pseudonym or do not have the name of their authors. These are about or from countries where to name the author is to risk the lives of local believers or of the Christian workers themselves.

Evan Davies
General Editor

Introduction

Setting the Scene

Evan Davies

WEC International is a company of God's children who have fallen in love with Jesus and want to share what they know of Him with people all around the world. Coming from many different occupations and Christian persuasions, this international community is dedicated to going to those who have never had the opportunity to know the transformation Jesus can make in the lives of ordinary people. You may ask, how did it start?

In 1877 a traveling American speaker was instrumental in bringing the news of salvation through Jesus Christ to the wealthy English Studd family. Father first, then three sons, made individual commitments to become disciples of Christ. Before long one sports-enthusiast son, Charles Thomas (C.T.) Studd was passionately concerned about the needs of China. While still a student at Cambridge University, he volunteered to join Hudson Taylor's growing band and as a result set sail for China. Upon his father's death he gave away his share of the fortune and recommitted himself to serve the Chinese for Christ's sake. Ten years later, with a wife and four daughters, he had to return to England to recuperate from some of the serious illnesses he and his wife had experienced.

Back in England, C.T. took part in an international ministry to students and to all who would hear his fiery talks about commitment to Christ and the needs of the world. Soon he was arrested by the needs of India, and the family spent six profitable years there. On his return to England, a sign outside a hall in Liverpool stopped him in his tracks: "Cannibals Want Missionaries." Of course they did—for more than one reason!

Learning of Africa's needs, and in spite of poor health and family limitations, he set off on an exploratory journey to central Africa. On the way out God spoke to him, "This trip is not only for Sudan but for the whole unevangelized world." After a tough and almost fruitless recruiting effort back in the UK, he finally left for the Belgian Congo with one companion to start a new enterprise. In 1913 WEC International was born.

Within the remaining eighteen years of C.T.'s life, thousands had a revolutionary experience of Christ, and eventually a growing group of international enthusiasts embraced the vision for the whole unevangelized world. As new countries were entered, churches were started and educational, medical, humanitarian and communication services commenced; many communities were positively impacted by the Christian message. Today more than eighteen hundred workers from a wide variety of nationalities continue to give dedicated service in over seventy countries.

The stories you are about to read explain some of the amazing ways that God has worked in and through many individual members of WEC during the past one hundred years.

Enjoy and be blessed!

1

Living on the Edge

It's great to accept a vision, but there is a cost to pay.
Ron Perschky

O let me go where things are hot,
And there's a sulphur smell,
I want to run a rescue shop
Within a yard of hell.

C.T. Studd

We love because he first loved us.

1 John 4:19

Killer Hurricane

Peter Horrell
Texas, USA, 1967

The angel of the Lord encamps around those who fear him, and he delivers them. (Ps. 34:7)

*E*verything was ready. Our equipment had been moved out of our trailers, and we were now settling into the dean's home to wait. No one was to be seen on the campus; all were behind closed doors and boarded windows, waiting. The campus property and personnel had been committed into the Lord's hands. This was His property, and we were His people. The time was five in the afternoon on September 19, 1967.

The hurricane was moving at ten miles an hour across the Gulf of Mexico straight toward the Rio Grande Valley in southeast Texas. Can you imagine an oval-shaped mass 100 miles wide and 250 miles long, spinning at 175 miles an hour at the center? Beulah, the killer hurricane, had already claimed thirty-three lives and caused damage running into millions of dollars and was now heading directly toward us. In ten hours' time we of the Rio Grande Bible Institute and Language School could expect to be in the eye of the worst hurricane of the century.

Thousands of people had left their homes seeking shelter in schools and churches which had been turned into refugee centers. Coastal towns were evacuated.

As I lay down that evening, wondering what to expect, the Spirit of God whispered Isaiah 26:3 to me: "You will keep in perfect peace him whose mind is steadfast . . ."

And then she struck. Winds tore through the campus with

tremendous force. The whole building we were in shuddered and groaned under pressure exerted upon it. All around us Beulah unleashed her fury.

After the storm had subsided and it was safe to venture outdoors, what a sight met our eyes! Most of the trees on the campus were down, yet not one building had been destroyed. A couple of cracked windows and one demolished carport was the only damage to property.

But in other areas it was a different story. The hurricane had ripped buildings apart, torn off roofs and blown in thousands of windows. Wind and flood damage reached billions of dollars.

What had happened? As this mighty destructive power was steadily moving toward us, a yet mightier power was also in operation—the power of prayer. God's people throughout the world were praying for the Christians of this Bible institute. As the hurricane neared the coast, it stopped and for a couple of hours remained in the same position, gathering momentum in speed as if preparing for the kill. When it started to move again, it suddenly changed its course and moved northwest, away from us. The eye of Beulah had passed us by seventy miles! God had answered prayer.

Taken from WEC Australia Magazine, 1968

Originally from UK and then NZ, Peter Horrell studied Spanish at the Rio Grande Language School, Texas, USA before heading to ministry with his wife Carol in Latin America and Spain.

Facing the Real World

Cecily Booth
The Himalayas, India, 1951

*T*he threesome set off—the leader, Barbara Summers, a veteran of two years in India; Grace Atkins, an Australian nurse of one year's experience; and I, who had been there for three months but was on my way due to my background and youth in the country. We left Abbott Mount with our new and totally inexperienced cook, Hayat Singh, aged fifteen. A five-day trek of twelve to seventeen miles a day took us to our first base for three months.

Who were the people we were setting out to reach? These areas of the Himalayas were home to the Bhotiya, a Hindu mountain people whose national origin and culture was a mixture of Tibetan, Nepali and Indian Rajputs.

It was now May, and the summer had come, with a melting of the snow and the opening of the passes, so we were to move up to Mansiari at seven thousand feet. The upward trek was to take a further five days and include the famous five miles of steps which alone took a whole day. After this was the ten-thousand foot pass into the Mansiari Valley. But we made it, led by Hayat Singh, singing at the top of his beautiful voice.

We arrived at the bungalow, so glad to relax while Hayat prepared a welcome meal of *dhal* and rice. As we sat down to eat, there was a kerfuffle outside—the noise of arriving mules with bells on their necks and the shouting of various people as they crowded onto our verandah. Hayat was sent to make judicious inquiries. A very ill woman had just come up the hill, as we had done, and was being installed in our compound for Grace to give her medical attention. But then came a different sound—the throb of a *puja* (Hindu worship) drum, accompanied by high-pitched muttering and screaming.

"Hayat, what's going on?"

"Oh, it's just a woman possessed by a *devata* who has been called to do puja over the sick woman." (The devata is a "goddess" to them, but we knew it was an evil spirit.)

That was the end of our lunch. Out we went to tackle this invasion. The sick woman had been set up in a tent, and the possessed woman was going around her, invoking the demons and putting rice on the woman's forehead from a brass plate in her hand. We started to pray—Hindi first and then English—"In the name of Jesus come out of her and go." As we prayed, she spoke louder and louder, screaming, and then suddenly there was silence before she said, "I can't do anything with these people here." Barbara bent down, picked up the plate and handed it back to the woman; with streaming hair and dripping saliva, off she went.

There was only room for worship—thanks to the Lord, who is greater than all demon powers. We were glad of the chance to speak to Hayat and the sick woman's family of a God who is all-powerful and who cares.

Cecily Booth lived and worked in India for twenty years with husband Ken, (pictured here with their daughter Karen) before returning to Australia as WEC leaders. Later they became regional directors in Asia.

London Bombing
England, United Kingdom, 1941

Doubtless many friends will be anxious to hear how our London base and the new hostel have been faring these recent weeks. Situated in a southeastern suburb, which often figures in the reports as a recipient of damage, we are, of course, right on the main route of the bombers making for the center of London.

Highland Road headquarters

Since the heavy raids began, we have hardly ever been out of the sound of the night bombers and the roar of the anti-aircraft fire. Our area had its share of attention, particularly from three heavy-caliber bombs which burst on different occasions north, south and east of us, one in particular springing most of us from our beds by the scream and crash of its concussion. But we have asked two things of the Lord: first, the preservation of our four houses and our lives as a testimony to His faithfulness; second, that human life may be spared if bombs do fall in our district. To His glory we say that, though these three heavy bombs did much damage, wrecked many homes and smashed acres of glass, there were only limited casualties.

Several of our local staff members had miraculous personal escapes. On the Saturday when the heavy raiding began, not yet realizing the seriousness of the attack, many were traveling as usual. Four of us were in a crowd awaiting a bus. On arrival it stopped, not in its proper place but some yards short, with the door just opposite where we were standing. As a result, we were among the first on the bus; normally we would not have got in at all because of the crowding. We had just settled into the front four seats and were having a laugh about it, little imagining what was coming. With a scream and a roar, a bomb burst just in front of the bus. Every window was shattered, except the two front windows close to our faces, and we were covered with splintered glass. No one on the lower deck of the bus seemed hurt, and all quietly took their turn scrambling out, the only sound being our praises to God. None of us was scratched.

Another WEC member reported this experience that same evening:

> When we left the prayer meeting at seven-thirty in the evening the sky was red with the glow of two big fires. Two of us were escorting a young lady who needed to get to her mother, who was alone at home. We managed to board a tram. We kept pleading the precious blood over the tram and ourselves.
>
> One passenger asked me, "What will happen if the tram is hit?" I was led to answer, "We, as His children are the guarantee to the rest that it will not be hit. They are safe as long as we are in it."
>
> The Lord tested our faith immediately. The tram stopped outside a station under a railway bridge. The driver yelled, "Down everybody. Here they come." We heard a bomb whistling down. In no time everybody was flat on the bottom of the tram. I only had enough room to kneel. The few seconds before the explosion seemed endless. I could hear the others praying, as on my knees I pleaded Rev. 12:11. Then came the ear-splitting explosion. We were just sorting ourselves out when the driver yelled again and we heard another whistling down. Automatically we all fell to the floor again. We recovered from the second explosion to find the tram had not been

touched. I believe we were partly sheltered by the railway embankment.

There was no further transport, so we decided to go into a shelter. We just got in when the bombs began to fall again. The warden led us to the back of the shelter where there was standing room only. We were praising the Lord for bringing us in safely when two ladies opposite said, "Oh, are you Christians?" We soon made ourselves known and found that one had been to meetings at the WEC center.

We started singing hymns and choruses, which seemed to help people tremendously. We kept at it for two hours! Some moved to our part of the shelter to hear more clearly. A few encouraged us by saying, "That's a good one. Sing it again." When we had exhausted our stock of tunes, one of us was enabled to give a word of testimony to those nearby. Slowly the hours dragged by. We were continually bombed and fires blazed outside. Towards morning the atmosphere became unbearable on account of bad ventilation. Everyone was bathed in perspiration. We began to pray for the all-clear, and about five o'clock the welcome sound was heard.

We arrived at the young lady's house at six in the morning to find it shattered. There was not one window left and the doors had been blown off. Tiles were missing from the roof. But as we expected, our friend's mother was safe and sound. Had we not unitedly trusted the Lord for this down in the shelter? He is faithful. We know more fully now that, "He is able to guard what I have entrusted to him" (2 Tim. 1:12).

A few weeks later another WEC worker, on a visit to her home, took opportunity to put God's faithfulness to the proof before a group of people:

One Sunday morning at half past eleven the warning was given, and I was asked to turn the gas off at the mains. At this moment the Lord spoke to me with the words "And they overcame him [Satan] by the blood of the Lamb, and by the word of their testimony" (Rev. 12:11).

There were five unconverted friends, who had come into our house for shelter. After about ten minutes bombs began to fall all around. Instantly I was strengthened by the Lord and said, "In the all-prevailing name of the Lord Jesus this house shall not be touched, nor a pane of glass broken."

A bomb sounded as though it was coming straight for the house as I proclaimed God's care over us. It fell twenty yards from our front door, heaving up large boulders of stone from the road. Two pieces went through the roof of the house next door. Windows across the road opposite and further up were broken, but ours were not even scratched. Four time-bombs were dropped in gardens nearby, but even after they exploded later, the windows were still intact. God was so gracious to us.

Story taken from the Australian WEC magazine, 1941

Bomber, crashed in London.

Stay or Leave?
Anonymous
Middle East, 2003

*W*hen war loomed in the Middle East in February 2003, expatriate Non-Government Organizations (NGOs) were faced with a dilemma: should they leave the country or stay with the people they were serving?

Did God want us to stay? "God's servants should always be ready for three things: to preach, to pray or to die—all at a moment's notice!" said one of the teachers at our college. As it became clear that war was inevitable, the challenge about being ready to die was no longer hypothetical.

Staying would be an opportunity to demonstrate our faith to the population and would be particularly important for young local believers in our city. At the same time we had to be sure that staying was a matter of obedience to the Lord and not due to bravado or any other false motives.

My wife and I wanted to give others (field leaders, our families, sending base and churches) the opportunity to be part of the decision-making process. As we set aside time for prayer, God showed both of us independently we could fully trust Him to care for us. We were touched to discover that all those invited to be part of the process supported us in our decision.

We were holding onto God and believing He would watch over us and keep us healthy in every way. However, we realized we could not be presumptuous. We had to face the possibility that God might allow us to be killed. We prayed, "Lord, if it is your will, we are ready to die for Your sake."

We found it a releasing experience to realize that God had prepared our hearts to accept death if that was His will. However, the fear among the local population was paralyzing. During a meeting with a hospital director, he suddenly burst out, "We should no longer talk about this problem. There is only one thing that we should be concerned about—protecting ourselves from the inevitability of death!"

The overwhelming fear among the population was that the president would use some of his arsenal of chemical weapons against their cities. Half of our city's inhabitants prepared to move in with relatives who lived in mountain villages. The other half prepared a room in their homes as a makeshift shelter against chemical weapons, using plastic sheeting, improvised gas masks and supplies of bleach for neutralizing toxic chemicals. Like them, we prepared our own inadequate room.

At six in the morning on Thursday, March 20, our telephone rang. The capital had been bombed—the war had started!

Isaiah 7:9 says, "If you do not stand firm in your faith, you will not stand at all." It reminds us that our faith will only stand when we trust the Lord completely. During the dark days of the war, we were not immune to the unsettling nature of events taking place.

There were many questions. "Why haven't the Allies reached their goal yet? Could it be that the president will win?" A sense of panic rose again within the population. The increasing anxiety and uncertainty affected us too, so the day came when we had to sit down together and discuss our fears.

As we talked and prayed, God reminded us that He was sovereign, working according to His plan and not according to the US-UK war plan. So it did not actually matter who won the war! Even if the president won, nothing could alter the fact that our God was working out His plan for history.

We were learning that not only had He called us to be part of His plan for the country at that time, but also that we needed to return to Him again and again to reaffirm our trust in Him. Looking to the maker of heaven and earth helped us to base our faith firmly in Him. His peace came back into our lives, holding us through the remaining times of insecurity. In the end God did more than give us His peace. He kept us safe, watching over us during the conflict and in our traveling around the country.

We are very glad we stayed. We had many opportunities to share the gospel, and we prayed every day with local people. Although we expressed our willingness to die for the Lord, we are thankful that we can go on living and continue in ministry for Him.

Two Brave Women

Pat Symes
Colombia, 1934

There was a time in the history of Colombia when many local people were denied an opportunity to own a copy of the Bible or to read it. Powerful church authorities made life difficult for any who came from different denominations. This resulted in hostility toward people who proclaimed an evangelical doctrine. But why should people be denied a copy of God's Word or the opportunity to hear that they could personally know Christ as Lord and Savior? Early WEC workers faced severe opposition but persisted in reaching out in spite of the opposition. This is the story of one courageous attempt.

Finally we decided the Lord's time had come to travel twenty minutes away by train to a place called Cajica and share the gospel. We had been waiting on the Lord for a long time, and He said, "Go."

We planned to sell Bibles. Four of us went down there for two whole days and covered nearly all the town and surrounding farms. We were given a very good reception and sold lots of Scripture portions. The only difficulties were when Nesta encountered the local priest and had a few tracts torn up, and I had a Gospel thrown in the mud. The mayor of the town gave us permission to have an outdoor meeting on Sunday, and he bought a Bible.

That Sunday morning Señora Matilde, Bill Easton and I went to Cajica. It all started well; we sang, and then I began to preach. The people listened for a little over five minutes and then began to harass us. A few small stones and some banana skins

Colombian market scene

were thrown. They would not let me speak and threatened all kinds of things. The mayor and the police came over and took us to the municipal building, where we stayed until the train came.

Yesterday we went again. We had to get another permit, and then started the meeting at nine in the morning. Señora Matilde spoke, and the people listened well. I did not feel much like being there as I had been in bed most of the week with flu and malaria, but I spoke again, and they listened. Just before I finished, the people came out of mass at the church nearby and angrily rushed upon us. I quickly finished what I had to say, and then it started.

The people covered us with all the filth they could find and then began to push us. When we tried to leave, they went out of control, punching, pushing and hitting. Señora Matilde and I were punched with fists all over our bodies while trying to get away and to help each other in the midst of a howling mob. I tried to protect Matilde, but when they nearly put me on the ground, she lifted me up and got the blows. Nesta was hit in the head by a big stone and bled freely. Finally the police came to our aid and held back the angry crowd. If they had not come, you might not have gotten this letter, for the rage of Satan was in the mob's faces. We praise God that He kept us safe but let us understand something of what suffering for Him can mean.

While we were being beaten, we never felt one little bit of hatred in our hearts, nor did we want to hit back. Nesta lost some blood and was weak from the pain. While I washed her head with my handkerchief and water from a pipe, Matilde preached again to the people gathered at the door of the municipal building where the police had taken us. She wept, saying we had only come out of love and loved them still.

Nesta and Señora Matilde are two brave women. God give us more like them!

Taken from the UK WEC magazine, 1935

Pat Symes founded the Colombian field for WEC in 1933, serving there for fifty-three years. Today the religious climate has greatly changed, and the Colombian evangelical church founded by WEC is going strong with its own missionary outreach.

The Real Robbery

Patty Toland
Venezuela, 2003

It was two in the morning when the "police" stormed the cabin, waking everyone up and forcing them to stand against the wall. Bags were searched and Bibles confiscated. "Don't you know that having Bibles and believing in God are illegal?" yelled the "police" at the sleepy students. The intent was to create an atmosphere of fear and oppression. It worked.

This scene occurred on the first night of a WEC missions training weekend in Venezuela, and the police raid was carefully staged to simulate the realities facing the persecuted church in other parts of the world. The theme of the weekend was East Asian communist countries, and we took it seriously. We believed God had given us very specific ideas for this missionary training weekend, and we had spent many days and meetings leading up to the weekend in prayer, asking God for guidance.

Venezuela Perspectives class

The second day of the training camp, we sent a guy that appeared to be "beat up" and who was supposed to have been a pastor that had been preaching. While he was trying to convince the group not to give up their faith, several of us acting as the "police" walked out with everyone's Bibles and laughed while we (supposedly) threw them in a big bonfire outside. Then we hid the Bibles for the four days to teach them to value the Word and to thirst after it. (It worked—several have said they treasure the Word now like never before.)

The second night we took the group outside to a secret place of worship. While they were there, "police" raided and took the pastor off to be "beaten." No one stood up for him. Later we asked why not, but no one could answer. We then showed a film of Christians in China and how they had all identified themselves and gone to death together.

A Bible had been given to the trainees to pass around so they could secretly try to read the Word without being caught. The third day, the "police" did a search that revealed four more Bibles among the women. A confession was demanded from the women. This time all the women rose up to protect their two leaders by piling on top of them so the "police" could not reach them. As a result, the mock police threatened to retaliate later that night. Little did we know that what would happen next would test us beyond our expectations.

We had just finished the ministry time that night when, at midnight, five people in black ski caps burst into the room, carrying knives and automatic rifles. They yelled at everyone to get on the floor. We were confused as to who these people were. Some students ignored the mandate to lie face down on the floor. To convince us, the intruders grabbed a young girl and put a knife to her throat. Only then did we all realize this was a real holdup. These oppressors were real, with real weapons and real intent to harm. They locked all the doors, and in the chaos one gun went off. I found it hard to pray intelligibly, but my soul groaned inwardly to God.

We lay on the floor for about forty-five minutes while they carefully went through everyone's bags. They took our shoes, jewelry, cell phones, documents, money, valuables, teaching materials and the last of all our food. Even though we all shook like gelatin on the floor, none of us was really afraid, as all the events of the weekend had prepared us for just such a situation. The men left as quietly as they had come, taking suitcases full of booty.

As soon as they were gone, I tried to pray out loud, but was shaking so badly the words wouldn't leave my mouth. I kept asking myself, *As the leader, what do I do? No one ever trained me for this.* We all spent the night praying, singing, hugging, crying and digesting what had happened—one of the most profound prayer meetings I've ever been in.

God did tremendous things during the weekend. We all realized that the deep healing He had done in lives could not be stolen from us. The weekend went better than we could have planned. God intervened and did things His way. The robbery was the grand finale and the final test of everything we had been teaching.

The experiences that weekend created solidarity and bonds that did not exist before. We were reminded that Satan was trying to steal the precious lessons we had learned. The testimonies that have come out of the weekend are incredible. Many pastors asked the people to testify in their respective churches about what God had done. This had never happened before. How beautiful when God gets the glory! How grateful I am that forty people went and forty people came home! God is surely our protector.

Years have passed. Of all WEC's missions training weekends in Venezuela, that one has had the deepest impact. Today, as a result, several from that particular weekend are either missionaries serving cross-culturally, still preparing to go as missionaries, or in positions of Christian leadership encouraging others toward missions. Whenever I meet up with any of them, immediately there is rapport, warmth and a brotherly bond that doesn't exist with others from similar weekends. Their testimony still is, "That weekend changed my life, and that's why I'm doing what I'm doing."

What started as a weekend full of staged persecutions, ended with a tangible example of God's protection. He used our planning to prepare us for the robbery, and He used the robbery to prepare us for a life of trusting Him.

Patty Toland is from the USA and has worked with WEC since 1990 in the Ivory Coast, Venezuela and El Salvador.

Through the Flames
Judy Raymo and others
Victoria, Australia, 2009

Just after five in the afternoon on February 7, 2009, the skies over Marysville, Victoria, turned a glowing red as grey mushroom clouds billowed up. The worst wild fires in Australia's history, fanned by "a fatal combination of scorching temperatures, tinder-dry leaves and strong winds,"[1] raged unchecked as trees exploded into flames and ash fell from the sky. In fact, several bushfires had joined to form a gigantic firestorm, with "huge fireballs in the sky and walls of flames."[2]

At the Mountain Lodge guesthouse, Betel's center for ministry to people with addiction problems, staff members called to each other to look at the awful sight. Earlier that afternoon staff had been told to pack and be ready in case evacuation should become necessary. (All guests had left after breakfast, so only the staff members and their families remained on the property.) Two hours earlier two staff members were outdoors and heard a faint siren in the distance; there was no other indication that the fire was close enough to endanger the center.

About five the power went out. Luis Rodriguez, one of the Betel leaders, went to staff members' rooms to tell them to keep alert in case evacuation became urgent. Shortly after six, several staff members who were outside noticed flames on the horizon heading their way and called to people to hurry to leave.

They rushed to their rooms to grab what they had packed and then ran toward the ten-passenger van and other vehicles even as thick smoke and ash surrounded them and a wall of flame exploded twenty meters behind them. As they turned into the road, firefighters in trucks heading past yelled at them to leave quickly. The wind had suddenly changed direction, sending the firestorm toward Marysville and destroying the entire town.

Mountain Lodge guesthouse, Betel, Victoria

The van, as well as two family cars belonging to Betel staff, headed for a golf course designated as a meeting place during any evacuation. As they drove, Luis rang the bus to ask if everyone was all right and if Bian Tan was with them. When they

Bian Tan

realized she was not accounted for, people began to cry, "Turn around! Turn around!" Since the road through town was jammed with fleeing vehicles, they were forced to continue on. No one knew where Bian was.

At the golf course, Luis transferred his wife and little boy to the other car and immediately drove back toward the guest house through black smoke and burning embers that had begun to fall all around. A fire vehicle blocked the road. Luis told the officer in charge that he thought there was still someone at the Mountain Lodge. The officer simply shouted, "Get out of here!"

A total of 173 lives were lost in the wildfires of February 2009. The Mountain Lodge Betel property was completely devastated. What happened to Bian Tan?

Bian Tan was the "sickly first-born in a Chinese family that craved offspring, and was loved and cared for by her younger siblings."[3] After she turned from Buddhism to Christianity, she committed herself to serving God and the world, as previously she had been served. She attended Bible College in Australia for two years and then was accepted as a worker with WEC.

Myk McKenzie, a Betel co-worker, wrote:

Bian joined the Betel work in Valencia, Spain, in 1990. This slightly-built and fragile woman shared the uninsulated, mouse-infested area above our old secondhand shop with twenty women and their children, with no privacy of her own, for many years. Her twenty-four-hour-a-day companions were prostitutes and drug-addicted women and girls from the streets.

Bian was a servant. She was the first to anticipate a need and would quietly set about getting the job done, without having to be asked. Bian nursed some of the women in their long battle against AIDS. Through long days and nights she was the one to volunteer to wash their wasted bodies with her gentle hands and ease their pain with her prayers and loving smile, until they passed into the Savior's presence.

She was particularly good with children. When she babysat, she would patiently get down on the floor and play with dolls for hours, or do whatever else took their fancy. Nothing was too much trouble. She cared for her neighbors and took a real interest in the people she met when doing the grocery shopping or travelling by bus. She was an excellent listener, preferring to hear people out rather than dominate the conversation. She knew how to laugh at herself and take her worries to her Heavenly Father.

Although Bian often mentioned "retiring," she simply could not settle. She could not bear not to be busy loving, serving, and helping others. Thus, at age sixty-three, Bian Tan was still serving as a counselor to people with drug problems at the Betel center in Australia.

Her brother Justin recalled,

Besides her constant contact with people in loving chats and Bible study, her most important tool and ministry was her prayer. She managed to bring everyone she was in contact with before the throne of God. One time she came to me, very angry indeed, and rebuked me. "I am really angry with you; I have been asking you how I should pray for you and waited for three days, and you still haven't told me!"[4]

On an afternoon of raging firestorms, the faithfulness of the Lord toward his servant Bian was clear. About five that afternoon, Bian was chatting by mobile phone with her sister-in-law in Perth. There was no mention of the bushfires: "Bian kept saying, 'I am so happy today, the Lord has been so good to me.'" Bian mentioned all her siblings, sisters-in-law, nephews and nieces, and unborn grandnephew by name and blessed them all.

Then she said, "The Lord has given me assurance from the Bible: 'Fear not, for I am with you!'" (Isa. 43:5). Amazing, especially now that we know what was going to happen in less than an hour. That chapter from Isaiah begins:

> Fear not, for I have redeemed you;
> I have summoned you by name; you are mine.
> When you pass through the waters,
> I will be with you,
> and when you pass through the rivers,
> they will not sweep over you.
> When you walk through the fire,
> you will not be burned;
> the flames will not set you ablaze. (43:1–2)

As Justin Tan explained,

It is our firm conviction, holding to the promise of God in His Word, that Bian walked through the fire and was not burned. In fact, we can piece together the last minutes or seconds of the event and know that because of the position of her room, facing the corridor, when the fire came, air and oxygen must have been sucked out through that corridor as through a wind tunnel. Smoke would have come rushing in to fill the space. Bian would have passed away in minutes or even seconds, before the fire could touch her. We know the Lord was there with her, comforting her and telling her gently to fear not, for He was there, and then He took her away in spirit to be with Him. No flame could consume her![5]

Jim and Judy Raymo (USA), with their seven children, served in mission in UK and then worked with WEC in Tasmania, Australia and Canada as well as in candidate orientation and national leadership in the USA.

When Danger Becomes a Reality

Martin Till
Guinea-Bissau, West Africa, 2001

I woke in the middle of the night. A quick look at my alarm clock confirmed what I suspected: it was two in the morning—exactly the time when "it" had happened. And again, whether I wanted it or not, memories of that situation kept flooding in and with them came the feeling of being at the mercy of something vague and dark that cannot be grasped. "What if they return?"

So often my wife and I prayed together, sang hymns of faith and turned our minds to the fact that we as Christians are under God's special protection. But the distance between reason and emotions, between head and heart, seemed so immeasurably long. In the stillness of the night, my soul was again like a little, fearful child, and I found myself checking every noise for its potential danger.

"Wasn't this a rustling? Wasn't that the sound of steps? Is our protection sufficient? No, not again! I don't want to succumb to these thoughts. Lord, I want to believe, I want to trust! Lord, help me! O Lord, why is this so difficult?"

After an armed robbery of our Bible school and mission center at N'tchumbe (Guinea-Bissau) in 2001, my wife and I went through the whole gamut of feelings, from taking a stand of faith to the decision to pack our suitcases and fly home. We tried to calculate the risks of whether such an incident could happen again, and we took precautions, like bolts on doors. We were grateful for Pedro, an experienced guardian who offered

his service, and we welcomed two dogs given to us. But it was neither reasonable thinking nor Pedro's gun under the windows of our sleeping room which really helped us to hold out and to find our feet again. We realized this in an instant one night when we were very discouraged and the Bible college students came over spontaneously. They encouraged us and prayed for our protection.

Guinea-Bissau Bible school student

"Surely God is my salvation; I will trust and not be afraid" (Isa. 12:2). This verse means so much to me now. Our Lord wants to provide for us shelter and protection in every desperate situation of our lives and, even more, glory and eternal life after death. Trust is the sudden awareness of God's overwhelming presence in the midst of the darkness of our fear. I have experienced that in the dark nights in N'tchumbe. However, fears do not only exist in the crisis zones all over the world. Whether our life is endangered by bandits' weapons or by depression, by a stroke or by cancer really does not make such a big difference to the soul. Isaiah 12:2 speaks to us "professional" expatriate workers no less than to all other Christians.

Martin Till went to Guinea-Bissau from his home in Germany and served there with WEC for fourteen years. Along with his wife Ingeborg and family, he is now on the staff of Cornerstone, the WEC training center in the Netherlands.

" What Would You Do if You Knew You Could Be Arrested for Sharing God's Word?

Anonymous
West Asia, 1996

*T*hey are waiting for you downstairs!" The shout came from the floor below.

A local believer and I were talking to a lady at the door to her apartment in Western Asia. We had just given her a copy of the New Testament, and she asked for prayer. We were reading to her from Philippians 4:6: "Do not be anxious about anything, but in everything . . . present your requests to God."

"We won't be long," we responded, thinking our friends were waiting for us downstairs.

Suddenly the lift door opened behind us and an aggressive policeman got out, spoke gruffly and waved us in the direction of the lift.

It was actually happening. We all knew that giving out Bibles, although not illegal, could lead to our arrest. But we had felt so burdened for these people who had no opportunity to read or hear God's Word. "Lord . . . ?"

A crowd had already gathered downstairs. After all, it was not every day you saw a police van taking four older foreign ladies away. Everyone was curious.

At one in the afternoon on September 19, 1996, we were taken to a room at the police station with many desks and policemen. The local believer was our spokesperson, as she was the only one fluent in the language. The extent of mine was "Hello" and "This is a gift for you." We produced our IDs, and the questioning began.

"Which organization are you with? Where do the funds come from?" They insisted we were handing out propaganda. The New Testaments were confiscated—we were intrigued to notice that the police not doing the questioning were flipping through them. They were certainly interested in this little green-covered book.

Because of the lack of space in the station, we were ushered downstairs and asked to sit outside on a bench. The day was sunny, but chilly, and we had only one coat among us. Some officers gathered outside to sip their small glasses of strong black sweet tea. They kindly offered us some, which we gratefully accepted as the wind whistled around us.

A guard continued to stand and walk in front of us with his large machine gun. We began to realize we would be there for a while. The officers told us that men from the Special Branch on the other side of the city had been called in, and we had to wait for them.

We prayed together, and knew our heavenly Father's peace. Our local worker requested and was permitted to make phone calls; we knew this would activate a prayer chain throughout the city.

After three hours the men from the Special Branch finally arrived. Our local friend was bombarded with loud, fast questioning. I prayed with my eyes open while she answered quietly and calmly. The attention then focused on me, which eased the pressure on my friend, as she could listen to me and then translate.

We were eventually taken upstairs to the office of the chief of police. He was a pleasant, smiling man, and certainly interested in discussing Christianity. Our local believer made every effort to share the gospel and explain what a good book the Bible was.

The chief apologized for detaining us, and said we could go. At our request he tore up the written report in front of us, although we knew they had another list of our names.

We were then given back the confiscated New Testaments. Imagine our delight when the chief asked for a copy! Soon there we were, the four of us, distributing God's Word to the police officers in appreciation for their kindness to us. They were literally clamoring to receive a copy.

We left the police station around five, having received an invitation to return on another occasion for tea. What a thrill, and how precious those four hours were. Who could have imagined that we would have the opportunity to distribute the New Testaments to all the men in the police station? How wonderful that each man knows that the others have a copy too, as they can now discuss the things they read.

2

TRAVEL

God will accomplish His plans for His glory. And He wants to take us with Him—but not as spectators.

Stewart Moulds

The vital relationship with Jesus is a walk of love and obedience. 'Being in me' is more important than the fruit. Love leads to obedience and vice-versa. Together real love and real obedience produce glory for God.

Sergio Santos

And God is able to make all grace abound to you, so that in all things at all times, having all that you need, you will abound in every good work.

2 Corinthians 9:8

All Things Are Possible

Anonymous
Central Asia, 2004

"

*T*his sickness will not end in death." During a time of harassment by the authorities, these were comforting words. Until, that is, I checked what happened next: Lazarus died! (John 11:4). I was shocked! Even so, I was not prepared for my "death": an EXPELLED stamp in my passport and a police escort onto the plane. But the "resurrection" followed too, and in less than three months I was back (with a new passport, of course).

"This sickness will not end in death." My second EXPELLED stamp came three years later. (I'm trying not to make a habit of collecting them). This time it was on the page facing the photo where it couldn't be missed! Or could it? In the four months that followed, I made five internal flights, having my passport checked at least once per trip. But I prayed like Brother Andrew—"Lord, you once made blind eyes to see, now please make seeing eyes blind"—and not once did the authorities notice it.

"All things are possible." We had sung this my first Sunday of internal exile, three days after getting that second stamp. My court victory had been overturned, and my one remaining chance was an appeal to the President. I waited. Although the chance was slim, I stood firm in faith and prayer. But the unthinkable happened—the appeal was rejected. What happens to faith then? I have to admit I nearly bought an air ticket to London.

Then I remembered another resurrection (Mark 5:21-43). Jairus must have been full of hope when Jesus agreed to visit his sick daughter. But the woman with bleeding waylaid Jesus, and meanwhile, the girl died. And what about Abraham, who kept on believing when there was no hope left? (Rom. 4:18). No hope—that's certainly how it looked. Thank God for some good friends who fanned my dying faith into flame.

"It can't be how it seems. Remember what God has said," one encouraged. "Why not say to God, 'I'm finished. I've no options left. So I'm asking You to help—no one else can'?"

"Admit that the final decision is with God and wait in faith," another suggested.

So, illogical as it was, I kept believing. We prayed and fasted, and the impossible began to happen—an audience with the prosecutor, a new investigation, victory in the court. And so I am left amazed, grateful, humbled. But it's sobering to think how different things would have been if I'd stopped believing too soon. As the local translation says, "He who keeps on believing (not being put off when things get worse) receives."

"This sickness will not end in death." Four years and another visa refusal later, I found myself making a sudden exit of a different kind—this time on a stretcher, having had major surgery in-country.

"Don't drop her!" Those words, combined with a slanting and falling sensation, were my first awareness as I regained consciousness. A few minutes earlier I had collapsed as I tried to make it to the ambulance on my own two feet. Now I was being lifted over the banister on a stretcher by three females and a skinny paramedic. But thankfully the operating surgeon was more competent than the paramedics, and a physical resurrection wasn't required. And so I am still here. Or should I say, back again in the place of my calling!

The result? My faith's grown for sure. But that's not all. I no longer am afraid of being expelled, nor of court cases or summons, nor even of having to set foot in a local hospital. That's real victory!

To Niangara
W.J.W. Roome
Congo, 1914

*E*arly days in WEC were fraught with difficulties and the possibility of disease and even death.

At noon on Thursday, December 17, 1914, after eighty-two days of travel, we reached Niangara in the heart of the Congo. Ocean steamer, rail, riverboat, ox wagon, sedan chair, bicycle and foot—all were requisitioned for various stages of our journey. Through fair weather and foul, health and sickness, the good hand of our God was with us.

C.T. with Alfred Buxton

We left London seven in number and arrived here the same numerically, but not the same individuals. A.J. Bowers became seriously ill with a tropical fever that proved too much, and he died on December 1 at Yei. At the early age of twenty-five, his work on earth was completed. While we mourn his loss, the call to press on only becomes more urgent. Our prayer is that his home-call will prove a field-call to many other young men who will more than fill the gap.

The addition to our number was Albert Buxton, who has been C.T. Studd's comrade during the past two years of exploration and foundation-laying. He met us at Mourdjian

and traveled the rest of the way with us, helping greatly with his knowledge of the country and language.

As we made our way overland from eastern Sudan to Niangara, about two hundred miles, the scenery im-

New arrivals by canoe

proved and interest deepened. Rolling plains of giant grass and scrub merged into forest. From scorching, shadeless grasslands we passed into avenues where natural green boughs interlaced overhead.

People became more numerous. Neat villages, half-hidden in banana groves, were generally bright and clean. Whether the folks understood our mission or not, they gave us a hearty welcome, making us feel at home in a strange land. The Belgian officials in each place were kind and willing to assist us in every way.

We praise our heavenly Father for His protecting care over these many weeks, bringing us in health and strength to our goal: the heart of Africa.

Taken from UK WEC Magazine, 1915

Rev. W.J.W. Roome was on the administrative staff of WEC in the early days of the mission.

Himalayan Mountain Danger

Ken Booth
India, 1954

*I*was living in Tiksen, a village situated about nine thousand feet above sea level in the Almora District of the United Provinces of India, right in the heart of the Himalayan ranges. One fine day in 1954 I planned to trek from our village around the *pakdandi*, the spur of a mountain ridge which descended sharply between our valley and the next valley south. I wanted to visit the people of Rachuhen to spend some days and nights bringing Bible picture stories and sharing the good news of Jesus with them.

So I packed my rucksack and asked a young local man to travel with me and carry some of the gear that was needed for food and ministry. We went eastward down along the side of the mountain spur and then aimed to cut around the lower section of it into the next valley. The spur was mostly used as an animal track, but some of the local people would take it as a shortcut. We traveled down easily because the northern side of the spur benefited from the sun, but once we hit the ridge line of the spur, we moved around to a section which did not get any of the afternoon sunshine. This was a very different scenario.

Gori Ganga river gorge

It was damp and slippery. As we went along carefully, we got to a highly unpredictable patch. The track would only have been two feet wide. Straight up to our right was sheer cliff and to our left was a frightening sudden drop right down to the Gori Ganga glacial river, which was three thousand feet below us.

Suddenly my feet shot out from under me toward the edge. My rucksack took me over backward and bumped the side of the cliff. I was flat on my back with a leg and an arm and part of my pack right on the edge of the precipice. The slightest move of the eighty-pound pack could have taken me over. My companion, pale with fear and shaken, came quickly to my aid and lifted me to my feet cautiously as we balanced on that ledge. Dazed and grateful, we completed our journey. God had protected us!

Ken Booth with his wife Cecily lived and worked in India for twenty years before returning to Australia as WEC leaders. Later they became Regional Directors in Asia.

Someone Else Was Driving!

Colin

Asia, 2004

*G*od had given our team access to a remote mountainous region in an Asian country where the people were poor, isolated and without knowledge of Jesus. A group of us were on a fact-finding visit with the long-term goal of planting a church in the area. We stayed a couple of days in a small village and had been well-received by the people there.

Early in the morning of our planned departure day, we discovered that an unexpected and heavy covering of snow had fallen overnight. The roads were deserted. The prearranged driver was not willing to make the return journey on roads that were now unpredictable. A search for someone willing to take us was fruitless. This was not a pleasant thought—snowed in, stranded indefinitely in that mountain village. We were not equipped for that.

Windy, snowy vehicle road in Himalayas

According to my morning routine, I took out the Bible and opened to the passage that followed from my previous day's reading from the book of Exodus. The first words I read were, "See, I am sending an angel ahead of you to guard you along the way and to bring you to the place I have prepared" (23:20).

It was the classic "words jumping off the page" experience. I took this as a word from the Lord—that we would indeed be leaving and that we would arrive safely at the bottom of the mountain. This was a here-and-now concrete situation into which God was speaking. A driver was found who, for an appropriate fee, was willing to take us. It was exciting. It was daunting. It needed action.

I felt compelled to declare aloud what God had spoken. I stood in the back of the jeep and did so. We set off, four people in the cabin and three in the open tray at the back. It was a five-hour trip down on the snow-blanketed road. There was no fencing on the cliff edges, narrow passes, steep descents and sharp bends. Beautiful scenery! That word from God was carrying us along. The foot of the mountain was safely reached and relief was felt all round. The tires were bald and had no snow chains. The driver (not a believer) just mentioned to one of the party, "At times it was as if someone else was driving!"

God's Goodness

Bev Harvey

Brazil, 1977

*The task of developing the Brazil sending base for WEC made
it necessary for Bob Harvey to spend many days traveling the
country, sharing the missionary challenge and opportunity with
Brazilian churches. His wife Bev stayed at the mission center, praying and wondering what was happening on each trip. She tells the
story of a few incidents on these journeys.*

At two in the morning, Bob was on a bus to Maringá in
Paraná State—sleeping peacefully, though a little uncomfort-
ably, after waiting twelve hours in São Paulo. Suddenly he was
jolted awake by an awful falling sensation. There was a sickening
crunch as the bus hit the ground. People were screaming; blood
was running down his face.

Outside, it was pitch black and drizzling rain; inside, confusion reigned. Those with broken legs and arms groaned; children
cried while distraught mothers screamed and frantically searched
for their children, oblivious of anything or anyone else. Only two
adults were virtually uninjured—Bob and a Christian lady sixty-
seven years old. Bob's cut lip, which needed six stitches, carries a
small but noticeable scar to remind us of God's goodness.

A week later, sleeping in the downstairs apartment of a pastor's house in São Paulo, he awoke to a strange noise not unlike the breaking of glass. Soon he saw a flashlight scanning the
room. Thinking it was the pastor who had come to check the
noise, he lay quietly in bed. After a few moments, he realized it
was not the pastor, but a thief!

Feigning sound sleep, Bob hoped the pounding of his heart wouldn't give away his presence in the next room. The man passed his doorway and began to climb stealthily up the stairs to the next floor. Criminals are not to be messed with, and Bob didn't know what to do. Actually, the only thing he could do was pray—and pray hard that God would in some way stop the thief. Halfway up the stairs, the burglar suddenly stopped and, for no apparent reason, left the house without shutting the door behind him—and without taking anything!

At Easter Bob traveled down to Santa Catarina to preach at a special conference. As he doesn't sleep too well in buses since the accident, he was praising the Lord that the church had offered to pay his air fare. As the plane taxied down the runway, passengers had their seat belts fastened in expectation of the imminent takeoff. Then without any warning the pilot suddenly braked, throwing everyone forward in their seats. Something was wrong with the plane, but fortunately the pilot had discovered it before leaving the ground. Praising the Lord for His hand of protection, Bob changed planes and an hour later was on his way.

Bob and Bev Harvey, from Australia, went to Brazil in 1966 for twenty-five years and were involved country-wide mobilizing the churches for missions. Subsequently their role has been to advise WEC missionary teams in Latin America and then provide an IT consultancy service worldwide.

"This man is not going to die!"
Jen Kallmier
Java, Indonesia, 1977

*I*t had been a good weekend ministering at a students' conference in southeast Java. Our small children had stoically endured the usual cheek-pinching and face-stroking because these lovely Indonesian young people were so much fun to be with.

As we began the long journey home, my husband Trevor and I were sharing anecdotes of different incidents from the conference, praising God for all He had done. Rounding a long, steep curve, we were suddenly confronted by a motorcyclist leaning the wrong way into the curve—and way over on our side. Trevor swung the car onto the shoulder, dangerously close to the steep mountainside—but it wasn't enough. We felt a bump, and then turned to see the cyclist lying on the ground, blood pouring out of his head, while the bike's engine raced furiously.

As we jumped out of the car and rushed to help the cyclist, two prayers were running through my mind: "Lord, please protect and heal this man" and "Please protect Trevor."

Within minutes a police vehicle pulled up behind us. Phew—what a relief! However, the two constables were more focused on justice than mercy. They took one look, and then ordered Trevor into the police car to be taken to the police station for questioning.

I was left with three tiny children, our family helper and a badly injured man on the side of the road. "This man is not going to die!" I cried as I brushed the flies from his bloody head. I grabbed the *selendung* (a strip of cloth for carrying our baby) and wound it around the man's head to stem the bleeding, wondering where the nearest hospital might be. A bus with very interested onlookers passed by, then another motorcycle drew up alongside us. "Oh no," I said to myself, "not more onlookers."

Instead, the two young men on the motorcycle proved to be our "angels." They carried the injured man to our car and one of them drove the man to the nearest town, where there was a small medical center. By this stage the injured, unconscious stranger had become my personal responsibility. I cared about his well-being, but I also cared about what might happen to Trevor if the man should die. We wealthy foreigners are usually seen as the guilty party unless proven otherwise. I wondered what was happening in the police station.

As I followed "my" patient into the treatment room, waving the flies away as we went, Trevor was being interrogated by an officious policeman over at the station. He was demanding Trevor's passport when the commandant walked in. This man was older and much wiser. He remembered a previous incident when a foreigner had been falsely accused. This time, after hearing Trevor's story, he suggested they return to examine the scene of the accident. There they saw the clear imprint of our car's new tires in the soil on the side of the road.

Meanwhile, back at the medical center, I continued to pray and wave the flies away. My makeshift bandage had been removed, and the wound was about to be cleaned with some undiluted disinfectant. But first they were going to give the injured man a raw egg.

"Why?" I asked.

"Because if he swallows it, we know that he'll be okay."

I didn't stop to ask what would happen if my unconscious stranger couldn't swallow the egg, but simply said, "No thank you." Many months later I discovered that this was an element of Javanese mysticism. Some people do survive, but not all—particularly if they are unconscious when the egg is poured down their throats!

The medical attendant then began to clean the wound and prepare it for stitching. I had many unanswered questions about the ongoing treatment of the patient but knew the time had come for me to entrust him to the Father's care and return to my family.

The children, with their white skins and blonde hair, had yet again been surrounded by many adoring fans. They were not bored. They had been fed and watered, and our faithful helper was keeping a watchful eye on them.

It was getting late, and it was unlikely that we'd be able to reach home that day. The town was small; where would we sleep for the night? Soon Trevor returned saying, "The police commandant has invited us to stay overnight in his home." What an amazing turn of events! From being objects of suspicion, we had become honored guests. Only God could do that!

Trevor made several trips back to that small town following the accident to sort out various details. He was able to connect a local Christian with the injured man who, amazingly, made a complete recovery. A situation that could, in so many ways, have been extremely difficult for us became, in God's hands, an opportunity to prove His faithfulness.

After a period in pastoral ministry in Australia, Jen and Trevor Kallmier joined WEC in 1975 and proceeded with their family to Java in Indonesia. This was followed by several years in leadership of WEC in Australia, then as Regional Directors and election as International Directors.

Encounter with Jesus

Eva
Middle East, 2009

At four in the morning, the house intercom rang. "Your taxi for the airport is here, Madam."

As I stepped outside the apartment block, I enjoyed the quiet in the usually noisy streets of the capital city of this Islamic country. The quietness agreed with me at that time of day as I am not a "morning person."

The taxi driver seemed to respect this for the first two minutes of the trip. Then he could no longer hold back his curiosity.

"Can I ask you a question, Madam?"

"Okay, why not?" I agreed.

"May I ask please what your religion is? I beg your pardon for asking such a personal question."

"No problem at all, sir; I am a follower of Jesus."

"I thought so!" he cried out. "I felt it immediately as you stepped into the car!"

"Why is that?" I asked, suddenly fully awake and a bit apprehensive, wondering if this was real or some kind of trap.

"Well, you see, I had a dream just recently, and in that dream I sensed an incredible peace, joy and love—unlike anything I had ever experienced before in my whole life. And as you can see, I have already lived for quite a while. And now, just as you entered my car, I experienced exactly the same peace, joy and love again! So I thought that you had to be a follower of Jesus."

I realized that if what he said was true, this was really the Lord's presence shining through me, in spite of my sleepiness when I got into the car. What an encouragement that would be!

An affirmation of the faith that we hold high in this country, where one cannot evangelize or share the gospel openly with others, believing we always proclaim the gospel even if we can hardly ever use words to do it.

"So, what did you dream?" I asked.

"Actually, my dream was very simple," he answered. "There was a Person who just looked at me. But the way He looked at me was so full of love! It went through my whole body and soul. It touched my entire being. It was a love that was greater than the whole world, and at the same time it was very personal— love especially for me! He loved *me*! He was dressed in white clothes, but the most important of all were His eyes and the way He looked at me. I knew immediately that it was Jesus. I don't know how I knew that, but He must have made that clear to me without words. I also felt that He knew everything about me and about everything that I have ever done, but that He loves me anyway with that very deep and accepting love."

When he stopped talking his eyes were filled with tears. He was definitely 100-percent sincere.

"Do you know what is so wonderful?" I asked. "All the imams that people talk about in Islam are dead, but Jesus is alive!"

"Of course He is," he replied. "I saw Him, so He clearly is alive! And the dream was so clear that I am certain it was more than just a dream. It was like a vision, and it has definitely changed my whole life. No dead person could have done that! I too am now a follower of Jesus. I want to get to know Him better."

After this comment we could hardly stop talking with and listening to each other. We both felt how the Holy Spirit was in charge of this chance meeting, and we used the unexpected opportunity to share and to encourage one another to the full. All too soon we reached the airport. We knew that after this intense time of getting to know one another and experiencing God's presence with us, we were going to say goodbye, and most likely we would not be able to meet again. However, we both continued our separate ways into the new day in the strength which the joy of the Lord brings.

God of the Never, Never
Valda/David Langton
India, 1966

Rain, more rain and landslides made the road home to Batote, India impassable for twelve days. Our family was trying to get home after visiting two remote Kashmiri villages and took the first bus out when the roads finally opened. Our three-and-a-half-year-old son, Stephen, wasn't doing well with a high temperature and distinct dislike for light and noise. The next day, he began twitching, which confirmed my diagnosis of meningitis. We made plans to go to the Christian hospital in Ludhiana, a town nearly two hundred and fifty miles away.

At nine in the evening, my husband David and I hitched a ride in the cab of a truck heading south to Jammu City with our kids. On arrival after midnight, we found there was no bus to Ludhiana for hours. By now Stephen was convulsing and screaming out loud. How could he survive the hubbub in the bus terminal, plus the trip to Ludhiana? We realized we had to admit him to the local government hospital.

When David and Stephen left for the local hospital, I stayed at the terminal and packed up the children's bedding and camp cots, all the time praying for God's overruling. His promise

"Never will I leave you; never will I forsake you" (Heb.13:5) was like oil on troubled waters. After David returned to take us to see Stephen, I found the children's ward intolerably chaotic. A nurse gave Stephen a penicillin injection, resulting in another convulsion. Couldn't we get a single room, I asked? We were taken to one with two beds, right next to the Men's Medical Ward.

The doctor in charge was a physician specialist, recently returned from the United Kingdom. He gave Stephen high penicillin doses in tablet form, crushed and mixed with jam. We supplied our own penicillin and jam from the bazaar. After five days of treatment, Stephen was declared well enough to travel back home. Though our son was just a shadow of his usual bouncy self, we were very thankful to the Lord. Folks told us that some children in the outer district where we'd been had died of meningitis.

A week after our return home, Stephen unexpectedly showed signs of a relapse. David was twenty-four hours away at a field leaders' council, so Ghulam, our cook, set off with us for Ludhiana. Before nine in the morning, again we crammed into the cab of a Jammu City-bound truck. The plan was to get a bus to the railhead at Pathankot in the Punjab region and take the next train to Ludhiana and the Christian hospital.

Reaching Pathankot just after five in the afternoon, I quickly joined the long ticket line for the five-thirty train to Ludhiana. When I reached the window, the clerk said, "No seats left." I told him my son was very ill, and we had to get to Ludhiana for treatment. He informed me that only the ticket collector could help, and his office was on the platform. I searched for it and discovered he wasn't there, but was out somewhere in the milling throng. There were now only minutes to spare. The next train would be six hours later. The platform was crowded with hundreds of people: soldiers going on leave or returning for duty;

village folks and town people; yelling sellers of tea and snacks; coolies jostling with baggage, plus me—one lone woman on a search for someone she didn't know. That search was an earnest "prayer-walk."

Halfway down the platform, I halted at a group of three men in conversation. I interrupted them and asked, "Can anyone tell me how I can identify the ticket collector? My son is very ill and we need to catch this train. No seats are available." One gentleman said, "I am the Ticket Collector. Come with me." My heart leapt for joy and was filled with thanks to the Lord, who had not forsaken us! We followed the ticket collector, who then arranged for us to find seating just before the train began to chug out of the station.

The train had to rattle along for five hours before we would reach Ludhiana. How would I spend all that time? The Lord knew. He kept me busy during the journey! There was only one other civilian in our compartment, a Muslim priest. The rest were soldiers, one of whom was a sergeant, a high caste Hindu. They were all interested to find out why we were traveling and then began asking questions of a spiritual nature. A lively yet serious discussion took place between the Hindus, Muslim and Christian. By the end of the five hours, I had given away all my tracts and Scripture portions in four languages. The bag was empty! Our arrival at Ludhiana station took me quite by surprise.

On reaching the hospital, I was told there was no room for Stephen in the children's ward! It was full of diphtheria patients. I then contacted a doctor and his wife whom I knew from Language School days. They gladly responded to my call even though it was after eleven at night. They cared for us after the pediatrician examined Stephen and prescribed more oral penicillin. Stephen improved daily and had his sight and hearing tested, with favorable results. The doctors thought the relapse was due to ceasing the antibiotics too soon. We were now able to return home.

We were learning that, whatever our circumstances, God will provide a way of escape that we may be able to endure. The "way of escape" for me, His child, was to rest on Him and His promise that He is, forever, the God of the "Never, Never."

From Australia, Valda and David Langton and their family lived and worked with WEC in India and Kashmir for many years.

Encounters in Desert Places
Ingeborg
Middle East, 1994

It was our free afternoon. Finally we could get out of the city and leave the business of our hospital work behind. How I loved the rough mountains, the high desert places and the quietness of nature—no one else around, only my friend and I. But then, after half an hour, we saw a tent in the distance. We did not know that there were Bedouins living up here. They had already spotted us and were waving us to their tent. It always amazed me how welcoming and hospitable these people were! What a surprise: they knew my friend from the hospital. She helped them during the delivery of one of their children. We were invited for a cup of tea in the shade of a big rock. The whole family gathered around us, including some goats. Next to their resting place we saw a radio. "Do you listen to the *Voice of Forgiveness* [the name of the Christian broadcast in their language]?" my friend asked them. "Yes, we do. They say that Isa [Jesus] is the Son of God," was their reply. We offered them a New Testament in their language. which they gladly accepted. "We have enough peace to read the book here," they said. When we left, we wondered if we would ever meet them again. But we were certain that they would read His Word.

Another day we were off into the mountains toward the east. We drove on rocky roads and followed a kind of trail up into the wilderness. Were we going to meet anyone up here? We must have been nearly in the neighboring country when we finally arrived at a stone hut. An old grandma greeted us. She was caring for her grandchildren while the rest of the family was somewhere in the mountains with the flock. While we were drinking a cup of tea with her, we got talking about *Isa Al-Massih* (the name of Jesus in their language). She eagerly listened to the stories we told her. Later she wanted to retell the stories to her grandchildren, but she got stuck. "What was His name again?" she asked. It was the first time that she had heard of Jesus. What a privilege to tell those who have never heard!

We were in the northeast of the country and wanted to stay overnight with some friends. We could not warn them that we were on our way (those were the days without mobile phones). We had arranged our stay elsewhere for the first night. But after two days of traveling, we were not sure if we would meet the people we wanted to visit. What a surprise—when we arrived at their place, they were expecting us! One of the daughters had a dream that they would receive visitors. So they finished all their housework in the morning and were ready to receive us as their guests. As usual, the whole family gathered around us, drinking tea together and talking about life. The man of the household had already received a Bible from someone and had many questions. But we did not get very far. The teacher of the mosque of the village suddenly appeared and our talks about Isa came to a sudden end.

The next morning we traveled on toward the main road to the capital. We stayed overnight with another family we knew from the delivery room. When we wanted to leave, the father of the family insisted on taking us in our car to the main road. So he was driving the car while we were sitting squeezed together in the seat next to him. We had just left the last village and were driving through a deserted area when we saw three men sitting under a tree. Taking them for hitchhikers, we told them that we were sorry, but there was no space left in the car. Well, they didn't want a ride, they wanted our car! A fierce discussion was started between our driver and the three men. All were carrying guns. We could only pray and try to convince our driver that we would rather lose the car than his life.

Finally, we all got out of the car. We were allowed to take out our luggage (including a box with Bibles in their language) and were left in the middle of nowhere. After a while we heared a car in the distance: a taxi on its way to the town where we had just come from and where we would be able to take a taxi back home. We got into the taxi and now traveled together with two soldiers who were accompanying their sick mother to the hospi-

tal. On the way she had such severe pain that my friend asked the driver to stop to be able to give the lady an injection against the pain. This certainly relieved her. Having reached the main road, we suddenly saw a car at a petrol station which looked familiar—yes, it was ours! We told the soldiers in our taxi. They asked the taxi driver to turn around and drive up to our car. When the thieves realized what was happening, they tried to race away. Our taxi followed, overtook them and stopped in front of them. All the men got out of the cars with guns pointing at each other. My friend and I prayed that no one would be killed because of the car. In the end the thieves agreed to let us have our car back. We swapped cars and the taxi driver took the thieves to the next check point. We arrived back home, quite shaky but thankful for the protection we had experienced.

3

Healing

There is a difference between greeting God's promise with a distant wave and hugging it.

David Macmillan

When we open ourselves to new things, we discover the God of the present is as good as the God of the past.

Stewart Moulds

I will remember the deeds of the Lord;
*   yes, I will remember your miracles of long ago. . . .*
You are the God who performs miracles;
*   you display your power among the peoples.*

Psalm 77:11, 14

How Much Faith Do I Need?
Caroline Pinke
Ivory Coast, 2006

My husband Bruce and I lived among the Malinke people of West Africa for twenty years sharing God's words with people who had never heard. "In Bible school," Bruce says, "God put a concern on our hearts to go where the people don't yet know Jesus. He sent us to the Malinke." There was one special lesson the Father taught me about faith.

Nochee, my colleague, and I usually walked all over town, stopping where the Master opened a courtyard to us. Building friendships, we prayed for the sick and shared stories from God's Word. One particular day God led us to a lame woman, Miriam. She sat on a mat on her front porch every afternoon. After the greetings we asked if we could pray for God's blessing on her and then if we could share some of God's words. She agreed. Every week we stopped at the same time. Her quiet smile and warm welcome won our hearts.

Several months passed. I always prayed that the Lord would give strength to her legs, but I went away feeling that I should take her by the hand and say, "Stand up and walk in the name of Jesus!" But my faith was weak. I felt ashamed and told Nochee my struggle. Then one day after a worship service, I spoke to Moussa, a gracious evangelist, explaining the situation and my problem.

"I have sinned!" I blurted out. "My faith is too small!"

He listened quietly and then warmly shared how others have struggled with the same thing. "For example," he chuckled, "the famous Korean pastor David Yonggi Cho had a similar experience. His faith was small. He agonized in talking over his problem with the Father. Finally his faith grew a little as he fixed his gaze on God and the truth of His words. One day he saw a crippled man in the market. He walked over to him and then passed him quickly, murmuring out of the side of his mouth, 'Be healed in the name of Jesus.' The man jumped up and walked!"

I was encouraged by his kind attitude and went home to dig into Scripture again. It was the words "faith as a grain of mustard seed" that arrested me. That mustard seed is very tiny. God is hugely powerful. I only need a small bit of faith. He has the rest! The power of that truth struck deeply into my heart. Walking back to our new friend's house that week, I shared with Nochee what the Father was teaching me. I felt so full of peace and faith. I was ready to take Miriam by the hand and speak those words of faith in Him.

When we arrived in the courtyard and faced the door on the front porch, we saw an amazing sight: Miriam was walking through the house toward us! Absolutely delighted, we asked her what happened.

"Well," she said, "every week when you prayed for me, I grew stronger in my legs, and I would walk little by little. Then

Undercover market, Abidjan

my family would bring me special leaves over which the shaman had done incantations. 'Bathe in these, and you will get well!' they said. But I always felt weaker again. So this last week I told them, 'No more leaves! I am going to walk in the name of Jesus!'"

Carolyn and Bruce Pinke, with their three children, have worked with WEC since 1988 in Ivory Coast and as acting regional directors for Africa.

Miraculous Healing

Mina Purves
Ivory Coast, 1951

*J*acques, a Christian man suffering from leprosy, attended our church service when he felt fit to walk the four miles from his village in the grassland. One Sunday we received a note to say that he was dying and wanted us to pray for him.

The local doctor, three male nurses, colleague Gwen Whittaker and my husband Will went to see what could be done for Jacques. They found him lying on a straw mat on the veranda of his hut. He was disheveled, dirty and suffering from pneumonia, jaundice and severe dysentery. He was unable to speak clearly and was evidently dying.

While the Baouli villagers crowded around to see and hear, the doctor made his examination. He advised that Jacques be sent immediately to the local hospital at Bouaflé for treatment and penicillin injections; failing this, he would die before the morning.

Here was a doctor with a team of three nurses and an ambulance to transport him safely to Bouaflé, but all this counted for nothing in comparison to the importance of Baouli tribal law. According to their social law, the elders of the village and the older relatives in a family are in authority, and their decisions are final. Jacques' uncle and the village chief refused to let him go to the hospital.

Although a married man with a family, and willing, no doubt, to go, Jacques had to resign himself to their cruel decision. They maintained that he would die if he were taken to hospital, *but that he would be healed if Will prayed for him.*

For some time Will reasoned with them to show them their responsibility and that medicine is a gift from God to be used for healing. They were as adamant as Pharaoh in their refusal to let him go. Will asked the doctor if he would like to be present during the prayer, and he stayed.

Two Baouli Christians, the doctor, Gwen and Will, got down on their knees beside the filthy mat on which the panting and emaciated form of Jacques lay stretched. In the death-like silence that followed, Will asked the Lord to override the selfishness and stubbornness, and to care for His hard-pressed child, to heal him and to raise him up for a testimony to the power and glory of God. Little Wilma, our daughter, also asked the Lord very earnestly in her evening prayers to heal poor Jacques.

The following evening Will cycled out to the village. The Lord had answered prayer. Jacques was washed, able to sit up, and pray too! The dysentery had stopped, and the pneumonia was easier. Although he couldn't remember anything of the previous evening, he had heard that they had been there, and he knew that God had answered prayer for him.

Since that day, he has been to church services several times, walking the sizeable distance to and from his village. The villagers acknowledged that God healed Jacques, and we are sure that His name and power were demonstrated to the not-yet-Christians among them.

Taken from WEC Australian Magazine, 1952

Mina Purves with her husband Will from Scotland served in Ivory Coast in the 1940s.

God Holds the Key to My Cancer
Jill Johnstone
England, United Kingdom, 1991

When told initially that I was likely to have cancer, my husband Patrick and I faced up to the issue: Does God allow His children to suffer? Is it always His will to heal us?

I had read of the anguish of the wife of a Christian leader dying of cancer. Her husband preached and believed that it is always God's wish to heal in answer to prayer. As she became weaker, and weaker she felt she was letting her husband down by dying of cancer, and she couldn't speak to him about it, at a time when she most needed his intimate understanding and strength.

As Patrick and I discussed it, we realized that all over the world people are dying of disease. Some have no loving family, no friends, no pain-relieving drugs or, most tragic of all, no knowledge of Jesus' love and hope for life after death. Surely we who have the love, friendship, peace and hope for the future that Jesus gives can find support and strength enough from Him at a time like this.

Scriptural Contradiction?

When in the hospital for my biopsy, I read Isaiah 48:16 and 50:10. The two verses seemed contradictory. First, "Come closer and listen, I have always told you plainly what would happen so that you could clearly understand," and secondly, "Who among you fears the Lord and obeys his servant? If such men walk in darkness without a ray of light, let them trust the Lord, let them rely upon their God."

So what did God mean? Was He going to tell me plainly what would happen—or would I walk in darkness without a ray of light? A few minutes later the hospital chaplain came to speak to me and said, "I would like to give you a verse from Isaiah 50:10." How good God is! From that moment on I understood that God was clearly telling me what would happen. I would walk in darkness without a ray of light, but I could trust the Lord and rely on my God.

Months Rather Than Years?

The biopsy showed I had secondary spinal cancer. Radiotherapy did an amazing work of healing on my spine, but I was told I would have months rather than years to live. Since then I have been able to work a fairly normal day in the office and also nearly finish a children's version of *Operation World*, entitled *You Can Change the World*.

Many friends around the world have lovingly written and prayed for me. In January 1991 the Bulstrode fellowship anointed me and prayed. Am I healed? This is where trusting in the Lord and relying on my God comes into focus, as I am still walking in darkness without a ray of light!

More recently my pain has worsened, and my condition has deteriorated. Scans have revealed secondary cancer in my spine and my brain, for which I am undergoing radiotherapy treatment. Some believe I must hold on in faith for healing, but I feel no urgency to beg God for something He has not actually promised me. Of course God can heal me, but is it lack of faith to be willing to rest in Him whatever He chooses to do? Recently the words of Isaiah 45:19 spoke to me: "I did not tell Israel to ask me for what I did not plan to give."

A Glorious New Experience

My children, Peter, Tim and Ruth (between the ages of 18 and 22 as I write), all sincere Christians, have been such a strength to me, and Jesus' love has become so real and encouraging that we are experiencing great joy, whatever the future holds. Living or dying no longer seems a very big deal, while God's kingdom, His purposes and fruitfulness in our lives seem far more vital. It is a glorious new experience to walk in darkness when we have a God like ours in whom to trust and on whom to rely!

I can hardly get up the stairs, but I am dancing in my heart!

Taken from the WEC Australian Magazine 1992

Patrick and Jill Johnstone founded the prayer guide Operation World, *were WEC's deputy international leaders and international research secretaries, based in Bulstrode, WEC UK's main center. Jill went to be with Jesus in 1992.*

Skulls and Miracles
Laurenz Gossweiler
Chad, 2000

*I*was alone. I felt so incompetent standing there with my chisel against her head, about to cut a hole in her skull. I looked down, raised my hammer and let out a prayer: "Lord, help me."

It wasn't supposed to be this way. I had arranged to come to Chad, Africa in 1999 with another Swiss doctor to jointly take over this rural hospital. Ever since I became a doctor, I made sure I was always paired with someone else because I knew my limitations. But God had different plans for me. Just before we moved to the remote village, the other doctor had to return to Switzerland for a family medical emergency. I had to start at the hospital on my own and confront a situation I always feared and wanted to avoid.

This hospital did not have running water or electricity. The next hospital was a five-hour drive away. My staff consisted of eight "nurses" who had very little training. There was no phone in the entire town that I could use for a quick consultation with another doctor. I was alone to make decisions and would cry out to the Lord again and again for help and wisdom.

After about three weeks in my new home, as I was still trying to get my bearings of the place and its equipment, a lady was brought to the hospital totally unconscious. The day before she had been working in the fields when she got into a violent dispute with her husband's second wife. The fight ended when the other woman hit her heavily over the head with a hoe.

The wound was initially stitched closed by a nurse and the woman appeared to be all right. However, she started becoming sleepy and confused, and by the time I saw her, she was deeply unconsciousness with no reactions at all. It was clear to me that she must have bleeding in her head that was pressing on her brain.

I consulted my medical books, which said: "Just don't do nothing, otherwise the patient will die. Try to open the skull in order to remove the intracerebral hemorrhage." I had never done this before. I didn't know yet what medical instruments were available. What about the anesthesia? What should I do?

After a lot of prayers, and sweating bullets, I finally managed to make up my mind to try the surgery. A new house for a co-worker was being built, and I asked our mission's team leader to get a hammer, chisel and drill from the building site.

I disinfected the instruments and started the procedure. I reopened the stitched wound on the lady's head. When I was on the bone, and after some trying, I managed to drill and chisel out of the cranium a five-centimeter large hole with my construction site tools.

I looked down and straight onto the brain. Unfortunately, I didn't find any signs of bleeding and didn't have the courage to drill another hole at another site (as was recommended in my books). I thought to myself, *At least I tried, but she will die anyway, either from the intracerebral pressure or from the infection (through my inappropriate instruments) and the following meningitis.* With the hole in the bone remaining, I just tried to close the skin again and prescribed antibiotics.

I went home exhausted and saddened by the failure of my intervention. It confirmed all my fears about not being capable on my own. When I returned to the hospital the next morning, my first goal was to find out what happened with the lady during the night. I asked the night guard at what time she passed away. He responded: "Come and see."

We went to her room—and there the lady sat on her bed, smiling, and wearing her white head bandage like a turban. I couldn't believe it! For the first time I could talk to her—her name was Isalla. Apparently, the hole in her cranium had decreased the pressure to her brain. In fact, after a very slight and transient hemiplegia (paralysis on one side of the body) because of minor brain damage I caused with my intervention, Isalla fully recovered and was able to be discharged after a few more days!

It was a wonder to me that she didn't develop an infection from the non-sterile way I operated on her. With my scientific thinking, I still can't understand why Isalla survived. From a medical point of view, it was an impossible thing. It really was a miracle done by the One for whom "nothing is impossible."

When I had to start my work in the village without another doctor at my side, I felt like Joshua after the death of Moses. It must have been an absolutely overwhelming task for Joshua to lead the Israelites after the blessed and gifted Moses. But God knew his fearful heart, and over and over again he encouraged him, "Be strong and courageous. I will be with you."

What I experienced with Isalla was the Lord telling me that He was in control, telling me not to look at my skills or the circumstances, but at His opportunities beyond measure. "I will be with you." It was a huge encouragement.

In the following years we saw Isalla now and then on the street, happily living her life. Sometimes, as a reminder, I used my fingers to feel the hole in her skull under the scalp. God is still the same as in the times of Joshua!

Laurenz and Marianne Gossweiler from Switzerland were members of the Chad team for nine years.

Lord, There Is No One Like You

Louis and Susan Sutton
Chad, 1992

During our first term in Chad, one of our twin daughters, Susan, became seriously ill. Louis and I didn't recognize at first that anything was wrong because the symptoms came in stages. We had just returned from a family vacation in early December when Susan began complaining of a sore neck. Assuming the soreness was from a poor night's sleep, we were not overly concerned in the beginning. But the pain did not go away, and over the next week she began to show signs of fatigue that went beyond what was normal for a seven-year-old. One night Susan woke me up to say that her neck was hurting again. I led her into the kitchen where I filled a glass from our filtered supply of water and handed her an aspirin for the pain. Unable to bend her fingers, the tablet slipped from her small hand and dropped onto the floor. My heart dropped with it.

Louis had already been watching Susan carefully for the past few days, his physician's mind running through all of the possibilities for her symptoms. He had even fasted that particular day, seeking God's wisdom on how to treat her. Once I told him about the aspirin, he gave her a complete physical the next morning. When he checked her eyes, he recognized signs of pressure on her brain and knew immediately that she needed help beyond what was available in Chad. At the time there was not a CT scanner in the entire country. We knew we needed to go home.

An emergency evacuation is not easy from the remote town of Adré, Chad where we were serving. It's a bush town on the Sudanese border, nearly 800 miles from the capital city and a four-hour drive over rough roads to Abéché, the nearest town with an airport. The only civilian flight from that town to the capital is once a week on Friday and this was Saturday afternoon—the Saturday before Christmas. Susan's condition was too serious to wait an entire week to leave the country. We would have to trust God to go before us and make a way.

Knowing that we would be away for a while, we packed up as best we could and left Adré on Sunday morning. When we arrived in Abéché, we noticed that Susan's eyes looked strange. They seemed unable to focus and were unusually bright.

Louis went to the French military base to ask if they could help us. We knew that their usual military flight leaves each Saturday, so it seemed as if we were too late for that plane as well. The WEC team was praying, and one member gave us a verse which was to be God's promise throughout the next four days: "Lord, there is no one like you to help the powerless against the mighty" (2 Chron. 14:11).

At the military base they said we were "in luck." Their Saturday flight had been cancelled due to a problem with the plane. They were now going to fly on Monday and, yes, we could be on that flight. God had already gone before and scheduled the flight we needed.

We were flown to the capital on Monday. Susan's physical condition seemed worse each day. By now she was unable to sleep through the night, was losing body fluid, and we still needed to get out of the country. It was Christmas week, an impossible time, we were told, to find extra seats on the one plane scheduled to fly to France. Would they be willing to let our entire family of five board on such short notice? Yes, we were all accepted on the flight. We later learned that Air France had at the last minute decided to send a larger plane to Chad for this flight to accommodate the Christmas crowd. "Lord, there is no one like you . . ."

At this point Susan was deteriorating so rapidly that Louis considered beginning her on steroids to relieve the pressure on her brain. This was not an easy decision because, without the correct diagnosis of her condition, it was unsure whether steroids would help or harm. He prayed for guidance, sought the long-distance advice of a neurosurgeon in North Carolina and made the decision to put her on steroids.

On Tuesday we were in France, and Susan was in a wheelchair. As desperate as we were to continue the journey, no connecting flights were available that evening. We had to spend the night and were booked into a hotel. Three long days had passed since we left Adré; it was very hard to wait another night before finally reaching home, family and a hospital. Louis and I put Elisabeth and Scott to bed but knew that Susan needed our care throughout the night.

Louis and I were exhausted. We looked at Elisabeth and Scott lying asleep in their beds and thanked God for how wonderfully they had behaved during the stress of the past few days. We looked at Susan lying in a fitful sleep, so different from the little girl we had known only a week before, and our hearts broke. All of the tension, uncertainty and grief that had built up during the past days finally caught up with us. We moved into the bathroom so the children couldn't hear and collapsed to the floor in tears. I had already cried at intervals throughout the past three days, but now I heard great, wracking sobs pouring out from Louis, who had been so strong and calm as a doctor, so capable as a husband and father in getting us to this point.

We held each other for nearly an hour until the tears subsided. Then we talked about Susan. We wouldn't know what was wrong until we reached a hospital where she could be tested. But we decided while sitting on the floor that one thing we did know and would hold on to was the goodness of God. No matter what was ahead, we would not stop believing that God is good.

The following morning we waited in the hotel lobby for the wheelchair van to arrive. Our two other children, Scott and Susan's twin, Elisabeth, stepped outside to pass the time blowing "smoke" in the unfamiliar winter cold while Susan lay on a couch inside, her eyes staring straight ahead, her body unable to move without help, but with a sweetness of spirit that made me want to cry every time I looked at her.

Time passed and no van appeared. After a half-hour wait Louis went to check at the desk. He returned shortly with a look of disbelief on his face. The van was not coming. The airline was on strike and no vehicles were being allowed in or out of the terminal. The airline wouldn't even receive calls so we could explain our situation. We looked at each other helplessly, and the verse came to mind, "I would have despaired unless I had believed that I would see the goodness of the Lord in the land of the living" (Ps. 27:13, NASB).

We knew that the team back in Chad and friends and family at home were praying, but we had no way to tell them this news. We bowed our heads and prayed, "But You know, Lord."

Another half hour went by before we were called to the hotel desk by the clerk who had been watching us with increasing sympathy. She had a smile on her face. The strike had "suddenly" been called off. A wheelchair van was on its way. "Lord, there is no one like you . . ."

Because of the delay, we reached New York with only fifteen minutes to go through customs, get to another terminal and board our final flight to North Carolina. It was the day before Christmas Eve, and everyone was helpful, but they all said we wouldn't make it. In spite of a slow crawl in a taxi between terminals, we rushed from the taxi to the plane just in time, with Louis carrying Susan in his arms. "Lord, there is no one like you . . ."

By the time we arrived home, Susan was losing vision in the left eye but had already stabilized in other areas due to the steroids. She spent that night and Christmas Eve day in the hospital undergoing tests but was home with the family for Christmas.

Tests revealed pressure spots on the brain but no tumor. Finally, doctors concluded that she had a rare neurological condition which needed treatment for several months. The required treatment for her condition? Steroids! "Lord, there is no one like you . . ."

Over the next five months, Susan's health and vision improved. Her pediatrician told Louis that the use of steroids in those early days saved her vision. Now Susan is left with only a slight visual impairment as a reminder of that part of her life.

We are left with memories of God's great care in a time of crisis. He had promised years before that He loved our children even more than we love them and that He would take care of them. At a time of great need, He showed just how worthy He is of our trust. He gave Louis wisdom as a doctor trying desperately to help his own child. He gave emotional strength when we looked helplessly at our daughter deteriorating before our eyes. He carried us over seemingly impossible hurdles each step of the way. He got us home.

Louis and Susan Sutton, with their three children, have served with WEC since 1987 in medical work in Chad and in national leadership in the USA, followed by election to the role of International Directors in 2011.

4

Prayer

And I will do whatever you ask in my name, so that the Son may bring glory to the Father. You may ask me for anything in my name, and I will do it.

John 14:13–14

I don't want to learn how it can't be done. I want to believe it can.

Elliott Tepper

We always maintain it as our objective not to go to prayer with a string of "maybes" and "hope-sos" and "if it be Thy will" but first of all to find (though sometimes it may take days or weeks) what we understand to be the will of God in a situation, conveyed to us through His mind enlightening our minds, through the weighing of the situation, through open discussion, through a word from the Scriptures, through general unanimity; then we go to prayer with the prayer of faith.

Norman Grubb in *The Four Pillars of WEC*
(Gerrards Cross: WEC, 1973)

Ask Whatever You Will

Ken Ward
Kalimantan, Indonesia, 1987

*L*ife was never easy in Indonesian Borneo. Whenever we had our three-month supply of shopping to take home, it was too much to carry in our long boat. The supply included drums of fuel, large tins of sugar, sacks of flour and rice along with canned goods. Our nearest co-worker, Bruce Rattray, would take us up the river in the houseboat Utusan Injil with our long-boat tied at the back.

The Utusan Injil only traveled six miles per hour, so it was very slow; in good conditions we would get home in two days. When darkness fell, we had to tie up to a tree on the riverbank to stay overnight. At first light each morning, the engine was started. We would travel again until dark, cooking rice and vegetables on a small cooking stove while traveling. There were four bunks that folded down from the side walls, but usually there were too many people for the number of beds, and some had to sleep on the hardwood floor. I usually lay behind the motor with my feet on the gearbox.

One morning on such a trip upriver, I was sitting at the end of a bunk having my devotional time while my colleague steered. We had traveled all the previous day up the winding Ketungau River and noted that the further we went, the lower the water level became. It was obvious that we were not going to be able to get right back home. The burden of my heart was to reach home with all the supplies. If we had to leave them in a Dayak village, it was likely that most of the stuff would be missing when we returned later.

As I finished my Bible reading and began to pray, God said to me very clearly, "What do you want me to do?" Wow! This was the first time God had given me a blank check in this way. Because of the burden to get our supplies upstream, my answer came quickly, "I want to get this load right to our house today." It was an impossibility apart from God.

We knew from experience the signs of lowering water. I did wonder how it could ever happen, but as we wound our way upstream, the brown water began to rise little by little until it was no trouble to get right up to Riam Sejawak before dark. Evidently there had been rain way upriver causing a temporary rise in the water level. While I was thankful to God for this amazing answer to prayer, I later thought that I should have given it a bit more thought and asked for something less temporal—like asking for the Holy Spirit's conversion of a key man in this area. God then reminded me of a verse from one of John Newton's wonderful hymns which I had written inside my Bible cover:

Thou art coming to a King;
Large petitions with thee bring;
For His grace and power are such,
None can ever ask too much.

Sometimes we ask for such small things when God wants to do so much more.

*Used by permission from
Ken and Colleen Ward,* Surviving Borneo *(self-published, 2009).*

Ken and Colleen Ward from New Zealand arrived in Indonesia in 1973 with their two children. They lived in Kalimantan among the Dayak people for eleven years.

Authority in Prayer
Bruce Rattray
Kalimantan, Indonesia, 1987

For though we live in the world, we do not wage war as the world does. The weapons we fight with are not the weapons of the world. On the contrary, they have divine power to demolish strongholds. (2 Cor. 10:3–4)

I had just arrived in Kalimantan (or Indonesian Borneo) from a scheduled home leave in Australia when I received a message on my two-way radio. "You had better get up to your home base quickly. You have trouble on your hands up there."

I quickly traveled to my home region and found that a national church, liberal in theology and politically orientated, was seeking to get into the area where we had been working and turn the young churches into their denomination. Their representative came up to my area twice and never contacted me. He clearly wanted to turn the people against us and try to get a stronghold in there for his group. When I found out about his actions and motives, I traveled to this remote area and arrived just before dark. I could hear the gong being beaten for the evening service.

I met the leader of our church on the trail a little bit outside of the village, and he was unaware of this other man and his actions. He had heard the gong and thought that it was being beaten for me.

At the sound of the gong, many people gathered for the meeting, and I walked in with my Bible and sat down. About five minutes later the other fellow walked in. He nearly fell over when he saw me sitting there, and when it came time to preach, I was asked to do it instead of him.

He said he was going to go home the next day, but he didn't leave. He decided to stay and have another meeting the next night in the church. This was a problem because I was going off to another village to do a bit of evangelism and would not be present like the previous night.

I'll never forget what happened next. The church leader and I walked through the jungle for about an hour and three-quarters to the village where I was going. When we arrived at the edge of the jungle and before we entered into the clearing, I urged us to pray together.

We immediately knelt together on the side of the trail and I prayed:

> In the name of Jesus Christ, who brought to nothing the works of darkness by His death and resurrection, I shut the mouth of this man from being able to say one word that would hinder the purpose of God in this young church. Satan, in the name of Jesus Christ I shut your mouth. You shall not be able to speak through this man and hinder the purpose of God. I claim that now in the name of Jesus Christ. Amen.

I quickly forgot about this prayer as we stood up and entered the clearing. I returned to the other village two days later.

Church members gathered and told me how the man stood up to give his speech, walked out to the pulpit and opened his mouth but not a word came out. He stood there for a moment and then sat down again.

They sang a hymn and invited him up front again. Once more, he stood up and opened his mouth and gave a brief word on "rejoicing in the Lord." They told me he did this three times before giving up.

Glory to God! Why did God do that? Because all authority is given to Jesus Christ, and Satan is defeated. Trust God and this same authority is yours to use in our spiritual warfare. That is the power of prayer.

Taken from WEC Australian Magazine, 1987

Bruce and Annette Rattray came from Australia and felt the strong call of God to serve in West Kalimantan, Indonesia. For thirty-three years they planted churches and trained leaders.

Delayed Results
Jeanne Buchanan
Colombia, 2010

Cast your bread upon the waters, for after many days you will find it again. (Eccles. 11:1)

After many years in missions, I have found there are times when the work seems to be bearing no fruit. However, we never know how God is working. He is faithful when we "cast our bread upon the waters." Here are two such examples from my time as a missionary in Colombia:

The first occurred in 1968, when my husband Alf and I drove down to the eastern plains in Colombia. We had been invited by a missionary to teach in a Bible course for Guaraní Indian church leaders. We arrived before the students and waited eagerly for them to show up. Only three turned up after several days of waiting, even though we had expected many more. The teaching was not easy as their Spanish was not as fluent as we expected. After a couple of days, one of the three went back home, then another one. The one remaining student stayed a few more days and then also went on his way. This left us very frustrated.

A full nineteen years later, I attended a conference in Bogotá geared toward bringing together Colombian evangelicals who were doing missionary work with unreached groups, whether within the country or abroad. One of the men talking about his work was a Guaraní Indian. He looked very similar to the last of the three pupils we had taught in 1968. He came up to me afterward and asked if I had been a teacher in that course.

"I thought I recognized you!" he said, and continued, "You know, those few days changed my life. God spoke to me to serve only Him, and that is what I have been doing ever since." Alf and I had thought that the trip had been a complete waste of time. How wrong we were.

The second example began when I was walking toward the bus stop after teaching at the Presbyterian Seminary and noticed a young woman walking in the opposite direction, crying. I walked on, but then turned back and caught up with her. She told me that her boyfriend had kicked her out of the house because she was pregnant, and now she had no money at all. She was going to stay with a relative while she sorted herself out, but it was a long walk.

I gave her all the money I had, which was just enough for a couple of buses, and gave her the phone number of a church near where she would be staying. It was a simple gesture, but all I could do at the time. (I even had to walk back to the seminary and borrow money to get home!)

I frankly forgot all about the woman until several months later when she called me. She now had a job, the pregnancy was going well, she was going to the church I had recommended—and she was trusting in Christ as her Savior. Praise His name!

Jeanne Buchanan left the UK to work with WEC in Colombia in 1959 and, after the death of her husband, continued there in theological education and writing until 1997.

El Monte

Ed Somerville
Mexico, 2010

You might think it a simple matter to buy property if the owner wants to sell and the buyer wants to buy—but not in Mexico and not if the devil is convinced you are a threat to his plans!

In 1991 Pruett and Linda Burnam moved to Mexico to open a new WEC field. Part of the vision God gave them was for a camp ministry, so they immediately began looking for a suitable property—one with adequate acreage, sufficient water and a legal deed.

Others joined the Burnams, and eight busy years passed as the team became established and ministries began. The group never stopped looking at properties but could not seem to find the right place at the right price.

Then in the autumn of 1999, the team met for annual conference at a lovely waterpark, and the vision for a camp revived. We held a prayer walk around the property, and for the first time the whole team felt this was the place to pursue. There were ten acres of land, plenty of water and a legal deed.

The property was owned by a family of eleven brothers and sisters, some of whom were interested in selling. What they couldn't decide on was the price!

As we prayed and discussed whether this was God's place for the camp, one church made an offer of $200,000 toward purchase of the land, and a long-time supporter matched that gift.

Some of the family who owned the property were quite happy with our offer of $600,000, but others were holding out for $1 million—200 pesos ($20 US) per square meter. Round and round the family went—making promises, breaking promises, calling meetings, postponing meetings. In the end we decided to walk away from the deal, after a whole frustrating year of negotiations.

Why did this happen? Initially, some of the team had reservations about buying a property; the Lord used the time of

El Monte planning

negotiations to deepen our unity and assurance that it was God's will for us to have a camp site. However, one of the hardest challenges is when God tells us to wait. As the situation dragged on, we did begin to wonder if He had abandoned us.

How surprised and grateful we were when in 2002 another property was located: twenty-five acres with a small river at the bottom of a hill, a legal deed and, best of all, just one owner, an eighty-five-year-old woman. The elderly owner asked her nephew to handle the negotiations, and we were pleased that her asking price was fifty pesos ($5 US) per square meter, or $500,000—half the million asking price of the first property. Perhaps this was what God had in mind when the first deal fell through: more than twice the property at half the price!

Things went well for four months, and hopes were high. The donors, who had been very patient, were thrilled to support the purchase. Then the public notary handling the deal called to tell us the nephew was asking that the payment for the property be deposited in his personal bank account in the United States. Apparently he was trying to cheat his elderly aunt. The notary advised us not to have any more to do with him. We had to agree.

Walking away from that property left the whole team discouraged and sad. Eleven years of searching and negotiating for a camp property and still nothing to show for it!

By now we had formed a camps department, dedicated to fasting every Tuesday and meeting for prayer in the evening. During those bleak times we hung on by remembering that God was good, that He was almighty, that He hadn't left His throne and that if He hadn't given us a property yet, it was for our good and His glory.

One Tuesday in 2003, I (Ed Somerville) headed out to search for property. I knew the entire state had been scoured, and my chances of finding someplace new, short of a miracle, were virtually nil. With faith even smaller than a mustard seed, I set off to search one more time.

I headed into the heart of the state of Morelos, toward an area famous for its waterparks. In the back of my mind was a large yellow sign I'd noticed, advertising land for sale. I finally found it on the banks of a small river, in a lovely valley filled with sugar cane. A rocky hillside rose up on one side, dotted with dramatic cacti and gnarled trees. A dirt road led invitingly into the property. The sign read, "Water. Views. Deed and—land." Lots of land. Seventy acres of it. I did the math. If the asking price for ten acres had been $1 million, what might the owners want for this place? There was no way we could afford to buy a property like this, but what if the purchase of a small piece could be negotiated? I decided to at least try and headed into the town of Ticuman to find a phone.

"Hello, is this the owner of the property that is for sale near Ticuman?"

"No, but I am his representative."

"Would you be interested in selling just a part of the property?"

"No, that would be impossible because there is only one well."

"Oh. Thank you anyway."

I was about to hang up the phone in defeat. Just then the representative added, "But the owner is selling the land at a very good price."

"Really?" I asked. How many times had I heard this line? I wouldn't rise to the bait.

"Yes. The owner is asking for only eighteen pesos per square meter."

I hesitated. Had the representative said eighteen or eighty? With my short time in Mexico, many times the language still confused me. Even if I'd heard eighteen, which was much less than the 200 pesos of the first property, or the fifty of the second, what if the representative was wrong?

"We may get back in touch with you later," I concluded and hung up.

Slowly what the representative had said began to sink in. I realized that if he had really said eighteen, this was a property six times bigger than the first one at one-third the asking price. Could it be true? I was afraid to get excited, but turned in the direction of the weekly prayer meeting with my heart racing.

"Guys, I'm not sure if I heard the gentleman correctly, or if he's telling the truth, but I believe he told me he had a seventy-five-acre property for sale at eighteen pesos a meter," I shared. I passed the representative's phone number to my co-worker Mike, son of Pruett and Linda, so he could verify the price. Mike dialed, and the rest of the group prayed.

"Yes," said the representative. "I talked to your colleague this afternoon. I told him the price, but he didn't seem very excited about it. So I contacted the owner in Mexico City and talked to him about the money. If you're interested, he says he is willing to reduce the price to fifteen pesos a meter."

Mike hung up the phone and with wide eyes began to share his conversation. Slowly it dawned on us that we were witnessing a miracle.

The team began the purchase process by letting the representative know we were interested. Then we waited . . . and waited . . . and waited. Several weeks went by, and the only thing we heard was that "suddenly" other parties were interested in purchasing the property.

Requests to speak directly to the owner were put off. Eventually it became clear that the representative was fishing for a bribe. In a move reminiscent of a detective movie, team members went to the office of the land registry and tracked down the deed for

El Monte new buildng

the land, only to find that a high-ranking government official in Mexico City owned the property, although it was registered in his wife's name.

The wealthy and aristocratic in Mexico move in completely different circles from the rest of society. This politician had been the governor of the Federal District and the right-hand man of a past president. In order to speak to him, one had to get past his security and personal bodyguards, secure an appointment with his personal secretary and find a rare moment when he was in the city and not at another engagement. This would take either substantial bribes or an act of God!

So the team prayed and, armed with a city map, headed to the address indicated on the deed. We found ourselves in an upscale part of the city, knocking on a heavily barred gate and speaking to a uniformed guard through a tiny window. As it turned out, the politician "happened" to be in town. He was gracious enough to give us a couple of minutes of his time and was surprised to hear of our interest in the property. He said he would be happy to arrange an appointment with us to work out the details. That was the last we heard of him for a couple of months.

Meanwhile, the church that offered to donate $200,000 had been unable to postpone use of its gift and diverted half the amount toward another project. The other $100,000 would also be withdrawn if we weren't able to sign a contract by the end of February 2004. As it was now nearing Christmas 2003, a special team prayer meeting was held, and together we called out to the Lord for His intervention.

After repeated phone calls to the politician's security guards, we finally were connected to the politician's personal secretary, who said she would try to arrange an appointment. No response. More calls to the front gate. Finally, another connection to the secretary and another promise of an appointment led to another disappointment.

After weeks of getting nowhere, the secretary told us we could meet with her boss if we were willing to drive seven hours to his home state of Guanajuato. By this point, with the countdown running, something had to be done, so along with another team member and a lawyer friend, I climbed into a cramped Nissan pick-up and headed off early one morning. After several hours, we reached Guanajuato and stopped by the politician's office. No, he wasn't in the office. In fact, he was at his home in a town farther down the road.

Two hours later, we knocked on the door of the politician's house. No, he wasn't at home. No, he wasn't at his campaign office. No, there was nothing on his agenda about a meeting with WEC.

Frustrated and exhausted, we three decided to look for some lunch. We headed back into town and entered a small restaurant. Sitting around a table in the shadows, we sipped Cokes and looked from one to the other in bewilderment. Now what?

At that moment, who should walk into the restaurant but the politician and several of his bodyguards! We recognized him immediately, and after a moment he noticed us. "What are you doing here?" he asked.

"You mean your secretary didn't tell you?"

"This is the first I've heard from you since we met in Mexico City. Are you still interested in buying the land?"

After I explained the many efforts to get in touch and the long day's journey to see him, the politician offered his apologies. He even paid for lunch! Better yet, he gave us his personal cell phone number, and within a few weeks the group was reunited around a table in his Mexico City home, accompanied by a public notary and a check for the full purchase amount. Five days before the end of February and the withdrawal of the $100,000 gift, the WEC team had a certified sales contract in hand!

When we'd reached the end of our rope and exhausted our resources, the Lord stepped in and did something none of us could ever have conceived. Discouragement and fatigue fell away, gratitude and praise took over, and El Monte camp center was born!

By August 2010 God sent an extra $120,000, the first four cabins were nearing completion, additional vehicles, recreational facilities and power outlets were in place.

"Sing to the Lord, praise his name! . . . Declare his glory among the nations" (Ps. 96:2–3).

Ed and Debbie Somerville joined WEC in 2000 and are serving in Mexico as deputy field leaders. They have eight children, one of whom also worked with WEC.

Lord, Heal Mary Jean

Mary Jean Robertson
Congo, 1996

Traveling from Nebobongo by bicycle for a visit to Ibambi, a village eleven kilometers away, I arrived uneventfully. However, on my way home I was descending a rather steep hill. Congo is notorious for its poor roads, so I was intent on choosing my route. Much to my horror I came to a place with no good choices and found myself stuck in a rut with a huge rock sticking out of it.

The next thing I knew I was catapulted through the air!

I landed in a ditch with my full weight on my chest. My chin struck the top of the ditch with a wallop, followed by my head; my glasses went flying. The ensuing pain and sound of cracking bones were ominous.

Gasping for air I rolled over. My ribs felt intact but pressure indicated a severely compressed sternum—it was painful to

Conference of missionaries and church leaders

breathe. I had blood on my shirt from a lacerated chin. I stood up—no broken legs, but dizziness and extreme weakness told me I had really "done a number" on myself!

As a colleague drove me home, I became aware of a growing pain and stiffness in my left wrist; by evening I knew it was severely injured. I couldn't move it, turn my palm up or down, or bend my fingers. After splinting my wrist and closing the three-centimeter cut on my chin with a butterfly bandage, I went to bed.

I was in agony all night and stayed in bed the next day. The team doctor was away, so Donna, the MAF pilot's wife, ran in and out to help me as she was able. That evening she and her two-year-old son Matthew came over to see what they could do for me. As they were leaving, Donna said, "Matthew, do you want to pray for Mary Jean?" In response he laid his hand on my splinted wrist and closed his eyes tightly. With deep emotion he prayed, "Lord, heal Mary Jean. Amen!" I smiled. He sounded just like his dad.

When I awoke the next morning I tried to budge my fingers—and they moved. No pain! I sat up in amazement, unrolled the bandage, shed the splint and clenched my fist—no pain! I turned my hand this way and that, and still no pain. Running to the door I found Donna on her doorstep. "Look Donna!" I shouted as I held up my hand and made a fist several times. At that moment I realized I was shouting, taking deep breaths with no pain in my chest! I ran to the bathroom to look at my chin. I peeled off the butterfly bandage. The laceration was completely closed with a solid scab covering it. God had truly done a miracle in response to a child's prayer.

Even more than being excited over a genuine miracle, I was touched by this mom and dad who had taught their toddler how to pray. On previous occasions when I had prayed with this family, I would hear Matthew's little murmur of agreement to what was being said. I found myself smiling at his imitation of his parents. Or was it?

What an encouragement for this child to see that God hears and answers prayer. What an encouragement to this mom and dad in a day when there is so much confusion and uncertainty in child-rearing. And what a joy to our Lord Jesus Christ when He heard one of His little ones crying out with trust, "Lord, heal Mary Jean. Amen!"

Taken from WEC Australian Magazine

Mary Jean Robertson (Canada) served at a medical station in Nebobongo in northeastern Congo. Mother to five grown children and grandmother to seven, Mary Jean is well aware of the importance of teaching little ones to pray.

Miracle Donkey
Bob Harvey, Brazil
Queensland, Australia, 1980

I don't know how you would describe a missionary on home leave armed with boxes of books and free literature, projector, suitcase, Bible and toothbrush; but like it or not, he must travel. And travel in Australia means long distances and needed transportation—and this involves telling Father about it.

For some three months we had been quietly "telling Father," and no car had turned up. The reason was obvious. He wanted us to slow down to a dead stop for a while till we had adapted to the Australian way of life again, attended to medical examinations and dental treatment, and related to family and friends.

My brother-in-law very warmly made his home and second car available to us as we waited.

Then it happened—my first car accident in twenty years! Exit one Chrysler Valiant, for a time. Complications plus! How would we do speaking tours now?

Then God stepped in! A car appeared for sale in the front yard of a nearby residence. It looked good: a 1965 Holden car for $300—about what we thought we might pay (obviously not a Rolls Royce!). The tires were good, the paint OK (a little rust—nothing serious). It was clean inside and had a sticker on the back window: "Tell it as it is—Jesus Christ is Savior."

I figured I had to meet the owner even if we decided not to buy it. His name was Don—a complete stranger to me but a keen Christian for two years who had just resigned his job at a gambling agency because God had challenged him about it, even though there was nothing else in view. God held the key to his heart, possessions, family, everything; for Christ was Lord in his life, not just Savior, as the sticker had said.

Little did I know I was answering a prayer! They told me a previous interested party had scoffed at the car and the price—reckoned it was a "bomb"—and Lorraine (the owner's wife) had prayed that a Christian would come along.

Sure, I was a Christian and I came in answer to her prayer, but I silently said to God, Lord, *I don't want a "bomb."* The fellowship we had was tremendous, but I said I wouldn't commit myself till a mechanic friend checked it over for me next day.

The next morning, as he meditated on the story of the donkey whose owner had released him for the Lord to use on Palm Sunday, the Spirit of God said, "Don, the Lord needs your blue and white donkey, standing in the front yard, for Bob."

I couldn't believe my ears when Lorraine told me the "donkey" was ours—for nothing! Don still hadn't appeared on the scene, so I promised to return next morning to meet him and check whether it was really true!

What lovely fellowship we had next day as we shared the Lord together; then Don said, "Are you taking the 'donkey' home now, Bob? It's yours to keep."

We fixed up some minor problems, but the "donkey" served us well for the whole year of our furlough. When it was time to return to Brazil, we felt the Lord was telling us to give the "donkey" back rather than sell it. We hadn't seen the family since picking it up, and when we arrived, they were the ones who had need of the "donkey." Lorraine was very sick, Don had lost his job recently, and they didn't have a car. They were over the moon!

How wonderful is our great God!

Bob and Bev Harvey from Australia went to Brazil in 1966 with their family for twenty-five years and were involved country-wide in mobilizing churches for missions. Subsequently their role has been to advise WEC missionary teams in Latin America and then provide an IT consultancy service worldwide.

Sold in the Nick of Time
England, United Kingdom, 1937

Fran and Elsie Rowbotham, believing God was calling them to Colombia in 1937, booked passage for August 6, in faith that the Lord would provide buyers for their shops and property in Birmingham. In June their faith was being tested, for they were still unsold.

The God of the Bible is also the God of business affairs to those who obey and believe Him. A block of houses was to be disposed of as one item, and the shops, which consisted of the frontages for several of these houses, was being sold as another. They were the property of Fran's father, their use given to his son for the purpose of carrying on the business. This made it all the more essential that a fair price be obtained for the sale.

Fran and Elsie Rowbotham

The Rowbothams' first act of faith was a public announcement of their sailing for Colombia by turning the annual WEC meeting in the City Hall into their farewell. The devil was telling them that a public announcement would hurt the business and the prospect of a good sale, but with the cat let out of the bag, interest was obvious when attendance at the meeting jumped from the usual 400 to 1,500!

The next test concerned the date for sailing. Once again the "Rows" walked straight ahead and agreed to book passage on the first available ship after the WEC staff conference—set to sail August 6. They knew the property sale must take place a month before they left to allow time for all the details to be settled.

Then came the real pinch—weeks passed with a few inquiries, but no results. The usual question they were asked was "But what will you do if it is not sold?" It was a question they refused to consider, for if no purchaser came forward, they knew the shops would have to go under the hammer and the stock go for an odd £100 or so. This they might not have minded for themselves, but they knew it would not be to God's glory when the property was their father's, and the proceeds would go to him.

At the same time they were not blind to the fact that with the advent of multiple store competition, it was difficult to sell a private business. They knew of several unsold. But they walked those weeks "strong in faith" and testified that God would deliver.

Only two weeks were left before July 6, the latest possible sale date. A man came to see the house property (not the shops). He asked to be given two weeks to think over the purchase. Two weeks passed, and July 5 arrived. Another man came to see the shops and stock. He said he would return the next day, July 6. He came, and in his hand was a check for shops and stock! While he was talking with the Rows, the phone rang. The man who had asked for two weeks to consider the house property was calling to say he would purchase it!

Two more items complete the perfect picture. The Rows also wanted to get rid of their car. The purchaser of the shops saw it standing there, asked if they wanted to sell, and bought it, even "lending" it to the Rows to drive down to the conference. The three assistants in the shops all found other positions, so no one could say God's call to the Rows meant loss of employment to someone else. They who trust Him wholly find Him wholly true.

Taken from WEC UK Magazine, 1937

This was the commencement of a life of faith for the Rowbothams. After two years in Colombia, they returned to the UK and were used by God to set up a WEC base, Training College and Conference Center in Scotland.

God's Double Surprise!

Junior Damasceno
France, 2008

On a hot day in July 2008, Marie was passing by our street and saw the sign in front of our church: Église Protestante (Protestant Church). She had been looking for a place where someone could tell her about spiritual things. She was searching for God and didn't know there was a Protestant church in our town in France.

That day we had twenty-two Brazilian Christians visiting us, including five pastors and other leaders from a Baptist church. They were visiting Europe to learn more about the spiritual situation on this continent and had lots of ideas about how to make the church grow. We had to explain to them that what works in Brazil doesn't necessarily work here! Their first surprise was to know that there were no other evangelical churches in the town (their home town had twenty-two Baptist churches), and their second was that our church consisted of only thirty-five members. "How can it be that you are so few, when you have been here for over a century?" was their comment. How could they understand the slow growth of the French church when they baptized 200 people a year? In seven years we baptized seven, I told their senior pastor.

While we were still talking, Marie, the lady searching for God, rang the bell. I introduced her to the talkative Brazilians and showed her around. She was curious about our church and what we believed. I wondered if I was dreaming, rarely does someone arrive asking about God.

The noise coming from the office, where we had left the Brazilians, brought me back to reality. The lady was asking questions about faith and about our church. This was real. "Can I come to the service on Sunday?" she asked.

She did come the next Sunday, but what she didn't know was that our church building had been inspected by the police, the fire department and a person from the town hall for security reasons. We were waiting for a phone call or letter and had no idea what would be the outcome of their visit. But we were worried. We were praying, crying out to God and waiting for a miracle.

Summer was ending when we finally got the phone call from the town hall. The security team who had inspected our church had decided to close the building. We knew that in the near future we would be officially asked to leave. Marie was there in church the Sunday we announced we were looking for a new place to meet. After many years meeting at the same location, we had to move, but we had no idea where to go.

"Why don't you write to the mayor and ask for a place to meet?" Marie suggested. We thought it was a shot in the dark. Ask the town hall for a place for the Protestant church to meet? *In France?* But we had nothing to lose. We were going to be out on the street.

The police came, just as they said they would—at nine-thirty in the evening, and they made a lot of noise to make sure the neighbors knew. They officially closed our church building forever.

One day a letter from the town hall arrived with the morning mail, telling us we could have a place to meet on Sundays for free. The miracle had happened.

We have been meeting at the Charite Hall since September 2008. The Charite, located in the historical heart of the town, used to be a Catholic orphanage in the Middle Ages. People who would never come to our previous building now attend our services at the Charite since it is a public place and less threatening to them than a Protestant church building.

Back on that warm day in July, what we didn't know when we welcomed Marie for the first time was that she knew the mayor well. We could not have guessed that her husband had worked for the town hall for many years as the administrator. The mayor was her friend and listened to her request on our behalf. We could not have known that. But God knew!

Junior Damasceno from Brazil felt God's call to him in 1989 and served in Senegal for several years. After his marriage to Sue from the UK, they transferred to France in 1998 where they have been engaged in church planting.

The Lost Son
Veronika Elbers with Titus Dima
Indonesia, 2009

*T*imes were difficult for Titus, the first Indonesian to join WEC. The mission was unknown in Indonesia, and he had no support. And when he announced that God wanted him to go to the African country of Guinea-Bissau, senior Western WECers in his home country tried to persuade him to consider an English-speaking WEC field instead. In spite of all this, Titus still felt the call to work with WEC in Guinea-Bissau.

When he shared his burden with his mother during one of his rare home visits, she reacted strongly. She was not ready to give him permission to go abroad. His father had died several years before, and she was depending on her children to support her.

Titus, her third son, was one of a few young people in the village who had been given the opportunity to go to the island of Java to study. The widow was proud of his master's degree in theology, especially as her second son was not well-educated and still lived with her, and her first son had been missing for years. Now Titus, her hope for the future, wanted to go away! She told him, "If God gives me back my lost son, I will give you permission to serve the Lord in Africa."

On his way back from the village to do the candidate orientation course with WEC in Singapore, Titus felt confused. Could God really bring back Benyamin, his oldest brother?

Benyamin had gotten lost at a young age, when the family lived on Sabu, a poor but Christian island. He and his friends climbed aboard a ship which had landed at the remote island.

Titus Dema

The ship left Sabu with the boys below deck as stowaways. Titus' mother and the whole village were desperate when they noticed that the boys were gone; nobody knew where the ship was heading.

Titus' mother could not accept that her firstborn was lost forever, and yet when the family moved from Sabu to Flores, they had almost given up hope of ever coming into contact with Benyamin again.

Titus fought with the Lord. "Shall I go to Singapore for candidate orientation, or shall I stay in Indonesia to help my mother?" After a long heart struggle, he decided to go to Singapore and trust the Lord to take care of his mother.

After a few months Titus was enjoying the course in Singapore. He was the first Indonesian WEC worker to prepare for Guinea-Bissau. During a prayer day he shared about his family and their problem with his lost brother. One Korean colleague challenged all of the others in the course and Titus himself to pray and believe the Lord would return the lost brother to the family. Titus himself had never trusted the Lord for a miracle like that.

But the Lord proved that He was a Father who really cared and that He could provide far beyond man's expectations.

A strange Javanese lady came to visit Titus' mother and the family, asking a lot of unusual questions: "Are you from Sabu? How many sons do you have? Where are they?"

Titus' second brother, who was present when the lady visited his mother, asked her, "Why are you asking all these questions? What do you really want?"

The lady replied, "I am Ratna, your daughter-in-law. I am married to your son Benyamin. We met in Sorong, in West Papua. He told me he got lost when he climbed onto a ship in Sabu, fell asleep and woke up on the way to Papua."

In Sorong the boys had to leave the ship. Benyamin became a street kid and eventually worked for a Chinese shop owner. "We met, fell in love and married. We have been looking for you for a long time. Because you moved from Sabu to Flores, it was difficult to find and contact you. I have come to you to get your blessing on our marriage. Although we have been married for a long time, we have no children. I am quite a bit older, and I feel the need for your approval of our marriage if I am to have children."

What a big surprise for Titus' mother, his family and even for him! Eventually the family met Benyamin. God had been so good to them all and had done more than Titus could have imagined. What a wonderful Father, who brought back the lost son and helped Titus' mother accept his call to service in Africa!

Veronika Elbers is from Germany and has been working in Indonesia in theological education since 1984. Titus Dima went to Guinea-Bissau from Indonesia in 1994 and serves in church outreach and mission leadership.

The Parcel

Jenny Carter
England, United Kingdom, 1970s–80s

"What do you do up at WEC?" someone asked me at a church weekend.

"I work in the finance office," I answered.

"How boring!" she replied.

End of conversation.

"Boring" is not a word I would use to describe my twelve years in the finance office at Bulstrode (UK headquarters).

For me, working there was:

Fascinating, as we met people passing through from all corners of the world; heard about their ministries and got to know their supporters, friends and families.

Interesting, as we communicated with the treasurers on the fields and sending bases.

Challenging, when finances were low and we were called to prayer.

Intense, with a monthly deadline to meet.

Stimulating, as we were involved in so many people's lives, leading to a deeper involvement in personal and corporate prayer times.

Faith-stretching, as we trusted God to provide for the needs of individuals, fields and projects.

A privilege to be part of the UK finance committee, which met monthly to allocate general funds to workers, often being able to pass on larger gifts to a person in need or a project.

Exciting, as we saw answers to prayer for the general fund, as well as for other needs, frequently at the eleventh hour.

For example, just as I took over responsibility for the office in 1979, the Bulstrode staff had committed to another phase of renovations of the building. Parts of the balcony surrounding the outer courtyard were in a state of collapse. One arch was filled with bricks to hold it up; decorative molding was missing from the top and needed to be replaced. Inside, the rooms on two floors would be part of the project, with new rooms being created in the attic space. The cost was £110,000, over and above normal income. Did we have the money? No. Did we have faith? Not immediately, but after prayer, yes.

The complexity of the outside work required that it be done by skilled professionals. Everything had to be restored to its original state because the building is a "listed" historical property. We had no choice. Our faith stance was explained to the builders, who were prepared to trust us to trust God!

During the course of the work, the bills had to be paid as certain stages were reached—about £10,000 each time. Each occasion warranted special prayer. Opening the mail in the finance office with expectation, we were amazed to see gifts come in designated for this work. Often the first few would be small amounts dropped into the letter box on our door in the corridor, obviously from Bulstrode residents. These would be like small holes in a dam, making way for larger amounts to follow.

God works in various ways. Toward the end of the project, a quite separate decision led to the sale of a large unused and unusable piece of land. The money received paid off the final balance for the renovations.

During my years in the finance office, there was rarely any money "left over" from the general fund for the next month. At that time we needed at least £30,000 each month toward the support of our overseas workers alone. The home staff trusted God personally for their own support. Only once in twenty years did we need to drop the overseas allocations by five pounds per person, and we were able to send that same amount as extra the following month.

The allocations had first call on the general fund. Money came in from faithful supporters, bank interest, legacies, covenant tax refunds (later named Gift Aid) and so on. When I first worked in the office in 1976, a card record was kept of people's gifts. One elderly man had sent £2 twice a month for many years. When he died, out of curiosity we added up his gifts— they came to over £1,000, a sum he probably never had at any one time in his life.

Often the end of the month was a cliffhanger experience as only after the final bank statements and post had arrived for the close of business would we know the final results. For that reason, in those days the finance committee met on the first working day of each month. On one such occasion, a Friday, we were £13,000 short! What could we do? We talked and prayed and agonized. Then Pauline Nicholas, who with her husband Colin was UK director, said she felt strongly we should meet again on Monday. Guess what? The first envelope opened by Colin in the

UK office on Monday morning contained a check for £13,000. God had done it again.

The most exciting event of all occurred in the late 1980s, also while Colin and Pauline were directors. The general fund was as low as it could be toward the end of the month.

On a Sunday morning, most of the staff members were at church, a skeleton crew covering the kitchen and other essential duties, listening for the phone at the unmanned reception desk in the front hall.

I came back from church and went to my room, where the phone rang. Colin asked me to go down to the finance office. Wondering if I'd done something wrong, I hurried downstairs.

Colin was sitting at my desk with a large parcel in front of him. Pauline had gone to the reception desk at mid-day and found this parcel which had been left behind the counter. Thinking it might be a bomb (parcel bombs were around at the time), she called Colin, who started to open it. Seeing what was inside, he took it to the finance office and called me.

The parcel was stuffed full of money, neatly folded in small bundles. When we counted it, we found £26,000, exactly what was needed for that month when other money had seized up.

Colin Nicholas

Who was it from? Who walked in on a Sunday morning and left it? We never knew. This may say something for leaving the front door unlocked! But it says a lot more about God's faithfulness and about the amazing sacrifice and generosity of His people.

Would I describe working in the finance office as "boring"? Far from it!

"[He] is able to do immeasurably more than all we ask or imagine, according to his power that is at work within us" (Eph. 3:20).

Jenny Carter worked in the finance office at the UK WEC center from 1976 until the mid-eighties, after which she served as administrator in WEC's international office, followed by a ministry to retired workers.

5

Family Focus

We are living with regular miracles.

Martin Walser

FAITH spells RISK. It is also spelt Fantastic Adventure In Trusting Him.

Brian Woodford

We will tell the next generation the praiseworthy deeds of the Lord, his power, and the wonders he has done. . . . Then they would put their trust in God.

Psalm 78:4–7

A Scary Step of Faith

Jim & Judy Raymo
USA, late 1980s

*I*think I need to go to the doctor." Little David's words spoken in quiet, sad tones reflected his five years of life with serious asthma: often being rushed to the hospital at midnight gasping and wheezing; innumerable needles, medications and breathing treatments; a child's intense fear of impending pain battling an experienced patient's knowledge that he required medical help.

Jim, Judy and family in the 1980s.

Despite our best efforts at following medication protocols for David's asthma condition, every month meant many clinic visits and usually at least one frightening and draining trip to the emergency department where we had to help hold him down as he sobbed, "No more shots! No more shots!" while the doctors injected epinephrine again and again.

We wondered about David's health in light of our family's future. After thirteen years working with a church-based tent-making mission organization in the capital cities of Europe, we had taken a break at home in the USA. Jim had found a reasonably well-paying job that provided good medical benefits, and we were renting a comfortable apartment in a southern California beach town.

But at every turn we seemed to bump into a WEC missionary, receive a greeting card with WEC applications enclosed or hear a missions speaker at church. We knew we were not prepared to walk away from our call to global missions. While in Europe, we had lived at WEC's main base in England, renting some extra space on the Bulstrode estate that no one thought would ever be needed for the mission's use! We'd heard many WECers tell stories about God faithfully meeting their needs in finances, family and ministry. We were always fascinated but thought tent-making suited us. Though convinced the stories of God's deliverances were real, and having seen God miraculously meet major needs at the headquarters, we still thought the "life of faith" must be a privileged experience for certain missionary saints.

Eventually we realized God was leading us into WEC, along the lines of Norman Grubb's words: "Once Caught, No Escape." We gave in and became willing to pursue this direction from the Lord.

Biographies of Hudson Taylor and George Müller, written with complete honesty and frank admission of human frailty in the midst of God's ability to do what He promised, encouraged us to begin our own pilgrimage of "living by faith." We began to grow in confidence that God could provide not only for these giants of the faith but for our family as well. As Mueller said,

It is the selfsame faith which is found in every believer. . . . Oh, I beseech you, do not think me an extraordinary believer, having privileges above others of God's dear children, which they cannot have, nor look on my ways of acting as something that would not do for other believers but stand still in the hour of trial, and you will see the help of God if you trust in Him.[6]

We took steps to join WEC and saw the Lord bless us with a financial gift that would launch us out into a new world of uncertainty and adventure. Just as we were preparing to leave for candidate orientation in Pennsylvania, Jim's fears about David's health bubbled up and caused his greatest personal challenge of faith. Were we irresponsible to take David away from the medical resources he seemed to need so desperately? Well-meaning Christian friends reinforced these fears by voicing their concerns:

"What about the medical coverage you have through your job? How will you pay for medication and treatment?"

"Why would you leave the doctors who know your son?"

"Does it make sense to go overseas, where there may be health risks and minimal medical care, with three young children, one who is chronically ill?"

When Jim prayed about this, asking the Lord to confirm His leading to us by healing David, we saw no answer. In fact, just two weeks before we were scheduled to leave California for

WEC buildings at Camp Hill, PA.

Pennsylvania, David had an asthma attack severe enough to force us to the local emergency room. Jim says, "I wish I could testify to being a man of faith and power, but as we drove east across the country to the WEC center, I did so with much fear and trembling." We knew God was asking us to take this step into missionary service, but we did not know where we would end up working or how David's medical needs would be taken care of.

Following our move to Pennsylvania, David never had another asthma attack that required a visit to the doctor or a trip to the hospital. Did the Lord heal him? Or did He know the environments where He would take us over the next twenty years, including Tasmania, Australia, and Vancouver, Canada, would be more conducive to David's healthy breathing? All we know is that David has not suffered from severe asthma since we set off for candidate training. We bless the Lord, for He knew we needed His encouragement in the early days of our adventure of faith and His confirmation that "your family is safest in the center of God's will!"

Jim and Judy Raymo (USA), with their seven children, served in mission in UK and then worked with WEC in Tasmania, Australia and Canada as well as in candidate orientation and national leadership in the USA. After growing up as a WEC MK, David works in construction and remodeling in Philadelphia, Pennsylvania.

All Things Are Possible with God

Graham Bee
Ivory Coast, 1972

For me, having grown up as a quiet country boy in South Australia, embracing the call of God to become a missionary and go wherever He would send me was a huge challenge. I felt inadequate, but the conviction in my heart and the assurance of His promises won through.

After training, serving on the staff of Worldview College, marriage and the birth of our first child, we prepared to head out to Ghana. God wonderfully blessed and encouraged us with His provision of both equipment and finance so that when we printed prayer cards, we included the verse, "Nothing is impossible with God" (Luke 1:37). Despite our own weaknesses and some trepidation about what lay ahead of us, we were convinced that God was completely trustworthy and His promises totally dependable.

Graham Bee, Marjorie and family.

We set sail toward Africa on the *Orcades*, which fellow passengers renamed the "Rockades," on its last voyage. Although workers usually traveled by plane, we had been advised by Greg Francis, the Ghana field leader, to come by ship and bring our equipment with us, as little was available in the country. We had lovely streamer-holding farewells with family and friends at each Australian port we touched, so we left on a high.

Reality soon set in, though, as the ship lived up to its new name, and we experienced a lot of seasickness. I contracted pleurisy as well. Our six-month-old daughter Julie hated being confined in the internal cabin, so we struggled to be out and about with her when we would rather have stayed in bed.

We finally reached Dakar in Senegal and watched and listened as our luggage was taken out of the hold before the ship continued on to England. Passengers questioned, "Why is someone getting off here? This is the end of the world!" We chuckled to ourselves as we disembarked and spent the next twelve days with WEC friends there, waiting for a cargo boat to take us around the coast to Ghana.

To our dismay, when the boat reached Abidjan, the crew decided they would spend the weekend there. We were still struggling with sickness and were desperate to get off the boat. The only faint contact we had was a post office box address for Alastair and Helen Kennedy, the first WEC workers in Abidjan, a city of one million. How could we find them? We had no residential address, no phone number, no visa or local currency, and spoke no French! As we prayed about what to do, I felt I should start walking and trust God to guide me, leaving my wife and Julie on board.

I came across a post office, and eventually found someone who spoke English, but was told this was not the place, and should get a taxi and follow a long list of directions that I had no chance of remembering. I left the post office and started walking, keeping an eye out to make sure I could find my way back. All the time I was praying, and telling God that I believed His promises and claimed that, even in this situation, "All things are possible with God."

Suddenly a VW Beetle pulled up in front of me. On the back window were the English words "ALL THINGS ARE POSSIBLE WITH GOD." I stopped, mouth open in amazement. The young driver got out, saw me staring and said, "Yes, do you believe it?" I said I surely did and had just prayed those words. After explaining my need, he said that if I would wait while he finished his business, he would take me to some people he had seen selling Christian books. I didn't know who they might be but had a sense God was surely leading me.

After a bit of a drive, we arrived at the CLC bookstore. CLC, an international Christian literature ministry, has close connections to WEC and the workers from both, enjoyed good fellowship. The bookstore managers, Doris and Lotti, called a taxi, asked the driver how much it would cost and put the money in my hand. They said, "when the taxi stops, give him the money, walk across the road, and knock on the door."

Thankfully the Kennedys were home and were amazed that an Aussie WECer had turned up on their doorstep! We hopped in their car, picked up my family and enjoyed a nice weekend together. We went on to Ghana to begin our work, greatly encouraged and wonderfully assured that as we faced the years ahead, God and His promises are absolutely dependable.

Graham Bee with his wife Marj, from South Australia, joined WEC in 1969 and served first in Ghana and then in leadership roles in Australia. After Marj's death he married Meryl, and they now continue in an advisory and teaching role.

More than Father or Mother

Byung Kook Yoo
South Korea, 2001

Mr. Yoo! It's a disaster! Our papers are all gone!"

"What? What do you mean, your papers are all gone?"

"The chief professor destroyed all the documents for our application! What will we do now?"

Months before, I had met Jihong and Sunmi. Jihong was a medical professor at the top university in Korea. The couple shared with me their calling from God for missions and instantly decided to begin the process to join WEC. Generally candidates spend a month or two filling out the forms and undergoing required medical and psychological check-ups. When this enthusiastic couple kept silent for months, I phoned Jihong to remind him of the due date for turning in the completed application.

His response was beyond my wildest imagination. Jihong explained to me that he and his wife had nearly completed their documents when one day he left all the papers on the desk in his office. On his return from a meeting, the pile of documents had disappeared. He found out that his superior, the chief professor, had broken into the office and taken the papers away.

"Why would the chief professor do this to you? Why is he not returning them to you?" I asked, puzzled.

Jihong explained that when he and Sunmi decided to join WEC after meeting with me, he immediately told his father they had dedicated themselves to mission work, obeying what God wanted them to do. In the beginning, his father did not take this seriously, but as time went by, he noticed that they were not faltering. The father called Jihong in and scolded, "What on earth are you thinking? It's nonsense for you to be a missionary, sacrificing a promising future as a medical professor! Consider how lovingly I've supported you! You've had remarkable success! What a waste if you leave it behind and go into missions! It's nonsense! Only over my dead body!"

The father was determined. His opposition was much stronger than anyone expected. Knowing he wouldn't change his mind, Jihong said, "I must, Father. This is what God is calling me to do. I'll do what He asks me to do, Father, no matter what!"

After a sleepless night the father visited the university to see if the chief professor could possibly stop Jihong. "I don't understand what my son is doing, sir. He's giving up his career to become just a missionary! I can't live without him. Do you agree with him? If not, please stop him!"

When the father had gone home, the chief professor sent for Jihong. "Is it true you are resigning from the school to be a missionary? You cannot be serious."

"Yes, I am serious. I'll soon resign and begin missionary training abroad. I'll serve God where the gospel hasn't yet been spread."

The chief professor became furious. "You must be out of your mind! How could you think like that? Look at your Bible. It says you should respect your parents. Where is your respect for your parents when your father says no to your decision? Don't even dream of being a missionary! I won't accept your resignation! I won't let you go! What you've studied is important to the school as well as to me. Don't you see that I've chosen you to succeed me as chief professor? What a waste! What a waste!"

Jihong left, and the chief professor, afraid Jihong would not change his mind, thought, *I should do something to stop him.* He went into Jihong's office and took the application files. With the files on his lap, he sat down on a bench near the university pond. He took one page and burned it. "I must stop him. It's ridiculous!" He kept burning pages until there were none left.

The next day when Jihong discovered the application papers were missing, he stormed into the chief professor's study and cried out, "Chief, please give the files back to me!"

"What files? I don't know what you are talking about."

"I know you took my files, please give them back. I must submit them to the immigration department today."

"I know nothing about your files."

"Sir, why are you doing this to me? You can't stop me by hiding my files. I'll go no matter what, sir."

The quarrel became bitter. Worn out by Jihong's persistent questioning, the chief professor finally confessed, "I did take them, but I don't have them. Give up! I burned them all."

Confused, Jihong called me. I too was confused, not knowing what to say. This opposition was far beyond what I had expected. Jihong needed to check his calling again. So I asked, "Are you really sure God is calling you to serve cross-culturally?"

"Yes, I am. God is calling us for cross-cultural ministry." His answer was sharp and clear.

"Okay. Forget about the lost files. We'll do everything again."

Jihong and Sunmi redid all the paperwork for joining WEC Korea. They requested all the documents for their visa applications again. Finally the application was complete, and the visa files were handed in to the immigration department. Upon receiving their visas, Jihong immediately booked plane tickets.

Two or three hours after Jihong informed me of their flight schedule for overseas training, he ran into my office with a pale face. "Byung Kook, my father took my children away! He disappeared with my children! As far as I know, he won't come back till I give it up," sighed Jihong. "What shall I do, Byung Kook?" His voice trembled with shock.

I've seen many candidates face resistance from family members, but this level of opposition beat them all. I couldn't find any words of hope for Jihong, because I was also beginning to get a bit discouraged. I felt I was in the middle of a spiritual battle. I decided it was time to ask the question again.

"Jihong, are you really sure of His calling for missions? Do you really want to go for the training after all this opposition?"

Even before I finished asking my questions, Jihong answered with assurance, "Yes, we are! We will! We have to! If we stop here due to this opposition, we will never take any step to be missionaries now or in the future."

His clear answer seemed to help win the spiritual war. I said, "Then you should go. Take the flight and leave tomorrow as scheduled."

"What about my children?"

"Don't worry. I will surely find them and bring them to you." I myself was surprised at my answer.

"Thank you! We will take the flight with your word of promise for our children." They went off to prepare.

I began to have doubts about my promise to Jihong and his wife. "What have I done? Who am I to make such a promise? How can I find the children when even the parents can't? If I do find them, how could I snatch them from the grandfather?"

I thought about all that had happened. I didn't understand the couple saying they would leave their children behind while they went abroad for training. I didn't understand myself saying I would find and bring the children back to their parents. "Lord, what are we doing?"

A chill when down my spine as I thought, *What if the grandfather loses his temper and takes it out on the children?*

Then the phone rang. "Hello, Byung Kook speaking."

"Hello, Byung Kook. This is Jihong's father."

"Oh. Hello."

"Byung Kook, you have to help me. Please stop my son! He is my life. I can't continue living if he leaves me. I won't let him go! I can't let him die!"

I could tell he was crying from the sound of his voice. Tears welled up in my eyes. Jihong's father reminded me of my own father grieving over my departure when I left for Africa.

"Byung Kook, are you there?"

I tried to reason with him. "Sir, I'm sorry for you. But think about this—your son is not a child. He has decided to live for the poor. He will not make lots of money, but his service will benefit people who otherwise could never dream of having proper medical treatment. Imagine the many sick and poor people who will thank your son for his help. He will definitely be working as a doctor. He will be a glory not only to God, but also to your family. Sir, let them go and serve God with what they have."

"What glory? I don't want glory. I want my son! Please stop him!"

"Sir, I have no power to stop them. They said they will take the flight even without the children. They are that determined."

"I don't understand them. Where is their filial piety? How can they do this to me?"

With a lifeless voice, he spoke his last words to me. I understood the heartbreak and pain of non-Christian parents seeing their children leave for a far-off country after giving up the world's security and honor. I could only pray, "Lord, give them your heavenly comfort."

Around midnight, Jihong's father came home with his grandchildren. He finally accepted the decision his son and daughter-in-law had made, knowing nothing could stop them. Jihong and Sunmi stayed one more week with their parents and then moved on to their missionary training.

"Anyone who loves father or mother more than me is not worthy of me" (Matt. 10:37).

Byung Kook and Bo in Yoo joined WEC in 1986 and served in Gambia, West Africa for ten years until they were asked to start the WEC base in South Korea. After pioneering this work for eleven years and seeing many Koreans join WEC, they became directors for international mobilization. They have three daughters.

He Tests Our Level of Commitment

Bruce & Annette Rattray
Kalimantan, Indonesia, 1983

Sacrifice? What sacrifice?

People have said to me, "You have sacrificed so much to follow the call of God to Kalimantan." I would have to reply, "Like what?"

He who offered the supreme sacrifice, and laid down the principle of life out of death for His followers, on one occasion said, "My food is to do the will of Him who sent me and to finish his work." Paul's attitude to his former attainments was that they were of as much value as garbage when compared to the experience of Christ's fellowship.

Once there is a total commitment to do the will of God as a rule of life, there are no more conflicts. Conflicts only come when there is an incomplete commitment, an uncrucified, self-assertive will or a clouded relationship with the Lord.

Of course, to bear the cross He has given us is no picnic, nor is it enjoyable when He tests our level of commitment.

It was 1983 and Annette and I, along with our only child Paul, had been in Kalimantan for nearly four years when the Lord chose to test our level of commitment. We both longed for another child, making frequent and earnest entreaty of our Father to this end. He heard and answered, so with expectation and joy we began to await the birth of our second child.

Labor Pains

When Annette had carried the little one for some six months, we embarked on a strange and eventful boat journey to the interior of the Upper Ketungau area. With Annette, Paul and myself were a Dayak evangelist and his family, a Timorese evangelist and our Dayak house girl.

Toward night on the first day, Annette complained of labor pains, which increased the next day. As we sought the Lord about this, His answer was, "Do not ask for the life of the child." The climax came on the third morning at a remote village church as I prepared to leave Annette to speak at the service.

"Let's sing a hymn together before you go," she said. God spoke to us very clearly as we sang, "He knows the way He taketh and I will walk with Him."[7] We both knew that we were bidding farewell to the child we had so eagerly awaited.

The Power of Praise

On the short walk to the service, I sought the Lord for His message to the people. "Preach on the power of praise from Second Chronicles 20:22" was His word to me.

At a time like this? I thought. However, in obedience and with much liberty, I gave His word.

When I arrived back at the boat, Annette asked, "What did you speak on?"

"If I gave you one hundred tries, you would never guess," I replied.

"You spoke on the power of praise from Second Chronicles 20," she said, "for from the moment you left the boat until your return, the Lord has ministered to me from that passage."

Then the Lord whispered ever so gently to us, "You can ask for the life of the child now; I was testing your level of commitment!" Slowly the contractions ceased.

His Presence

Sacrifice? We didn't think so; there was such a sweet sense of His presence through the whole experience. We only know that our lives and ministry were immeasurably enriched through it.

We interpreted the experience as the "death/life" principle of the corn of wheat dying that it might produce a much greater harvest, but honestly did not feel that we would call it sacrifice.

Three months later God gave us a lovely boy, Simon.

Taken from WEC Australian Magazine, 1983

Bruce and Annette Rattray came from Australia and heard the call of God to serve in West Kalimantan, Indonesia. From 1967 to 2000 they planted churches and trained leaders. Bruce died in 2002.

Something's Wrong with His Arms and Legs

Joann Young
Middle East and United Kingdom, 1960

*T*here's something wrong with his arms and legs, isn't there?"
I asked tearfully. My husband was sitting by my bed. Although I had been anesthetized for the birth and was only half-
awake, I knew all was not well with our newborn son.

"Yes, all of his limbs are affected, but he has the sweetest wee
face," Harry replied.

As if a soft ray of sunshine fell on my sadness, I felt the
warmth of Harry's welcome for his firstborn as a dearly beloved
son, despite the disabilities.

When the nurse first brought baby Terry to me, I saw the
truth. His little arms were short, with no elbows or hands, only
stubs. He had no leg on one side and a twisted one on the other. His limbs were bent or missing, but his face was round and
handsome, and his body perfectly shaped. I loved him unasham-
edly from that moment.

At the same time my heart ached for him. What lay ahead?
This was not a child with ordinary prospects. Somehow, though,
over and in us we sensed the powerful presence and grace of a
loving heavenly Father. He had not forgotten us in this "trial."
Though we could only see a day at a time, He had plans and
purposes He would unfold.

Harry and I were on our first time home from serving our
Lord in Lebanon, where we had met and married. This home
leave meant meeting each other's parents and families in Ireland and in America, where Terry was born. We could see no

way of continuing our calling. We wondered if our first term of language learning and getting to know the people had been in vain.

We followed up on several leads for places where we might get help for Terry. Some doctors shook their heads. Others kindly suggested we leave Terry in the care of others. They meant well, but nothing could induce us to part with our son.

One of our supporting churches was located in Detroit, Michigan. Friends there told us of a hospital that catered to child amputees. From our first visit, we were overwhelmed. The staff, many of them Christians, had enthusiasm that was contagious. Their proposals for what could be done for Terry surprised and delighted us. When they found out we were Christian workers, they started outlining a program whereby we could go again to the Middle East and take Terry with us. The plan was to return in three years, when Terry would be old enough to be fitted with artificial legs.

We talked with our pastor. What seemed feasible in one sense seemed foolish in another. To take a child as handicapped as Terry far from home, to subject him to travel and to curious stares, was surely a desperately rash proposal. Would it demonstrate courage or foolhardiness? As we prayed together, we found the indefinable awareness of God's leading. We could step out and trust Him to guide us in what was an unknown path. The church never tried to stop us or make us reconsider, but stood behind us, supported us and, with great warmth of faith, encouraged us forward.

Harry, once his mind was made up, was not troubled by misgivings. I, on the other hand, pondered how I would face the questioning and probing of friends and neighbors in another culture. Going back to our first field location would have been less foreboding, but we were going to a completely new country to be part of a small medical team in the Buraimi Oasis in Al

Ain in the United Arab Emirates. In those days the area was a primitive, out-of-the-way place where amenities were basic, and the wealth created by oil had yet to come.

I pleaded with God to give me a word to steady me and enable me to embrace with calm the coming move. A verse from John 11 caught my attention: "If you will believe you will see the glory of God." God, in His goodness, reassured my heart.

Later, we were overseas on our way to the Gulf when a dear local woman came up to me and said, "This boy will one day have a tent of his own, and people will come to him for his wisdom."

When we left the States in February 1961, Terry was ten months old. Questions were asked, and superstitions surfaced, but as Terry grew and could talk, laugh and sing, he gained a measure of acceptance. We had five other children while we lived in the Emirates. This big family of four boys and two girls gave Terry even more credibility. When we returned after Terry was fitted with legs, the surprise and delight of our friends and neighbors was obvious.

The Young family in the 1960s

By this time we were living in Dubai, the first resident Christian workers in that sheikhdom. We had *carte blanche* permission from the sheikh to live and move among the people. We didn't know it at the time, but we had a ten-year window in which to take advantage of this liberty. As Harry walked the market places and sat with the men in the evenings by their courtyard fires, he found them full of questions. Conversation easily and naturally turned to religion, and people listened with interest. A man who knew some English attached himself to Harry and to us as a family, opening doors to our witness. And with an open home, all kinds of people came to us.

Some of the foreign business people were Christians and urged Harry to start a meeting. After a shaky start this prospered. One couple had a large rooftop room where we met. There was a British army and RAF base nearby, where an influential Christian major would round up men and bring them to our meeting. Although other expatriates attended, none of the locals did, except when we had our Christmas-carol service in an outdoor courtyard, with festive lights and joyful singing.

Knowing Terry would need many changes of prostheses during his teenage years, we moved to Britain when he was ten years old. We settled in Birmingham and joined three Australians in a new venture of communicating the gospel to immigrants in communities in the Midlands.

One day, about four years after we came to Britain, Harry got a call from a British businessman. He said, "You don't know me, Harry, but I've just returned from Dubai, where I worshiped at the Dubai Christian Assembly. I want you to know that seven other groups have grown out of the original one!"

And the prophecy that Terry would "have a tent of his own and people will come to him for wisdom"? Words of prophecy were not common in those days, and I don't know what I actually thought at the time, but I did think enough of it to write of the incident in a letter to my mother. (I would have forgotten about it completely except my mother saved all my letters and years later gave them to me—a diary she had preserved for me at a time when I was unable to keep one.)

When I was reminded of those words spoken by a local woman so many years ago, I couldn't but marvel at how the prophecy had been fulfilled. Terry went on to grammar school and to Birmingham University, graduating with a PhD in Physics. For sixteen years he worked as a research scientist for Marconi, traveling the world lecturing and giving seminars. Today Terry is a professor at Brunel University, Uxbridge, with a chair in healthcare systems. He is married to Danielle, and they have three sons.

Joann Young from America, and her Irish husband Harry, served many years in the Middle East before moving to the UK where they joined a team working among immigrants. The team later changed its name to Neighbors Worldwide, reflecting the changes in the status of the local population.

6

Reaching People

But you are a chosen people, a royal priesthood, a holy nation, a people belonging to God, that you may declare the praises of him who has called you out of darkness into his wonderful light.

1 Peter 2:9

As we lift Jesus higher, the light is thrown wider.

Jenny Carter

O let us not rust out—let us not glide through the world and then slip quietly out, without having even blown the trumpet loud and long for our blessed Redeemer. At the very least let us see to it that the devil holds a thanksgiving service in hell, when he gets the news of our departure from the field of battle.

C.T. Studd

The Village in the Valley
Elizabeth
Central Asia, 2010

Our language teacher told us about her home in a high mountain valley in Central Asia. For a long time the people there had little contact with the outside world, and city dwellers called them "the wild ones." The summers were lovely with flowers and wide green pastures, but the long, hard winters held temperatures of forty below or colder.

After some time, the teacher invited some of us students to visit her family in the village where she was born. We brought with us much of the food we would need, including vegetables and, of course, lots of cookies and sweets, since few of these things were available in the mountains. We set off in a minibus that struggled up narrow, serpentine roads. Often the driver stopped to fill his water bottle from a mountain stream to try to cool the overheated engine. Our teacher entertained us with stories of cars going over the side of the cliff, sometimes due to carelessness, but once in a while out of revenge. The many rusty wrecks we could see below verified this.

Finally we saw the wide, high valley, framed by snow-covered mountains. Snow from an avalanche lay next to the road, but further down buttercups and forget-me-nots covered the green slopes.

Our teacher's older sister and her family received us with joy. Their table was laden with homemade bread, sour cream, jam and pieces of dough fried in oil. We talked about our families and home countries as we enjoyed the food together.

Next we visited the home of our teacher's stepmother. Her sixteen-year-old son was in the courtyard, a sheep with its legs bound together in front of him. After saying a blessing he slit the sheep's throat, and the stepmother collected the blood in a basin. With sure strokes the boy took the hide off and cut the sheep into pieces. The sisters took the intestines and washed them in a small irrigation channel, to be filled later with liver and other inner organs and rice.

The next day in another house another sheep gave its life. We tried to stop them, saying we were not used to eating so much meat. "We must!" Hospitality dictated this feasting.

After this first contact with the mountain village people, we began to pray regularly for them. How could we share the good news with our new friends? They had never heard that somebody paid for their release from the powers of darkness that for centuries seemed to have such a tight and uncontested rule over this area.

A friend and I decided to go to the village during our vacation in January to study language and culture for a week. Our driver, who brought us in the very old minibus over that icy mountain road, was aghast. "What, in winter, to this cold place! You don't even have a proper hat!" He took his own fur hat off and said, "Use this while you are there!"

We again stayed with the kind family of our teacher's sister. We slept in the living room. In the morning we sat around the low table in the one heated room. The grandfather was keeping the baby happy. The mother sat and drank tea with each member of the family. She taught us how to make dough and showed us the felt carpets her sister had made. One son, a policeman, taught me how to hold the broom properly when sweeping the living room.

The snow was almost a meter deep. The contents of the toilet were frozen and reached above the hole like a little mountain. When we opened the door at night, our hands nearly froze on the handle. Our hosts joked, "Can't you see, the weather got warm, only minus thirty, just for you!"

Someone brought up the idea of going sledding. The mother cut up an old plastic table cloth. Each one of us, including the sons and daughter-in-law, took a piece of it and went up the hill under a beautiful, starry sky.

The next day the mother had a brilliant idea. The family got the horse and sled out, borrowed a second horse and sled from relatives, and then we raced along the long straight road, again under a beautiful starry sky.

We had prayed a lot and tried to share with words, but mostly we were sharing our lives. How could we reach this village, still so isolated from the rest of the world?

We developed a plan for visiting, organizing cell groups, training leaders—but our team said: "No way! Too far, too dangerous, impossible for us! And you have other tasks to do." We did have our work in the capital, and that road did frighten me.

But I couldn't forget the mountain village people. Life was extremely difficult for them. The former collective farms had been closed and abandoned. How could the huge fields be cultivated when there was no tractor, no fuel, no seed? People saw no future, no hope; the only release was alcohol. Most of them resorted to this comfort. Even the babies were quieted with alcohol. Funerals were the social events. Several animals had to be slaughtered to feed the village after a death. People met to eat and exchange news.

We began to pray for the mountain valley in church. One Sunday, when first-time visitors introduced themselves, one was a lady from the mountain village. I invited her to our home. We talked for a long time, and she left the house with some good literature.

Later our church sent two young men as evangelists to the village. They stayed with our friend, the school teacher, and helped her build a little shack where they slept. But when they tried to share the good news, people beat them up and soon forced them to leave the village.

Later the teacher came to a three-day prayer seminar and was deeply impressed with what she saw and heard. So many of her own people group who followed Jesus were there! When I next visited in her home, she showed me a tiny corner behind the bedding she piled up every morning. "This is my altar!" she said. She had started praying for her village.

I don't know exactly when the teacher had put her trust in Jesus, but soon she shared all she knew with a friend who owned a little shop. The shopkeeper became a fervent evangelist. Many people who came to that shop, even from villages far away, heard the good news. If someone had a headache or other pain, the shopkeeper sat them down behind a curtain and prayed for them. She also opened her home to two other evangelists.

People came mainly after dark to hear what these young people had to tell them about God, who created heaven and earth—and who was interested in each one of them. "Through Jesus' death on the cross, you can be set free from the power of sin! He paid for you with His own life!"

They shared the message with people who were obviously oppressed and even tormented by Satan. They prayed with them for hours, drove out evil spirits in the name of Jesus, fasted and prayed again. And, step by step, a few people were moving toward freedom. The expression on their faces began to change. Fear was replaced by joy as they put their trust in Christ.

Then my husband and I, together with two other workers, were finally able to offer three-week English courses for schoolchildren in the village during their summer vacation. We made all the arrangements with the director of the school and had lots of lessons prepared. After loading provisions and bedding on top of a little jeep, off we went with great expectations.

The shopkeeper took us into her home. The two young evangelists were already staying there, as was her daughter, with a newborn baby and two older children. My husband and I were given the luxury of privacy: a little wooden shed in the court-yard.

Meeting the schoolchildren was a joy. They were eager to learn and practice English. Their English teacher sat in the classroom too, and was excited to watch our new teaching methods.

One evening, to our great surprise, the old van from our church arrived at our gate. The pastor and his family had brought a grandmother home to the village. A musician who had re-cently put his trust in Christ had come along and brought his accordion. Soon everybody was sitting on the floor, worshiping the Lord and sharing the Word with the little group of believers, who had been called together in a hurry.

That same night another driver announced his arrival at the gate with loud honking. The son-in-law came to see his wife and kids and new baby. He and another son-in-law who came with him were not happy to find the house of their father-in-law full of foreigners, those traitors who led people astray. They got very angry, yelled at the guests and with their fists drove them out of the house. They were half drunk and didn't listen to the explanations of their father-in-law and the calming words of others.

The pastor and his wife took their children and ran back to their van. The others quickly followed. A window shattered, then the van slowly started, backed up and drove off through the open gate. The road through the mountains was already closed for the night, so they had to sleep at an altitude of four thousand meters in the old van with the broken window.

In the meantime the shopkeeper's family tried to calm down the more aggressive son-in-law. But he was too angry and went after one of the evangelists. "It's all because of you! I'm going to kill you!" we heard him yelling behind his truck. The evangelist went silent. Later, the son-in-law, still shouting at his wife and children, left for the house of another relative.

Would he return? What would he do? We sat in the dark behind the fireplace. Suddenly we heard a hushed voice: "Quickly, you must go away before he comes back!" Our teacher was at the back door. We grabbed our most important luggage and hurried out into the dark.

Quietly we moved along the wall of the abandoned collective farm, rushed along behind the local mosque, through the shadows of the school building and then over the river, all the way to the teacher's house. Her husband wasn't too happy about this invasion well after midnight. Their little girl began to cry. Finally we were all lined up on the floor of the little living room, the evangelist who had been beaten groaning in pain. Dry mud and straw trickled from the ceiling.

"Lord, what's the meaning of this? What do you want us to do?"

We decided to get up early, try to get back to the shopkeeper's house, pick up necessary items for teaching and be at the school at eight in the morning as usual. Of course, word of last night's events would have already reached the farthest mountain dwellings. As soon as a car could be found, the badly injured evangelist had to be taken for treatment and safety.

When we got back from English teaching, the shopkeeper's house was deserted. Our little hut was still there, not burned down as we had feared. We'd just started resting when someone began banging at the door and demanding that we open it at once. The older son-in-law stood there yelling, "Where is the evangelist? I'm going to kill him!"

Honestly, we didn't know where he was at that moment. The son-in-law was furious. We tried to overcome our fear and talked with him. Then we heard a voice in the street: "Fish for sale, buy fresh fish!" That was a good excuse to escape. We surely needed fresh fish!

"I'd like to get some fish too but I don't have any money," said the son-in-law. My husband remembered Jesus' advice and gathered up all his courage: "OK, let's go together. I'll buy you some fish!" The son-in-law calmed down, and they left together.

We had hoped that children who came to our classes would invite us to their homes, but that happened only once. Even though the children enjoyed the lessons, the adults were fearful and distrustful. We didn't know they had been ordered not to talk to us.

Then the village mayor came with the school director to our lessons. We were singing "He's got the whole world in His hands."

"You cannot teach here anymore! You have to stop right now!" the mayor demanded.

"But why? We have all the necessary papers. The children like the lessons and are learning a lot." No explanation would do, so we had to pack up our books and leave the classroom.

"If we got permission from the Minister of Education, could we continue to teach?" The mayor agreed; in that case we could of course continue to teach. He knew it was impossible for us to get such permission. What he didn't know was that we knew the Minister of Education personally and hoped she would help us out. What we didn't know was that there was turmoil in the government, and the minister we knew had just been replaced.

We waited for permission, which never came. Every morning we went to the school to talk to the few kids who gathered outside the gates. We practiced English and played games with them. We forced ourselves to walk the streets every day and greet people in a friendly way so that they might see we were not as dangerous as others had made them believe. But as soon as we spoke to anyone, one of the Muslim activists, who went from house to house to bring people back to Islam, would come and involve the person in a long talk. These young people seemed to wait at every street corner.

Another week passed. A rumor circulated that the highest Muslim leader would come on Saturday with a delegation from the capital. There would be a big meeting because of that "sect" who hadd left the true way. The community should get rid of them.

The delegation arrived as planned and went to the meeting place. Would the believers be called in? Rain was pouring so hard no one dared leave his or her house. The fierce storm was unusual for this time of year. We huddled together in our hut, praying for the young believers in this severe test.

Watching the black clouds, lightning and thunder, we remembered Psalm 18:

In my distress I called to the Lord;
I cried to my God for help.
From his temple he heard my voice;
my cry came before him, into his ears. . . .
The Lord thundered from heaven. . . .
He shot his arrows and scattered the enemies,
great bolts of lightning and routed them. . . .
He reached down from on high and . . . rescued me.

(18:6, 13–14, 16–17)

Later we heard that the uncle of the angry man who wanted to kill the evangelist had been struck and killed by lightning outside his house.

In the afternoon as the rain continued to pour down, I sneaked out of the courtyard to go to another believer's home. The mother, her daughters and a friend were huddled fearfully in a corner. Why were we so fearful? Aren't we told these things will be part of the lives of Jesus' followers?

> Do not be surprised at the painful trial you are suffering, as though something strange were happening to you. But rejoice that you participate in the sufferings of Christ. . . . If you are insulted because of the name of Christ [which was happening daily] you are blessed. (1 Pet. 4:12–14)

The more we read about God's perspective on suffering, the more we began to relax. This is normal. We don't have to be afraid. We don't have to be ashamed. We can continue to do good and even love our enemies. The atmosphere in the small, dark room changed as the heaviness and fear lifted.

That afternoon when the shopkeeper came home, she told us she had been taken to stand before the delegation from the capital. "They took me in my old clothes and galoshes." For many hours she was interrogated, accused and threatened. "They asked me many things. I told them I'm a brand new Christian. I do not yet know God's Word well. But I know that you must repent and believe in Jesus if you want to go to heaven! The Holy Spirit gave me the answers, just as He has promised!"

The rain stopped. A beautiful rainbow hung above the valley. We ran outside, down the hill to the river and praised God, singing songs and laughing.

One day we went for a hike. We couldn't teach anymore, but we would stay through the end of the three planned weeks, until the driver who had brought us would come to fetch us again.

We walked a long way. How glad we were when a farmer and his wife stopped their tractor and let us ride for a while on the wagon filled with cow dung. After we jumped down we thanked them and said, "God bless you and your family!"

(Years later, visiting the village again, we met a new woman in the church meeting. "Oh, I know you," she said, "you rode with us on the dung wagon, and you blessed us! God has blessed us since!")

On the way back from that hike, we stopped the only car going our way. It was very kind of the driver to take the four of us in his small vehicle. He asked us many questions about God and our faith. He asked for a Bible. We didn't know, but our friends told us later he was the local mullah. What? We'd said we would give a Bible to the mullah? Wouldn't he use it to fight the Christians? Not many Bibles were available. Better to give them to seekers.

Months later we went back to the village to teach a course about God's covenant with His people. We didn't know we needed to get permission to do so. Toward the end of the week, we were taken to the police station. But when the policeman heard that the great God wants us to be covenanted to Him, he was touched. He sent us to the village hall, where everything could be settled. At the hall a man who seemed to know us came over. "Where is the Bible?" he asked. It was the mullah, and how glad we were that this time we could immediately give him what he wanted.

The few believers started to meet together to worship God, study His Word and pray. They didn't have a leader. They were only seven or eight people, struggling, some with husbands who couldn't stop drinking in spite of their desire to be reconciled with God. There was opposition from the village people and the religious leaders. "You have sold your faith! Traitors! *Baptists!*" (This was about the worst thing that could be said about anyone).

The shopkeeper's husband had put his trust in the Lord Jesus too. When he was tormented by evil spirits, he put the Bible on his chest and called out to the Lord. He became a diligent student of the Word. But he was still addicted to the bottle.

The whole valley was watching. "Can the God of the Christians really set him free from alcohol?" He battled for a long time. He wanted to be free, but fell back again and again. All his colleagues drank. He loved the Lord. He loved to study His Word. He was free for a while. We rejoiced.

We drove up the mountain another time. Our driver found out whom we were visiting and said, "He is drinking again!" It was true. The shopkeeper's husband had fallen again. But God didn't give up and finally set him completely free!

One of the village women had often been called to help cook at funerals. She was a heavy drinker. Nobody thought her life could ever change. But she met the Lord and, with much prayer, slowly became more and more free from alcohol. Her life changed. When the community realized that she too had become part of the "sect," they didn't allow her to take part in the funerals anymore. She became an outcast.

Still only a handful of people meet regularly in that village. They have gone through much persecution—slander, threats, personal weaknesses and attacks from the powers of darkness. They witness quietly and they pray. Early in the morning they meet to pray for their neighbors and the other villages in the area. Many people have heard the good news, but are afraid to be exposed as "Baptists," afraid they might lose too much.

Our brothers and sisters are diligently studying the Word and doing Bible courses by correspondence. A worker from our church visits them regularly. Their vision is to see in every village in the valley a group of people following the Lord Jesus, worshiping Him and reaching out to others who need Him so desperately.

Some of this small group recently visited our church in the capital city. What a joy to see those faces, once distorted by the powers of darkness, now beaming with the joy of the Lord!

7

First Encounters

It has always been my ambition to preach the gospel where Christ was not known, so that I would not be building on someone else's foundation.

Romans 15:20

Believing that further delay would be sinful, some of God's insignificants, nobodies in particular, conscious of our own impotence and ignorance, but trusting in our omnipotent God to bring it to pass according to his Word, have decided in simple lines, according to the Book of God, to make a definite attempt to make the evangelization of the whole world an accomplished fact.

C.T. Studd

There is no place here for discouragement or fear.

Rosa Ribeiro

A Raid in the Devil's Den

C.T. Studd
Congo, 1918

C.T. Studd

*O*n trek in the Congo: Another start found me after half a mile with a damaged valve and a puncture on my bicycle, so back I went to the rest house, and sent back a man to Niangara for tubing and patches and rubber solution. No more cycling that day, and it was a long trek. We only got into Chief Aboramasi's village at dark, and all were pretty tired. We only thought of food and bed.

But God had something better in store than bed in a hurry. I had some rice. The chief came and his people. We sang hymns, and then worshiped, and the chief asked if he might remain to worship with us; we were in the open with a bright fire and moonlight. The chief and people were so interested and appreciative; they stayed talking of the things of God and themselves. We forgot our weariness in the joy of telling of Jesus, and finding Him appreciated, so that when at last all had returned to their homes, and I could have a quiet time in my

Chief, wife and troops

blankets, the hour was half past one in the morning, yet I felt as happy as anything.

The chief had said he would call all his people together to hear, if I would stay longer, so I decided to do so, and to give them a slide show in the evening.

The next day the chief, and his brother chief, and crowds came and occupied my house all day, and one could not but remember those Jews spending the whole day with Paul, speaking the things of the kingdom of God. We now have some simple hymns to easy tunes, the hymns containing the main facts of the gospel. We spoke and sang all day.

Taken from WEC UK Magazine, 1918

"I Want God"
Mary Harrison
Congo, 1930

When my husband went out on his motorcycle to visit various places in the Congo, I joined him. While he was holding a meeting, I had a good time walking. At one place in the forest, quite a number of folk were working in a cotton garden. I spoke to them, but they were too busy, they said, so I called all those who were Christians, and we had an open-air meeting.

Two women who had put me off came near to hear the singing. Later I spoke to

Jack Harrison

them again, and one said, "If I follow God's road I will have to be holy." I agreed with her, and after some more teaching, she said she would believe. Then another woman believed.

We went to another place, and again, while my husband taught the people, I went scouting. I met a man coming along the road and when I asked if he was a Christian, he said, "No, I am a follower of our old religion, but there is no reason why I am not a Christian; I know your words are true."

So I said, "Well, come along with me. My husband is just going to have a service," and so I walked with him to where Jack was sharing the good news about Jesus.

On another occasion in 1930 one of the women at the mission center said she would like to come if I went out teaching, and I happily took her with me. One old, old woman with badly leprous feet was very surprised when I asked to shake hands with her. She was cleaning in her garden. At first she did not seem to understand why we had come. But after talking to her simply, she said she would pray with me, so I took her hand in mine while I prayed. Then we passed on and met another woman and a boy who wanted to turn their hearts to God.

But I think the best time we had was with a man and his wife who were working in their cotton garden. At first they said they would believe another day. They kept on saying this, and I was ready to leave them when, quite suddenly, the man said, "I will believe now; pray for us."

So there and then I prayed, and the joy of salvation got the man at once. He kept on saying, "I want God, I want God," and after I had gone some distance I turned round, and still could hear him shout, "I want God." We pray that he may get truly all he wants and that both he and his wife have been born from above.

It is impossible for me to make you understand how terrific the need is. Again and again I think to myself, if we only had about fifty more workers we could really tackle the evangelization of this part of Africa. People all over are clamoring to be taught. If young people only tasted the joy of speaking to these people, they could not rest at home.

Taken from WEC UK Magazine, 1930

Mary Harrison went to the Congo in 1923 and married Jack, who became the leader of the work on the death of C.T. Studd in 1931. After Jack's sudden passing fourteen years later, Mary continued to serve the Congolese people until the horrific days of the Simba revolt in 1964.

Paulo's Faith and Courage
Lily Gaynor
Guinea-Bissau, 2010

I want to enter God's way," said the young man who came to my house late one night in 1961.

"Why?" I asked.

"Because I want to have my sins forgiven and go to heaven when I die," he replied.

His name was Paulo, and he was sixteen years old. He looked so shy and insignificant that I had misgivings about him standing up to the persecution that would surely follow. We told him what had happened to four others, who, on different occasions had entered "God's way" and how each one had not been able to follow through. Paulo was quite determined, reasoning that even if they killed him, he

Lily Gaynor

had nothing to lose and everything to gain. We knelt together, and he prayed his first prayer, asking the Lord to forgive his sins and come into his heart.

Threats of Death

Two days later he came back to us, very frightened. He had told his family they were not to make any more sacrifices for him and that in the future he wanted to be excused from all ceremonies. What followed was even worse than we anticipated. The elders of his Papel village gathered together, counseling and threatening him (for a young man to refuse the counsel of the old men is unheard of). When Paulo stood firm, his relations gathered from far and near, wailing a funeral for him. His elder brother had gone to the fields that morning after threatening him that if he had not left "God's way" when he returned that night, he would beat him until he either recanted or died. His uncle too threatened to kill him and then take his own life. Paulo left the wailing, excited mob and ran to us.

Victory Gained

What could we do? We felt we dare not keep him at the mission center. After praying for him and trying to encourage him, we accompanied him to his home, hardly knowing what to expect. As we entered the compound, the Lord seemed to put a hush on them all, and they gathered round to hear what Domingos, a local evangelist, had to say. He preached powerfully for about an hour while they stood motionless, hardly even noticing the mosquitoes. When he finished, Paulo quietly but firmly confessed his new-found faith and told of the joy the Lord had given him even in the midst of the persecution. He went on to say that God had told him to obey and respect his parents, and he wanted to stay with them and work for them until they too accepted Christ as their Lord and Savior. A victory had been gained.

Now all eyes were on him to see if the spirits of the tribe would have their revenge. Paulo was the first convert in Biombo who had made such a clear testimony. We felt if he continued, he might well be the key that opened the door to the Papel tribe.

Significant Sequel

Paulo's story stands out in Papel church history. A week or two after his conversion, he came up our path dragging a homemade toy car on a string. My heart sank. *He's only a child* I thought. *He'll never stand all the pressures.* I was wrong. He did stand. Later I taught him to read, and he helped with translation of the New Testament. He also assisted in the little clinic we ran where his vibrant testimony, together with the miracles of healing the Lord gave us, laid the foundation of the Papel Church.

Eventually Paulo was conscripted into the Portuguese army in the fight for independence. There was no possibility of conscientious objection, but he trusted the Lord that he would never have to kill. God answered prayer, and he was taught to drive and spent all his time driving jeeps, never firing a shot.

Later he settled in the capital city and, together with others, won many Papels to faith in Christ. Today (October 2010) he is still a pastor and an active member of the church council.

The church in Biombo has grown through the years, reaching out with several daughter churches. From a tiny beginning there are now more than two thousand Papel believers in Guinea-Bissau, plus a few in Portugal.

Lily Gaynor from UK worked in Guinea-Bissau for thirty-seven years. She was a nurse and served in the Biombo Clinic. She also worked on translation of the Papel New Testament.

Secret Visit

Kevin Thomas
Nepal, 1970s

Nicodemus . . . Nicodemus . . . The name kept flitting into my mind as I listened to the man's story.

It was nearly nine in the evening on a dark night, not long after we settled here. Our visitor was short and stocky, even for a Nepali, and about forty years old. He was evidently quite poor, although he was a Brahmin by caste.

He told how he had been drawn into contact with believers by hearing sweet singing as he passed by their meeting place one day in far-off Shillong, Assam. They led him to faith in the Lord Jesus Christ.

"Outwardly I am still a Hindu," he told me, "but in fact I am the Lord's. I am praying that my wife will be saved, so we can all be baptized together. My wife used to rip up any good books I brought home and would not allow a Bible in the house. But now she doesn't mind."

"Isn't it strange how he always manages to come at the most awkward times?" we said to ourselves as he came again and again for prayers and fellowship, following that first visit. But the Lord blessed those times to our mutual benefit.

"I want to come and live here, near believers, so my family can become 'convinced,'" he said, as he prepared to leave for his village deep in the Nepali jungle—home of tigers, leopards and elephants. "But first I must go to my village for a year and try to raise enough capital to start a tea shop and small business here." We took the little family in our borrowed Land Rover with their goods and chattels to within three miles of their village on a jungle road, and they walked the rest of the way.

"Some disease epidemic came and killed the buffaloes of our village," he told us some months later when he came in for supplies, "except mine. It became very sick, but I prayed and God saved it. When the children cried for milk, I prayed, and my buffalo even started giving milk again, for of course it had gone dry when it fell sick."

Their village is extremely poor. During one hot summer the people existed for weeks on roots and leaves from the jungle. When their new baby developed fever and running ears, this man taught his relatives to pray instead of sacrificing their precious few chickens to the demons.

"You were right in what you told me last year," he testified. "God has indeed made my faith stronger by means of difficulties."

Nepali villagers carrying grain

Taken from WEC Australian Magazine, 1971

Kevin and Patsy Thomas from Australia worked in India and Nepal in the 1970s.

A Satanic Scene

Rose Robertson
Burkina Faso, West Africa, 1939

At last I was in Bourum-Bourum, the heart of Lobiland. The devil gave me a real welcome in the form of a death ritual. It was Satanic and sent cold shivers down my spine. Jack and I went over to the marketplace, where honor was being paid to the dead man. Never shall I forget the experience.

As we drew near, one of the local people told us to go over and see the corpse. We went. But I must confess that I was totally unprepared for what I saw. The dead man was sitting bolt upright—tied to a tree. He might have been alive, had we not known this was really the corpse. Three women sat before him, wailing and talking to him as if he had been alive—yet occasionally smacking him to keep the flies off!

While we stood there, the final homage was paid. Three chief men of the village filled their mouths with red betel juice. This they spat over him, each taking his turn. As he was considered to be a brave man (having killed someone), a hen and another bird were killed, the blood being allowed to fall on his chest. Had we not had the knowledge that we are under Christ's precious blood, we could have closed our eyes and imagined that we were in hell! At least that was how I felt as I watched this sad but real scene of Lobi life and death.

We are in the midst of a tough tribe! The Lobis have to fight against hard odds in order to live. For six to eight months of the year, rain is not seen; everywhere is parched and burnt. Their "staff of life" is millet, a kind of brown corn, which is so difficult to cultivate that it takes all their time during the wet months. As a result, they have a tough life, which creates a typically hard and independent character.

Yesterday a woman came carrying a four-year-old boy. He was paralyzed from the waist down. Her face wore a look of pity as she asked if we could do anything. At first I thought treatment would be useless, and she said to me, "What am I going to do with him? I shall throw him away." The mother knew what a fight it was for able-bodied folk to live, so her heart went out to her

little son. Every day now I am massaging the paralyzed legs with olive oil. If God heals this boy, which is our constant prayer, we know we will gain the hearts and confidence of this tribe. The medical work is a valuable and worthy means to an end.

Among the believers there is an old man, blind in one eye and also deaf. Formerly he was the noted witchdoctor and a very bad character. Four years ago he threw away his idols and was beaten for doing so. But our hearts are thrilled as we listen to him praying. He says, "The blood of goats is not good, nor the blood of sheep, only the blood of Jesus can cleanse from sin."

When a witch doctor has learned that truth, we are encouraged and say with assurance that God can and will save the Lobis.

Taken from WEC UK Magazine, 1939

Rose and Jack Robertson pioneered a mission to the Lobi people and founded a church there. Today (2010) the Lobi church has 10,000 believers whose lives show what God can do. The conditions for survival are still harsh, the power of the fetish and animistic ritual are real, but when Jesus is allowed to enter a life, the miracle is great to see—fear is gone, forgiveness is genuine, and a life of purity and freedom is the result.

The Glowing Testimony of Old Solomon

Mary Harrison
Congo, 1932

I went out for a weekend to a place called Bunzago. I had a great time. The drums of my ears actually tingled during the services, there was such a crowd packed into the little village church. I sang myself hoarse, but the folks were so bright and cheerful that it was a joy to go.

A white-haired old man had been named Solomon by Bwana (C.T. Studd), because he seemed to know such a lot about God and the Bible. He was always quick to answer any questions when the people gathered at Ibambi for the big weekends. I called to this old man and asked him how he first heard the gospel.

I can see him now standing in front of me, with a look of wonder in his big black eyes that I should want to know anything about him. He was wearing a tiny straw hat, with bark cloth round his loins, and had his books with him. "What is your real name?" I asked.

"Matuba," he replied.

"Tell me how you first heard the gospel," I said.

"I was a very bad man. I belonged to three witchcraft cults. One day I was ill, and the flesh on my body began to disappear. My body looked as if it was drying up. I had no strength and I could scarcely walk. My knees knocked together with weakness, and all my body shook. I was so ill my friends feared to have me near them. They cut me some palm fronds and laid me outside the house, and I slept there. Each day I used to hobble about to collect a few sticks, for I was cold at night.

"One of my relations from another village came to see me and told me to pray to God and repent, but I said, 'What good will repentance do to me? I am so ill.' Then your people sent a teacher to Bunzago's village, and one day, bit by bit, I crawled there. When the worshipers saw me coming, they were amazed. I repented of all my sins and prayed to God, and God gave me His salvation. Little by little, the flesh began to come back onto my body, and I began to feel stronger. I never had any medicine. God Himself healed me, and I have thrown all my sins away and just love Him. I had a desire to learn to read God's Book, and every day I came to school. I am an old man, but God helped me, and now I can read from God's Book and sing from the hymn book. I have only one desire: to love Jesus and serve Him, and not to sin any more. I want to go to heaven to be with Jesus."

By this time quite a few people had gathered to listen. My porters were waiting to take me back to Ibambi, but I said, "All shut your eyes, and we will pray." In that one-time heathen village, dark with sin and witchcraft, we lifted our hearts to God and gave thanks for this old man who had found the Light.

"Is it worth it?" people asked me at home. "A thousand times," I replied, for Matuba/Solomon one day will walk with Him in white. Truly there is glory in this work, and we are sorry for those who cannot be out here to share in it.

Taken from WEC UK Magazine, 1932

Mary Harrison went to the Congo in 1923 and married Jack, who became the leader of the work after C.T. Studd's death. After Jack's sudden passing fourteen years later, Mary continued to serve the Congolese people until the horrific events of the Simba revolt in 1964.

A Happy Ending
Birte Papenhausen
Mongolia, 2006

*E*veryone knows there is a good ending to every fairy tale. Only the central character is unaware of this, and has to go through all kinds of testings and sufferings until in the end we all breathe a sigh of relief and are able to smile again. Let me tell you about a fairy tale in my own life.

In Mongolia in the first decade of the third millennium, I, the main character, didn't know that my situation was going to turn dramatically bad or that it would finally take a turn for the better. All I knew was that I was exhausted. Weeks of intense work lay behind me. The last task, a youth camp, had just finished, and we were on our way home. I was hoping to tidy things up and then have a time of rest.

Instead, outraged parents entered my *yurt* (tent). They had been looking for their daughter since Friday and had found her with us! She had not told her (Buddhist) parents she was going to a Christian youth camp. A terrible struggle broke out. I sat in the midst of a Mongolian extended family, all yelling at me, reproaching me for kidnapping the girl and brainwashing her—threatening to go to the press, TV, police and provincial governor, assuring me that our aid organization and church were going to be examined and closed down, and I was going to be thrown out of the country.

I was in tears and worn out. When a young boy unknown to me later asked me whether it was I who had kidnapped that girl, I realized my reputation had been destroyed.

What could I do? Summertime had begun. Public life in Mongolia ceases during the summer months. Although tired and sad, I realized a life-long dream: I took lessons in archery.

Mongolian villagers.

After I started to become proficient, I enrolled for the province archery championships in July 2006, where the fairy tale took place. Surprisingly, I won the championship!

The provincial governor hung a medal around my neck; reporters from newspapers, radio and television asked me for interviews and reported on the foreign winner in Mongolian dress. People I didn't know came up to me in the marketplace, the post office and the streets to congratulate me and express their joy.

To me the archery medal does not symbolize victory in a sports championship; rather it is a wonderful demonstration that God took my side, fought for me and did not allow His child to be dragged through the mud. People "intended to harm me, but God intended it for good" (Genesis 50: 20).

Birte Papenhausen comes from Germany and has worked in Mongolia for more than ten years.

The Midnight Call
Eliki Drodrolagi
Chad, 2010

The mobile phone buzzed loudly on the table next to me. Looking at the time, I realized it was after midnight and lazily asked myself, "Who could be sending a message at this unearthly hour?" Staggering out of bed, I picked up the phone and read the text message, which to my surprise and amazement said, "Eliki, I want to be a Christian, can you help me?"

Coming from Fiji—a green island surrounded by water—to the semi-desert, parched land of Chad in Africa was a shock.

For twelve years my family and I worked in Abeché and Adré, in northeast Chad, in a church planting ministry. We learned the language and culture, and worked on building relationships with the people, who are normally quite hostile to the gospel. We were encouraged to see Muslims ask to study the Bible. But it was a greater joy to see these men believing in Jesus and meeting regularly to worship the living God.

In February 2009 we moved to the capital city to help strengthen team dynamics and help with church planting. In moving to N'djamena, we knew church planting would be a challenge because of the vastness of the city and the different lifestyle from the rural setting that was familiar to us. N'djamena is much bigger than Abeché and Adré; its population is two to three million. This cosmopolitan city has a modern lifestyle and a faster pace of life. People are more scattered. Meeting together regularly was quite difficult, as most people had to catch two to three taxis to reach their final destination.

I remember praying, "Lord you love the people, and I would love to see Your name glorified and worshiped in the lives of the people here in N'djamena. Show me how I should be moving forward in planting Your church." With peace in my heart, I continued my daily chores with an expectancy about what God was going to do.

Three months later at midnight my mobile phone buzzed. After I read the message, "Eliki, I want to become a Christian. Can you help me?" my mind woke up. I replied, "With pleasure I will help you. You can come tomorrow."

He quickly replied to my message, "I can't make it tomorrow. I will be coming to N'djamena on Wednesday."

"Great, I will see you on Wednesday afternoon."

"Inchallah [if God wills]," he replied. I waited eagerly for Wednesday afternoon to meet the midnight caller.

On Wednesday as the sun was sinking away and the call to prayer from the minaret was echoing through the city, I heard a knock on our front gate. By the gate stood a young man we had met previously. He was once one of my wife's faithful English students. He had moved to Abeché for further studies in the university a few years earlier. In Abeché I had read the Bible with him a few times. When he moved to N'djamena a year before to look for a job, he got involved in smuggling motorbikes across the border from Cameroon to earn a living.

I invited him in to sit with me on the veranda, then asked him, "Why do you want to become a Christian?"

"I went to Mongo to sell one of my motorbikes," he said. "During the night I had a dream. A man appeared to me as I was sitting by the river. He handed me a book and asked me to read a passage that says, 'So don't worry about what you eat, drink or wear. But seek first the kingdom of God and his righteousness and all these things shall be added unto you.'

"'I have already read this passage with Eliki,' I told the man. 'OK, then stand up and follow Me,' the man replied. I followed Him, and we walked across the river. The feeling was good as I followed Him. On the other side of the river was a big and bright mansion. I woke up thinking that it was all true, but to my disappointment I was still lying in my dry, dark mud-brick house. I knew that man was Jesus, and I would like to follow Him. So I sent you a message, not realizing it was midnight."

I had the privilege of sharing the gospel with the midnight caller and hearing him surrender and pledge to follow the Savior. He grew in his faith as he gave up worldly desires and developed a hunger for the Bible. God brought two other men who wanted to follow Jesus. By the end of the year, six men were meeting together regularly to study God's Word and pray.

In February 2010 three of them were baptized in N'djamena's Chari River.

God is sovereign. Over the years I have learned not to do things for God but to do things with Him. I don't have to be frustrated, running around trying to make things happen, but in prayer I can wait patiently for God to lead and guide.

Eliki and Lavenia felt God's call to leave their homes in Fiji, train in Australia and serve God in Chad, central Africa. They were there for over twenty years before returning to their own country in a mission mobilization role.

"Full Steam Ahead to the Heart of the Amazon!"[8]

David Phillips
Brazil, 2010

*A*n intriguing and currently popular book, *The Lost City of Z*, tells the tale of "generations of scientists and adventurers" who entered the vast Amazon rainforest in the area of the Xingu River searching for a fabled civilization reported to be hidden within the dense jungle.

In 1906 Colonel Percy Harrison Fawcett undertook his first South American expedition. After five further explorations and attempts to locate "Z," he was awarded a gold medal by the Royal Geographical Society in 1916. In 1925, on a trek up the Xingu River, one of the longest tributaries of the Amazon, he vanished.

He was not the only one. Believing there was immense treasure to be found, "For nearly a century, explorers have sacrificed everything, even their lives, to find the City of Z."[9]

But did you know that contemporary WEC team members braved the same biting flies and mosquitoes, tropical fevers, predatory animals, rushing rapids and poison arrows as the explorers, all because they wanted to take the treasure of Jesus to the lost peoples of the Amazon?

An exploratory trip up the Rio Negro in 1913 by Kenneth Grubb made C.T. Studd, founder of WEC, aware of the desperate spiritual need of Brazilian river dwellers and indigenous tribes being exploited by the booming rubber industry. A two-day prayer session in May 1923 convinced his colleagues in the UK that God's Word to them was Exodus 14:15: "Go forward" into the Amazon. Three WEC team members sailed for Brazil on June 12, 1923, aiming to begin evangelizing the whole of Amazonia, an area the size of half of Europe, with a population estimated at five million.

These pioneers began work in the interior of Maranhao, a coastal state, but soon trekked

Ticuna tribal markings

to the great tributaries of the Amazon, seeking Indian tribes. They endured not only hacking their way through impenetrable forests, but also shipwreck on the rivers and violent attacks, when they were beaten and left for dead. But the most costly sacrifice of this early work was the disappearance of the missionary team known as "the three Freds."

Our first Fred, Fred Roberts from Australia, served with the WEC team in Brazil for eleven years. After a long wait, his fiancée Mabel had joined him. They were married and began to work among the Guajajara people, but four months later, Mabel was dead. Fred had to conduct the funeral service himself and see that Mabel was buried next to Fenton Hall, another young worker who had died in 1924 of a tropical disease.

Fred continued to pursue his vision for reaching the ferocious Kayapo people living up the Xingu River. Another Australian Fred (Dawson), who as a farmer had felt compelled to stop his tractor in the middle of a field, kneel on the earth and commit himself to God's will, joined the first Fred. Then a third Fred (Wright) from Northern Ireland arrived in Brazil.

The three Freds left Belem in early 1935 to travel by boat up the Xingu. Eventually their boat was found at the foot of the Smoke Falls, but the men were never seen again. Were they clubbed to death by the very people they were seeking to reach? No one knows, but for almost seventy years after that incident, the Amazon ministries initiated by the pioneer work of the "Heart of Amazonia" team were left to sister missions.

In 2001 Ronaldo and Rossana Lidorio, who had been working in church planting in Ghana, caught a vision for starting a new WEC field to evangelize the many unreached tribes in their home country, Brazil. Although Brazilian evangelical churches have increased phenomenally in the last thirty years, the percentage of Brazilians engaged in cross-cultural missions is small. Evangelizing the growing indigenous population is still unfinished. Much remains to be done despite diligent work by Wycliffe Bible Translators, Unevangelized Fields Mission and New Tribes Mission. In fact, it is still unclear exactly how many people there are or where each tribe lives in the vast, mainly uncharted Amazon rainforest.

Others agreed with the Lidorios that WEC should once more play its part, and Project Amanaje began work on the 1000-mile long Rio Negro in northwest Amazonia. This fast-growing team has forty-one members today; almost all are Brazilian. The group includes twenty-eight WECers, five of them trained at MTC Latino Americano, and local workers with a thorough knowledge of the region. Amanaje now includes eight social projects, medical and dental work, and four churches, catering to different tribal languages. The team works among twelve different ethnic groups.

In the twenty-first century, reaching the tribes of the Amazon is still pioneer work, with conversions and backsliding, the challenge of syncretistic mixing of the gospel with pagan traditions, and the social tensions and suspicions of people both heavily demoralized by the worst civilization offers and proudly fighting to maintain their own identity and culture.

The WEC team has been involved with encouraging and organizing nationwide networking of Christians, facilitating two conventions of the Evangelical Indian Pastors and Leaders' Council, when hundreds met for worship and consideration of further evangelism and their rights and responsibilities as indigenous peoples. Ronaldo Lidorio's concern about the prevailing problem of syncretism encouraged him to hold seminars on Anthropology and Church Planting.

The Anthropos Institute (www.instituto.antropos.com.br) has been established with three websites and two electronic periodicals as a forum to help outreach workers understand Brazilian Indian and other worldviews and culture, so they can anticipate the misunderstandings and distortions of the gospel that may occur and be able to identify the appropriate biblical teaching to counter this.

Like Kenneth Grubb and the three Freds in the previous century, current WEC workers undertake perilous survey journeys deep into the Amazon to try to establish the extent of the unfinished task of reaching those who dwell in the endless forests. The vision for "Full Steam Ahead to the Heart of the Amazon" continues one hundred years later!

After serving with Unevangelized Fields Mission in the Amazon, David and Freda Phillips from the UK eventually joined WEC and worked in the International Research Office on the book Operation World *and in the UK center's front office. After Freda died, David served on the staff of the Brazilian WEC College.*

8

When There Is No Hope

We can know about unreached people groups and the latest movement of missionaries on the field, but knowing isn't what counts. We need to carve out time to pray, to not just talk about praying, but actually pray—to commune with God, to hold different issues before Him, to discern His will and to pray in faith.

Jeremy Ellis

I don't want to learn how it can't be done. I want to believe it can.

Elliott Tepper

We are not in the hands of others, not even ourselves, but in God's.

Traugott Boeker

I can do everything through him who gives me strength.

Philippians 4:13

Son of the Samurai
Anonymous
Japan, 1986

What a grim day! All the other students had new clothes for starting high school; I had only a ragged uniform, and one of my classmates laughed at me.

At noon one of the teachers found me hiding—pretending to be studying. The fact was I had no lunch. He kept asking me, "Why aren't you eating with the other boys?" I refused to answer, too proud to admit my family had lost everything through my father's bad business management; too stubborn to say I'd been going without lunch through most of primary school.

As I trudged home after school, I refused to give way to the bitter tears boiling up. I was too big to cry—and besides, the direct descendant of a Samurai warrior must never be weak.

Sliding the door open, I started in surprise. I had expected the house to be empty as usual; instead, a stranger was there waiting for me—a priest from the temple where my mother had recently been serving day and night, trying to gain favor with the gods. He told me that she had suddenly collapsed while praying.

I rushed over to the temple, where she lay before the altar at which she had been praying, covered with a sheet. Nothing could be done to save her.

In grief-stricken rage I vowed, "If this is what such a god does to those who serve him, I don't need him! I will devote my life to making money."

After completing high school I became a salesman. I worked hard and won most of the prizes my firm offered as incentives. I had money to spare for clothes, a car, parties and pleasure. But after each round of excitement was over, I was left flat and unsatisfied. My money seemed to go as quickly as I made it.

One day, wondering half-heartedly if Christianity had anything to offer, I visited a Christian pastor. Instead of him telling me of Christ, I sold him a sewing machine!

During the next few months, I went from sin to sin and bitterness to bitterness, until my firm sent me to manage a branch in Shiga Ken. Then a miracle began.

One day a customer told me about Jesus Christ. A few weeks later I met a foreign Christian teacher, and I started going to church. Many people tried to explain the way of salvation, but I couldn't grasp it. I was too embittered by all that had happened: how can they speak of a God of love?

Then one night God revealed to me my utter sinfulness. In tears I sought forgiveness, realizing that, no matter what the cost, I would have to make restitution for as many of my past sins as possible. That included returning money I had misused to my firm and reporting myself to the police after a false statement made on one occasion. I was quite sure that I would be imprisoned for the latter, but to my amazement no charges were made!

Proud and bitter, I had resolved to live a life separated from the god that I knew. But in love and mercy, the real God sought me out and revealed Himself to me

I could not escape from sin—God delivered me from it. I was restless and unsatisfied—God gave me peace. My aim in life was to make money. Now it is to please God.

Taken from WEC Australian Magazine 1986

This story took place twenty-five years ago. The author was baptized and received into membership in a church in Nagahama. He resigned from his job, sacrificing a good promotion to work with a Christian firm where he could have Sunday off for church. He became an elder of a church in

Nagoya and continues to live for Christ.

Saved in a Wheelbarrow
Howard Sayers
Guinea-Bissau, about 1980

We thought we were simply paying this remote village in Guinea-Bissau a normal courtesy call. However, as my co-worker and I trudged our way through the twisting bush paths in the heat and approached the village of mud huts, we saw an unusual heap of something lying in the center of the village. We were shocked to discover it was a man on the dusty ground, coughing up blood and surrounded by scrawny dogs and cows. After a moment we recognized him as the strong village chief that we were coming to visit.

Obviously he needed medical attention, yet as we greeted him and expressed our desire to help, he did not ask for medicine. To our amazement, all he wanted was an explanation of his recent, repeated dreams. Between fits of coughing, he told us in a weak voice about traveling down a long dark tunnel and coming out into a beautiful land. What did these dreams mean, he begged to know? We suggested that God was telling him, when he died, He wanted him to come to a beautiful place prepared for him. We explained how Jesus is the only way to that place. We knew as the village chief he was in touch with the evil spirits and responsible for using their powers to protect his extended family. Would he risk the wrath of his ancestral spirits by turning away from them to Jesus? Yes, he said, he wanted to turn to Jesus.

We agreed to give him a day to think about it and promised to return the next day to transport him to the clinic where we could give him a medical assessment. But how would we carry him along the miles of bush path that were impassable to any four-wheel vehicle? The only answer was to load him up onto our wheelbarrow.

In this unusual ambulance, with cushions and blankets to soften the rough ride, he arrived at our clinic. We checked him over and then had to gently tell him that he had advanced tuberculosis (TB), and there was little we could do for him. Despite this bad news, his main concern was still his dreams. We had arranged for the local pastor to be there to help us out.

Sitting in the wheelbarrow, this sick village chief explained his dreams to the pastor. The pastor told him simply how God's Son came to die in our place, take our sin upon Himself and open to us the way to God. Did he want to turn to Christ? Yes, came the reply! Hunched up in the wheelbarrow ambulance, the village chief asked Jesus to be his Savior! He is quite possibly the only person ever to be saved in a wheelbarrow!

Was it real? Did he truly know what he was doing? These questions worried us for the next couple of weeks until we received a message from his village. The chief requested that the local Christians come and witness as he burned all his charms and idols. Now we knew he was putting all his trust in Christ. The next Sunday a crowd gathered in the center of the village for the occasion. Our pastor preached and explained to the village folk how their chief had turned from his idols to Christ. The old chief then instructed his sons to bring the sacred items into the open space. As we all gathered around, they set fire to them. What a bonfire! The Christians rejoiced, but the chief's extended family was terribly afraid.

A couple of weeks later the old chief died. We had prayed that other members of his family would follow his lead and turn to Christ, but none had. Only years later did the good news reach us that seventeen members of the family had turned from their idols to serve the living God. Although we did not see it at the time, the Holy Spirit was working, silently convincing those villagers of the superior power of the Lord Jesus over all the powers of darkness. One old man, dying of TB, saved in a wheelbarrow, was the beginning of God bringing salvation to many in that village.

Howard and his wife Gill worked in Guinea-Bissau from 1975, returning to the UK for health reasons. They continued in the UK as candidate directors and then deputy sending base leaders; later they administered a retreat center.

Kaori's Story
As introduced by and told to Elaine Kitamura
Japan, 2006

M aking disciples for Jesus is a special challenge for those who respond to God's call to live and work in Japan. A highly complex and integrated society affected by an insatiable economy, the demands of long working hours and strong spiritual powers and obligations in the home make it difficult for people to abandon centuries-old practices for a foreign God. Churches are rarely bigger than thirty members, and the work of evangelists and church planters is hard and full of discouragements. Stories like Kaori's, which she shares below, are rare.

I came to live in Kinomoto in 2000, straight after my marriage. I knew there was a church in Kinomoto, and I was a little interested but didn't have the courage to make a move. Then in 2004 I saw an advertisement for annual English classes arranged by the church and led by a visiting Australian teacher. That was just the excuse and cover I needed! My husband and I both attended and were greatly attracted by the teacher's calm and gentle manner. I sensed it was because he knew God, and this awakened in me a desire to know God too, especially as I was exhausted with the effort of trying to be good. I started Bible classes with Pastor Shuichi, but I got stuck on the need for repentance. I just couldn't see it!

My father was an alcoholic. As the eldest of three sisters, I often found myself protecting my mother and my younger sisters from the unreasonable actions, yelling and violence of my father. I hated him for putting me in this position, though all of us suffered greatly. Whatever happened at home was our family secret and had to be kept from the world outside. As children, we couldn't admit the chaos, hurt and distress even to our parents. We had to pretend that everything was OK. Being able to talk frankly with my sisters was a relief.

Mostly my mother was concerned for us, but occasionally she weakened and put herself first. Then I had to take over her responsibility. One night when I was in my early teens, she asked me to put my drunken father to bed and get him to sleep. In extreme anxiety and distress, I managed to do it and then crept quietly out of the room and returned to my mother. I found her asleep and snoring! I felt betrayed and unloved. My one remaining refuge had gone, and I was in despair. But I continued my role as if nothing had happened. My mother would gladly boast that I was more of an adult than she was, but every time I heard this, anger would well up within me. Now I hated not only my father but my mother too.

I longed to be a good person, to have a pure heart, to be calm, to be understanding of others, to become a strong adult, but it was completely elusive. I felt I did not know how to love others or to be loved. Even after growing up and leaving home, I always felt a sense of being inwardly bound.

I became a kindergarten teacher, and during this time I realized I hated my parents. I kept control of my actions and words, but I couldn't control my heart. I disliked myself for this and spent many a night in tears in my flat after the day's work was done. I loved the children, and somehow my background enabled me to understand their hurts and to help them. Experiencing this was a comfort to me. But I still struggled to be perfect.

When I got married, I put all my effort into being a good wife, a good daughter-in-law, a good sister-in-law (the extended family lived partly with us and partly next door). I was trying to be good enough to earn everybody's love. The effort was too much, and I became exhausted. Adjusting to the local traditions and dialect, which differed from the area I came from, added to my stress. I was able to pour out my heart to my husband, and this enabled me to keep from going under. At this point I started going to church.

I wanted to believe, but somehow I couldn't. One day I had the opportunity to tell my background to Elaine, wife of Pastor Shuichi. Together we prayed, and the peace and love of God reached back into all my past and brought healing and release. My pride in wanting to depend only on myself was broken, and I was able to open my heart to God. I was able to tell Him everything just as it was—the pain, the guilt, the distress—and leave it all with Him. After that the things I had been learning from Pastor Shuichi from the Bible became real to me.

As I experienced the love of God, I was able to see and admit the sinfulness of hating my parents, of hypocrisy in my attitude to them, of blaming others, of resenting my sisters for having to protect them, and of my anger toward God. I saw the wonder of Jesus' great love in dying for me—taking all my sin upon Himself and taking my place when I should have been the one to be punished.

I was also enabled to look back and see all the ways God had helped and protected me before I even knew Him. My eyes were opened to see that perhaps my sufferings had been necessary in order for me to know God. I know He has a plan to bring good from it all, and that good includes my parents.

Elaine Kitamura originally came from Australia to Japan, where she met and married Shuichi. They have worked in pastoral evangelism for over 30 years.

Delivered from Demons

The story of Joia Nascimento, as told to Isa Arthur
Bijagos Islands, Guinea-Bissau, 1966

With superhuman strength I threw myself upon the door of the village temple. The door gave way; I fell inside on top of it and remained there, rolling on the ground. An evil spirit had come upon me. I was not conscious of any pain at the time, but afterward I stayed in bed for days, aching all over. On another occasion I fell on top of the fire and had to be dragged off by other women. I felt nothing then, but suffered long afterward from terrible burns on my shoulder.

Devilish Dances

I was in the *Defuntos*, a women's society. We met at certain times for ceremonies and dances, and at such times I would feel the evil spirits come upon me. Sometimes, even when I was alone, I would be attacked by these demon powers. I was an important person in the ceremonies, having inherited the right to carry the pole belonging to our lineage. This pole had been made by the temple men and was kept in the temple, but on ceremonial occasions I would carry it on my head and lead the other women. This position of honor would be passed on to my eldest daughter.

When the Word of God began to be preached on our island, I attended the meetings and thought much about this new message, becoming more and more convinced that it was true. But how could I give up my honorable position? At last, during a visit by two foreign evangelists, the Word entered my heart. I was unable to sleep that night. Plucking up courage, I rose and went to the house where all the Christian workers were staying and knocked on the door. After sharing my fears and burdens with them, I entered the Jesus way, and a new life began. Never again did the evil spirits trouble me. The desire for worldly fame and glory was conquered as I came to know the One who left the splendor of His heavenly home to come to earth and die for my sins.

Furious Relatives

Life was not easy, however. The trouble began the morning after I burned the cord which had been tied around my body to protect me from evil and to ensure that I would have children. The people in the village gathered together against me. There seemed to be no end to their reproaches. My mother was crying bitterly, saying I had rejected her. She was afraid of what would happen if I refused to carry the pole any more.

My husband was not at home (I was one of four wives), but he soon returned. He and his relatives were furious. Why had I done this behind his back? Why hadn't I waited to tell him first? "Had it been anything else," I replied, "I would have waited, but I couldn't wait to enter into God's way when He was speaking to me. How could I be sure that I would still be alive when you came home?" But their anger was not abated, so my husband sent me away. I returned to my mother's house.

All the women met together and called the temple man to come and perform certain ceremonies for them. Each age group presented a chicken for him to kill while they brought forward their petitions. I was to be brought back to the old way and take up the pole once more, or if I still refused, I was to die. Even members of my own family took part in this, no one having the courage to resist.

Fear of the Curse

Days lengthened into weeks, and I neither returned to the old ways *nor* died! Many of them, including my sister, became possessed by fear that the curse would fall back upon their own heads. The persecution gradually died down in the village but continued at home. When I gave thanks before my meals, my family rose up in anger until I could hardly swallow my food. I was given no peace to pray at home, so I had to find a quiet place in the bush. But as my sister saw no harm befell any of us, her fears subsided, and she began to defend me. Bit by bit the family became resigned to my new way of life and even began to listen to the Word. At one time I became very ill and was unable to walk. The people thought I was going to die at last. My mother wanted to have ceremonies performed, but I refused. Instead, I continued praying and trusting God. The Lord heard and answered, and I was soon well again.

God's Abundant Blessings

After staying for a time on another island, I returned home. The women gathered to look at me. They were amazed to see that I was strong and healthy—perhaps more so than any of them. This made a deep impression on several and was a link in the chain which led to the conversion of at least two women, one of them being my sister.

God has done great things for me. I am now married to an evangelist, and God has given us three little girls. He has kept me and helped me and blessed me abundantly. To Him all glory belongs!

Taken from WEC Australian Magazine, 1966

Happy though Blind
Betty Singleton
Ghana, 1968

The eye specialist looked grave. "I'm sorry, but nothing can be done for this young man." Dakori's sight was severely damaged from a long-standing tropical eye disease. "It's all right," Dakori replied. "Even though I go blind, I will still trust God."

Dakori's eye damage and his faith in God both began in his childhood. One day, when he was seven, he suddenly complained that his eyes were sore. "A snake must have spat in your eyes," his mother reasoned, and took the small boy to the witch-doctor. After making an offering of chicken's blood, the witch-doctor assured them that now the child's eyes would get better. Dakori's sight grew worse, and he was sent to the bush to mind his mother's cows every day.

Dakori

A foreign person came to Dakori's village and sang in the Vagala language about the living God and His gift of eternal life through the blood of his Son, Jesus Christ. Dakori loved the singing but got angry when he was told that everyone had sinned and that the fetish could not save them from their sin.

A school was started in the village, and Dakori wanted to go, but the people gave him no chance. They cursed him saying, "You are a boy with no eyes. Go out and look after the cows!" He waited till evening classes by lamplight were begun and went along. He quickly learned some English, for he was still able to see enough to read and write a little. In the daytime Dakori weeded and hoed on his brother's farm and wandered in the bush with the cows. His eyes and head ached, especially when the sun stood overhead each day!

Every time Dakori thought of what the WEC worker had said, he got angry. His fathers had followed the fetish way all their lives. Why should they turn to another way?

The young African loved the village drums; he loved the singing and dancing. He learned to beat the rhythms for the night dancing, which often ended in immoral practices. The boy's heart was full of fear: fear of darkness, fear of snakes, fear of spirits and fear of the fetish.

He knew that he often lied. But everybody lies. He knew he had stolen yams. But all the boys steal their mother's yams to roast a bit in the bush when they are hungry. He knew many things in his life were not good.

His head ached. His body was hot. He tossed on his grass mat, feeling he would die. Dakori seemed to hear a voice: "You

know that what you have heard from the book of the living God is true. The fetish cannot save you, but Jesus Christ will save you. His blood will wash your heart clean and set you free from the power of sin." Dakori had never prayed before, but in the darkness of the night, he cried out, "O God, if you are true, forgive my sin and come and live in my heart." A new peace came into his heart. The drums began to lose their attraction, and Dakori spent time with the Christian worker when he visited. He was quite sure God had changed him and given him a new direction for his life.

New foreign workers arrived in the area, and bright-faced Dakori came to see them. An interpreter was needed in the clinic so mothers and children could get medicine. Would Dakori interpret and tell the people what the living God had done for him? He gladly agreed. Some laughed at the message, but others asked, "How can you, with no eyes, be so happy?" "Jesus is in my heart. I have eternal life through Him" was Dakori's glad testimony. His mother and blind sisters accepted the Lord through his witness. How happy he was!

Friends prayed that Dakori's eyesight might be restored. What should be done—an operation or eyeglasses? Examination proved that the eye doctor could do nothing to help. The young man's trust in God never wavered.

How could a blind man learn from God's Word in order to grow in the knowledge of the Lord? Dakori saved enough money to buy a transistor radio. Now, wherever he went, he could tune in to Radio ELWA and hear the Word of God. He was given an old piano accordion and learned to play it. As his own darkness grew, he found joy in singing and playing and teaching Christian songs to others in their own language!

Still, Dakori wanted to read the Bible for himself. By now he was twenty years old. In a wonderful way provision was made by some Ghanaian women in Accra for him to enter the school for the blind as a special case to learn Braille. After six months he came home, carrying a big book borrowed from the school library— John's Gospel. He sat and read with great delight.

"Come and play the drums, Dakori. Come and dance and sing."

"No, I will not come. I have given my life to Jesus Christ. He is calling me to preach and teach His Word. Eternal life is more to me than the pleasures of this world. I will be an evangelist for Him who loved me and gave Himself for me."

Dakori playing his accordion

Eventually Dakori became a pastor in the WEC-related Evangelical Church of Ghana. For more than forty years, he has served as pastor and held added responsibilities, including Bible school teacher, regional superintendent and a member of the Vagala translation team. He is married, with eight children and three grandchildren, and continues to be a highly respected and appreciated Christian leader.

Taken from WEC Australian Magazine, 1968

Australian Betty Singleton and her English husband Norman served on the Ghana field for many years before retiring to England. Betty retains a prayerful ministry for the people of Ghana and many other parts of the world.

The Man Who Saw Heaven

Georgina Stott
Thailand, 2008

During my first year (1968) on the Thailand field, Else Petersen and I were at our usual Sunday morning service in the country village of Bantak.

Else was the preacher, and it seemed like every other Sunday, as chickens and dogs wandered in and out of the open home, but it was very different. The village headman, Phu Yaiy Kaew, was dying, and his coffin was being lovingly hammered together just outside our room while the sermon was given and hymns were sung.

This elderly, ill man on his mattress on the floor loved the Lord, and others knew the Lord because of him. The church service with his presence was special for all of us, and we had time to talk with him and eat together before Else and I made the long return journey to our home. Traveling in a borrowed pick-up truck, the trip took a long time as the road was under construction, and it was very difficult to negotiate with many boulders and potholes.

We had just arrived home and made a cup of coffee when we heard the sound of a motorcycle. A breathless member of the Bantak congregation popped in our door and exclaimed, "Yaiy Kaew died right after you left. He saw heaven and then came back to life. He told us all that he had seen in heaven, and it is true! He told us to keep believing, and then he stopped breathing once again."

Bantak church

We quickly gathered our black funeral skirts and white blouses, plus other clothes for the night, and got back on the road again. That night, we slept in a row on mats in the Bantak house with our heads not too far from Phu Yaiy Kaew's simple coffin. I remember being so excited to have this message of seeing heaven, but at the same time I was almost sick from the stifling heat and a decaying corpse right there by our heads. Some people stayed up and talked all night.

Because in those days we did not have a Christian burial ground, in the morning we gathered together around a funeral pyre in the forest for a simple service of thanksgiving for one of the first to believe in the area. We sang and talked as the flames leapt high, and we kept adding more wood until the body was cremated.

More than forty years later, I stopped by Bantak as I drove from Bangkok to our field conference in the north of Thailand. We had recently received news that one of the older Christians had died, and people were preparing for the funeral. We sat and talked with those gathered around making flower arrangements in their own church building. As we remembered many people together, I asked if they remembered Phu Yaiy Kaew. It took a few minutes, but yes, all those over fifty remembered his wonderful story. We recounted the history for the younger ones to hear and rejoiced together. The legacy of Yaiy Kaew—the man who saw heaven—continues to encourage and change lives in his remote Thai village.

Georgina Stott moved from Tasmania in Australia to Thailand in 1967. She has been involved in Christian radio work for most of that time.

God Alone

Detmar Scheunemann
Indonesia, mid-1960s

The Timorese congregation gasped as their pastor stood before them and opened up his shirt, revealing the red protection belt he wore. Leaders in the town had been fighting with each other. In the midst of the arguments and threats, the pastor had been trusting in both God and his protection belt to keep him safe. Now he tore off the belt before the church members as he found liberation in trusting God alone.

Before the Communist revolution of 1965, the Reformed Church on the island of Timor had invited a team from the Indonesian Bible Institute to conduct evangelistic meetings.

This team, which I led, found that people stayed behind each night to receive counseling from team members. Many of these people had used occult powers in the crisis situations of their lives. Now they renounced these practices and bondages and experienced God's full salvation. Even the local pastors were convicted of the need to be free from even the slightest dependence on any power other than the one true God.

From this beginning, evangelistic teams and prayer groups sprang up throughout the island, with the gospel reaching even remote villages in the interior and the mountains. God's fire is still burning in the hearts of thousands of Timorese Christians and sixty outreach groups who move throughout the country, as I was thrilled to observe on my visit in 2009.

Only God could have sent this blessing and a wider move of the Holy Spirit which has continued for so many years in Indonesia through regional Bible schools and home prayer groups. Once when my father was visiting, I accompanied him to a Sun-

Old Timorese houses

day morning service in the church where the revival had started. It was decided that I was to preach, but before I could stand up, I experienced such a severe attack of malaria I had to leave the service. The next morning I was still suffering when two Timorese women visited. They wanted to pray for me, but one of them said, "We cannot pray for you yet. You are sick because you are being proud."

As the woman spoke, I realized my pride stemmed from a desire to bring my father to the place where revival had started during my ministry in that church. Immediately I repented. The two village women knelt at my bedside and prayed a simple prayer of faith, committing my sick body to the Lord. Then they left, praising God. My fever went down; I got up and washed my face. The neighbors noticed, and the news spread that I was well. When they heard this, people gathered, and I spoke to them as I had been unable to do on Sunday morning.

In 1959 Detmar Scheunemann from Germany, along with Heini German-Edey from Switzerland, founded the Indonesian Bible Institute in Batu at the request of Indonesian Christian students. Today thirteen hundred graduates are serving the Lord in Indonesia, Asia and Africa. Detmar and his wife Gisela worked in Indonesia till 1989.

Naren: Boy from the Streets
Timothée Paton
Cambodia, 2010

The phone call came at seven in the morning. Naren's father, calling me from the slum, reported, "Naren had a very bad accident last night while collecting rubbish on the streets!"

This fourteen-year-old boy is one of the hundreds of poor children in Phnom Penh who are forced to go out every night to scavenge through bags of trash along roads and around markets, looking for any recyclable items from scrap metal to plastic bottles. The poorest children, some as young as four or five, carry large bags with them. Others pull carts. The "better off" ones may cycle or drive an old motorbike to pull their carts.

Naren's dad earns a bit of money from his old dusty billiard table, his only valuable possession. Young men from the slum come over every day to have a game. Naren has seven brothers and sisters. Their mother left for Thailand when she couldn't take any more beatings from her husband.

"Where is Naren?" I asked his dad on the phone.

"He's here with me."

I jumped into my car and rushed to the slum, less than ten minutes' drive away. Bong Tampon is one of the few slums left in Phnom Penh. Over the years many of the poor have been chased away. Sometimes their community has been burned to the ground so that wealthy and corrupt men can take over the area. Thousands of displaced families now live miles outside town in what look like refugee camps.

Naren, like everybody else in Bong Tampon, lives in a small shack made of cheap wood with a corrugated tin roof. Rats, cockroaches and other ugly creatures make their homes there too. Thankfully, there is a small church a Korean missionary built some years ago.

I went straight to Naren's "house." The boy was lying down, curled up, eyes bloodshot. His face was covered with bruises and cuts.

"What happened?"

"Last night my son was out with his brother on the road scavenging when suddenly a van drove straight into their cart. Naren was thrown onto the road and left unconscious."

The van, of course, didn't stop (a driver in Cambodia who causes an accident usually keeps on driving). Naren's brother managed to get him back to the slum.

"But he can't stay like this," I said. "He could die from the injuries!"

Child with handcart

His father helped me carry the boy to my car. Naren looked lifeless. I took him to a local clinic. The doctor feared Naren might have an internal head injury. "We can't do much here. He needs to go to the hospital for a scan. It's on the other side of town."

A few minutes later Naren, his brother and I were in an ambulance van with emergency lights flashing and horn blasting. I've never before crossed Phnom Penh in such a short time! Naren was waking up. His eyes were hurting so much he couldn't open them fully. He wasn't sure what was going on. I looked over to him and said, "You should see what I see. All the cars, even the big expensive ones, are moving out of the way to let us through. It's like when the Prime Minister is on the road!"

At the hospital medics got Naren out and took him for the scan. One hour later the results came: "No internal head injury."

In the ambulance on the way back, anger built up in me: anger against the evil system of child labor; anger that a child has to go out every night and work like a slave to earn about a dollar; anger that thousands of boys and girls are out on the streets day in, day out, scavenging through stinky rubbish bags, while the rich and powerful in town have no shame about building the biggest villas and driving the biggest cars I have ever seen.

I turned to Naren and took his hand. I looked into his bruised eyes and said, "Naren, I'm going to promise you something. You will never, ever go back to work on the streets again."

He didn't know what I had in mind. A few days later Naren's father signed a contract promising he would not send his son on the streets again and would allow him to go to school every day. In exchange the family would receive the same amount of money Naren used to earn working on the streets (thirty US dollars a month). The moment his dad signed the paper, a new chapter of freedom opened for Naren.

Scavenging on a garbage heap

From that day he has never gone back to the streets. Every day he goes to a small Christian school around the corner from his home. He even studies English and computer in the evenings. Every two weeks, on Saturday nights, he (along with about thirty other young people from the slum) attends New Life Church. When the worship band is loudly praising God, you'll find a young boy right up in the front worshiping God, hands lifted up, singing to Jesus from the bottom of his heart. He could have been scavenging rubbish. Instead, he's singing in church.

Naren told me he has been a follower of Jesus for two years now. When he grows up, he would like to be an architect. I asked him a month ago, "What would you like people to pray about for you?" He replied, "That my mum and dad and my brothers and sisters would be one family again."

Recently, Naren's mum has come back from Thailand. A week ago mother and father held hands and gave their lives to Christ. Last Sunday I took Naren and his parents to church.

Timothée Paton (the tall man in the back), after working with the Salvation Army in France, has focused his attention on the children of the streets in Cambodia and presenting a missionary challenge around the world.

Bishu—Follower of Jesus and Unstoppable Man of Faith

Evan Davies
Bangladesh, 2010

A paraplegic was inquiring about the possibility of being a student at WEC's Missionary Training College in Tasmania. We didn't know what to do with this remarkable application. We had never accepted a student in a wheelchair. Missionaries needed to be fit, able to go anywhere and cope with all aspects of the college program. Soon we wrote back briefly stating that our college was not set up for people like him. A few weeks later another letter came, asking us to reconsider.

This letter told his story. Born into a Brahmin family, grandson of the former Maharajah of Mymensingh in Bangladesh, he had a privileged background and the best of university education. Eventually he gained a position in India's fledgling nuclear industry. But something went wrong in an experiment, and he ended up paralyzed in a hospital bed with many hours to contemplate an uncertain future. He was given the best of treatment, and the medical staff was helpful and attentive. One of his caregivers even offered him a Gideon New Testament, explaining that it was the Christian holy book. The stories he read spoke into his soul, and eventually he came to faith in Christ. A Christian nurse was assigned to his care, and they found themselves falling in love. Rehabilitation therapy in Perth, West Australia offered him the chance to improve his medical condition, meet other Christians and solidify his convictions. During this period he heard of the college in Tasmania and felt he should apply.

Again the staff responded that we could not accept him. We fully expected this would be the end of the inquiry. But some weeks later another letter came stating that Bishu (Bishwanath Chowdhuri) was still convinced God wanted him at our college. Could we please reconsider our decision? It now threw the initiative back to the college staff. What was God saying?

We investigated and determined that with a minimum of fuss, small ramps could make all entrances navigable for a wheelchair. We heard of Bishu's understanding with Vijaya, the Christian nurse from the hospital in India. If Bishu and Vijaya married, there would be no hindrance to them both becoming students at the college and he would have a built-in caregiver who understood him and his history.

The staff could only acknowledge that God was in this situation in a way we had not previously recognized. Application papers were sent.

Bishu and Vijaya arrived and from the beginning embraced all aspects of the college program. In a residential course, which involved an academic curriculum as well as a hands-on commitment to daily duties and participation in the life of an active community, they showed their humility and maturity. They were devoted to God's will and service. But what were they going to do at the end of their training?

We thought they could return to their homeland and become active participants in the life of the church. They felt God had a special task for them to do. An exploratory visit to Bangladesh convinced them this was where God wanted them to serve Him. They wanted to join WEC, but at that stage WEC was not intending to start work in Bangladesh. Could they not do the WEC Candidate Orientation Course simply for what they could gain from it?

They could and did, and with minds stimulated and fixed on the challenge before them, they moved to Bangladesh. Moving around the country was seen to be too difficult for Bishu, and with advice from Christian friends, he was encouraged to set up the first residential training program for Christian workers in Dhaka.

The Christian Discipleship Center started small, but as the years went by, dozens of people came and trained. God helped them to erect suitable and substantial buildings. Overall the center provided a remarkable service in developing leadership for the Christian church in Bangladesh. Men, women and married couples were all given equal opportunities to train. Courses were devised to make the students competent to serve the needs of rural society. God sent additional staff to share the load. From an initial four students, the center graduated up to forty in later years, and in December 2009 Bishu wrote that a total of 689 had been involved in the training program.

Who can know how many lives have been touched and changed because of the ministry of the training center? Many are serving God today in different parts of Bangladesh and beyond as a direct result of Bishu's obedience and determination to follow the call of God on his life. Pastoral leadership has been provided, media work commenced, schools set up and committed servants of God have met the needs of the Christian community and rural society. Twelve adult literacy programs have seen many people come to faith in Christ and new churches established. One couple, working in a potentially volatile area, recently reported more than a hundred people baptized, despite the risk of persecution.

Bishu and Vijaya would not accept the obstacles in their way nor be daunted by the heavy challenges in front of them. Determination, faith and perseverance were their trademarks. In dependence on God and conscious of His call on their lives, they moved forward to see the impossible become reality. They were God's servants and followers of Jesus. Even though Bishu went to heaven in early 2010, Vijaya continued to lead the ministry, and God promises to bring in the harvest.

"If you have faith as small as a mustard seed, you can say to this mountain 'Move from here to there' and it will move. Nothing will be impossible to you." (Matt. 17:20–21)

Evan Davies was born in Congo to WEC missionary parents. With his wife Jenny he carried responsibility as principal of WEC's Training College in Tasmania, Australia and as international director of WEC.

Out of Nothing
Keith Bergmeier
India, 2010

The first verse in the Bible gives us amazing insight into the ways of God. Out of absolutely nothing He created the universe (Gen. 1:1)

God never changes. Throughout history He's been the one that creates out of nothing. Speaking of Abraham, the Bible says that out of one old man who was as good as dead, God brought forth descendants as numerous as the stars in the sky (Heb. 11:12). Paul wrote that God chooses the things that are not, to confound the things that are (1 Cor. 1:28).

Why would He choose an overweight, shy accountant, who'd never even met a heroin addict in his life, to work in a ministry like Betel?

For most of my life, I couldn't stand heat. My sister reminds me that, as a child, in the summer I would often return home from playing tennis with a headache and bleeding nose. In later life those headaches developed into insupportable migraines. Who would consider sending such a person, fifty-two years old, to spend the next eleven-plus years in Delhi, India—one of the hottest places on earth?

In all those eleven years in India, I've not experienced one migraine, and the Father has given me the privilege of observing many of His "out-of-nothing" creations.

One of the first heroin addicts to enter Betel India in January 2000 was Ayo Lolly. He was a sad-faced, dejected-looking figure with long hair, denim jacket and several pieces of metal hooked into his ears.

As he stepped into the house, he glanced around, suspiciously checking out his new surroundings. As his eyes momentarily met mine, his lips remained closed, and he gave me a "Don't think you'll change me" stare.

In those early days for Betel in India, we were still feeling our way. Several had come into our eighteen-month rehabilitation program, but the majority had left within a few days, some within hours. As I looked at Ayo, I wasn't encouraged to expect anything different. *Hmmm, two or three days . . . no more*, I thought, and continued with my other duties.

Ayo had become nothing. Many years of drug use and associated criminal lifestyle had made him unwanted in his beloved mountain village in northeast India. He was evicted by the residents and for a time lived in the nearby state capital. Eventually his insatiable desire for drugs led him to make the twenty-five-hundred-kilometer journey to Delhi. There he went from bad to worse. Ayo himself later said, "I had

Betel, India guys

lost all hope, I was dirty, I lived as a beggar in the streets of Delhi, no one cared about me, I wanted to die. I was nothing."

For a few months he found himself in a Delhi rehabilitation center, but to no avail. He left, went back to the street and back to drugs.

Ayo didn't leave after two or three days. He was still with us in January 2008, having known a marvelous freedom from his habits, when he received a mysterious letter. He did not usually receive letters in the mail (cell phone calls and text messages, yes, but not letters!).

He opened his mail with amazement. The letter was from the president of the Residents' Association of his mountain village. A special celebration dinner was to take place; all the residents would be there, and Ayo was invited.

Such a profound change had taken place in Ayo's life over those eight years that the scourge of the village had become the guest of honor!

Ayo was chauffeured to the dinner, publicly welcomed and presented to all the guests before being asked to address them. As he stood looking out over the audience, he noticed that many were staring back at him in puzzlement, some shedding tears. Many hadn't seen him since his school days. Later, as he chatted with old friends and acquaintances, one person kept staring and asked, "Is it you? Is it really you?" Not only had God completely changed Ayo's life, but now he is being used as God performs miracles in other "nothings" of this world.

After leading teams to establish Betel in three different states of Northeast India, Ayo served as founder and director of Betel in Nepal until his death in 2011. Subsequent to years in Spain and back in Australia, Keith moved to the Indian sub-continent to commence the Betel drug rehabilitation ministry in Asia.

9

Change of Plans

*Prayer is an expression of our total dependence on Him in our life
and ministry with the acceptance we cannot make it on our own.*

Young Choon Lee

God can see around corners.

Evan Davies

*May the God of hope fill you with all joy and peace as you trust
in him, so that you may overflow with hope by the power of the
Holy Spirit.*

Romans 15:13

An Unusual Way into Missions

Luise Läufer
East Timor, 1990s

I grew up in a Christian family with an elder and a younger sister. As a child, I was quite ill and finally diagnosed with tuberculosis. At that time the remedy was a long period of rest— an everlasting punishment for a lively child. One day we had a visitor, a deaconess from far away. My parents told her about their "sick chick." She was silent for a while and then said, "Let us pray." After a prayer in a foreign language, she pronounced with certainty, "She will be well and will become a handmaiden of the Lord." I was astonished—how could she be so sure of this? I did not get better in an instant, but slowly and steadily my health improved.

The dos and don'ts of our local church fellowship did not make Christianity attractive to me. My illness seemed to be God's punishment. Nevertheless, at the age of sixteen, I invited Jesus into my life during an evangelistic campaign led by a visiting preacher. My happiness was indescribable.

Our father retired early, so I had to help with the family income, working as a secretary; later I trained as a medical technician and worked in the local hospital. During those years God spoke to me, pointing to missions: "The Lord has come and He calls you"; "Sing a new song unto the Lord, His praise from the end of the earth"; "Go to my vineyard at the eleventh hour."

Where and when was uncertain. I went to missions meetings, expecting the place to become clear. Sometimes missionaries came to stay with us. One of them felt called to East Timor and was looking for a co-worker. While doing the dishes, I felt God saying, "You will go to East Timor." I had no clue where East

Timor was, only that it was a closed country. I thought this idea quite unrealistic and tried to forget it. But God did not forget.

After taking care of my mother until her death, I visited Indonesia and traveled with that missionary to West Timor near the border of East Timor. The region seemed lonely, spiritually dark and depressing. Back in Kupang, West Timor, I spent the afternoon at the beach and again heard the still, small voice: "He felt pity on the people and healed those who were sick." I prayed, "Lord, if You really want me for medical work in such an isolated region, please let me train in a mission hospital first." From that time on the WEC clinic in Gambia was on my mind.

Back in Germany I had to care for my father in addition to my work in the local hospital. After my father's death I put out a fleece: "Lord, if all of this is really from You and is not my own idea, please give me an invitation from the Gambia hospital." This was unlikely; rarely was anybody invited to a mission field. You were expected to have an assurance about which country to go to. Two weeks later an invitation was in my hands! Modou Camara, who ran the laboratory of the WEC clinic in Gambia, was going to Bible college and needed a successor.

I applied to go with WEC to Gambia first and to East Timor afterward—apparently a slightly absurd undertaking, as I was already past my fiftieth birthday.

I was able to go to Gambia and enjoyed the wide range of medical work there. Three years later I reached Kupang in West Timor and worked in a government hospital, getting to know the culture and language. Several years later, East Timor's borders were opened to foreign workers, and I seized the opportunity to move. From the time God called me right up to that moment, over twenty years had elapsed!

The twenty years God gave me in East Timor were highlights in my life. With no Western co-workers I immersed myself in

Timorese culture and, with two Timorese ladies helping me, started a polyclinic.

Soon patients were brought to us, some transport taking hours of night-time marches. In this situation we were totally dependent on God's help, and we indeed experienced it.

While visiting a village, we were called by a man to come to his hut, where he showed us a sick boy about seven years old. The man obviously was a witch doctor to whom the little patient had been entrusted. He seemed at the end of his wisdom. We took both of them to our clinic. The boy suffered from TB, but he refused to take any medicine. We were given permission to pray. Instantly the boy took the tablets—and soon got well.

Another time parents came with a seriously ill toddler. They too had seen the witch doctor first, without success. He finally said, "We can do nothing but wait for the boy's death." Again we were allowed to pray, and miraculously, the boy recovered.

A couple came with their eighteen-month-old daughter who was desperately ill. They had been in hospital and elsewhere with

Clinic Immanuel in Timor

her and finally had asked for the witch doctor's help. He said, "Next Tuesday the child will die." The parents were desperate.

They willingly accepted our offer of prayer—and on Tuesday we thanked God together for the restored health of the child.

Our God is trustworthy and able to help.

Luise Läufer spent twenty years in East Timor, running a clinic, preaching, giving broadcast messages and experiencing danger and warfare before and after the country's independence in 1999.

Blazing a New Trail of Patient Care

Ilse-Marie Neuroth
Gambia, 2009

_D_r. _Gisela Schneider joined WEC in 1984 and worked in the Sibanor clinic in Gambia until 1997. From 1999 until 2004, she developed the AIDS project "Hands on Care" in Gambia and later trained health staff in Uganda. In 2007 she was appointed director of the German "Institute for Medical Missions" (Difäm) in Tübingen, Germany._

Only a few people in Gambia know Gisela Schneider's real name. Most call her Jainaba Cham, a name given to her by women in Chamen, a village where Gisela lived for two years. This is a high honor, as it was the name of the leader of the local women's group. What did she do to deserve this honor? She blazed a trail of care for the most desperate of people.

The Gambian Ministry of Health had asked Gisela to set up a primary health care program in the Nianija District, a forgotten district in the eastern part of the country that was not easily accessible. Gisela accepted the challenge. She lived in the house of the village teacher, drew water from the same village well as everyone else and ate the same food.

Issues such as clean water, nutrition, prenatal care, obstetrics and the management of infectious diseases are essential in primary health care, and the area lacked this basic knowledge. Gisela knew that nurses and village health workers needed to be trained in this very remote area to improve the health of people and found herself to be the only Christian in the midst of a nearly 100 percent Muslim community.

In the early 1990s the first AIDS patients came to the Sibanor clinic that Gisela ran from 1990 until 1997. It quickly became clear to her that this disease had more than a medical dimension. Stigma and discrimination, fear and death needed to be addressed. AIDS was not the problem of an individual but included whole families, villages and clans. In particular, the local women were stigmatized and isolated.

The vision was clear: as Christians, we needed a holistic response—not judgment but love and healing for body, mind and spirit. So together with other partners, a holistic HIV care program emerged called "Hands on Care." People with chronic diseases and HIV found care, even though when they began, there was no drug treatment yet available.

Since then, AIDS has changed. Patients can live despite their illness due to anti-retroviral therapy. After the initial five years of

Sibanor clinic

the program, the first drugs came into the country, and today hundreds of patients receive care and have a hope and a future thanks to "Hands-on Care."

One specific patient still stands out to Gisela. This woman was diagnosed with tuberculosis. Nobody visited her, and she was unable to eat; her body was so emaciated that even the nurses thought her life was coming to an end. But God had other plans for her. Once the treatment had started, she gained strength and finally could be taken back to her family. But things did not go well there, and she kept calling Gisela to inform her that her family did not want her anymore. In the end her father made her move to a neighboring compound.

One day, this lady said to Gisela that she wanted to be a Christian. Gisela was astonished, because apart from some prayers that had been prayed on her behalf during her illness and some cassettes she had listened to, she did not know anything about the Christian faith. But her decision was firm—she wanted to become a Christian because it had been the Christians who had helped her when nobody else did.

Along with some African pastors, Gisela tried to accompany her friend on her way toward Christ with all the ups and downs in-

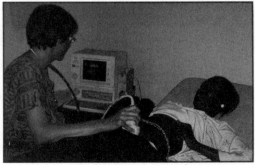

Gisela using ultrasound

cluded. This journey included a continued search for a place to live, an arranged wedding and a difficult pregnancy. In the end she asked to be baptized.

On the day of her burial, her oldest boy clearly said, "Our mother was a Christian, and we are Christians too." Her five children are now cared for by a local pastor and his wife, and Gisela keeps up with annual visits to Gambia to see "her" children grow up as young people who love the Lord and have a hope and a future.

Ilse-Marie Neuroth has been on WEC Germany's administrative and editorial staff since 1990.

Evicted!
Diana
China, 1992

"You have five days to leave China," said the angry policeman as he returned our passports to us. Surrounded by policemen and government officials in our small room in a large Chinese city, we had just refused to sign a confession admitting to crimes we didn't commit. This refusal infuriated the policeman and resulted in an immediate cancellation of our visa and the order to leave. The officials were conducting a purge of Christians in the area and wanted us out by any means necessary. We were helpless and could do nothing but pack our bags.

We were officially invited to China by two professors to teach English in a college for physically disabled students. These young people in their late teens came from poor backgrounds, mostly in the countryside, and had been refused admittance to universities because of their disabilities. They were intellectually quite bright and would have passed university entrance exams, but the policy in those days was not to admit them to university, as officials believed they wouldn't be able to find jobs after completion of their studies. Without this school, the only prospect for the young women among them was to be married off to old peasants.

Standard practice was to enter the country on a visitor's visa and then apply for a visa suitable for staying and teaching. The leaders of the college sent off our passports for the visa change but became concerned when they were not returned to us. After a few weeks they were more and more worried. We tried not to dwell on this too much and started teaching.

We grew close to our class of forty students. We had opportunities to speak to them privately and talk about our faith. They initiated conversations with questions like, "Why did you come to our country and live in difficult conditions, just to teach and help us?" Each day that winter we had to walk to a bus station, travel to the foot of a steep hill and climb the hill to the school, sometimes in snow, and there was no heat at all in the classrooms. The Lord gave us a deep love for the students, and they responded.

Then one day with no notice, armed guards surrounded our guest house. Officials came in demanding that we leave. We were told it was because they had heard we were Christians. The teachers at the school were extremely upset, as we were. We were told not to tell our students the reason we had to go, but they guessed and asked if it was because of their government. The following days were a blur as we prepared to leave. The students wanted to give us an official farewell and arranged a meeting for our last day on campus. They prepared songs, poems and speeches, and most of them were in tears. We had trouble holding back our tears too. A group of young women had gone to the top of the mountain early in the morning and collected a huge bunch of wild azaleas to present to us. Sadly we waved goodbye to the students through the windows of our train as it chugged away.

Why had this happened? Wasn't it God's will for us to be there teaching these students? Why had He called us and paved the way for us, only to have us kicked out less than a month later? We had to trust the Lord and believe He would work out His purpose for the college even without us.

A few years later we became leaders of our team of co-workers and had an opportunity to visit the couple who started the college. Because we were blacklisted in that province, we made only a brief visit and had to be careful when meeting with our friends.

After we were evicted from China, the college for disabled students had been forced to close because of its Christian emphasis. However, those with the original vision for the school were still meeting privately with groups of students, teaching and sharing their faith. Because of their stand, they were watched by the authorities and needed to be extremely cautious. Their boldness and commitment were inspiring to us. The husband had previously been a card-carrying Communist Party member, but now he was "on fire" for the Lord, even using his computer to copy large portions of Scripture and circulate them. At that time Bibles were not easy to obtain. I remember sitting on the grass in a large park with their son and a young woman, being bombarded with questions about "spiritual warfare" and the role of the Holy Spirit in our lives.

We later found out that a young local Christian teacher took our place, and a number of students became Christians and were baptized. We also found out that almost all of the students were able to get good jobs, some doing translation work.

In retrospect, we can see that what Satan meant for evil, God turned around for good. Recent stories of what God is doing in that city in China and of young people coming to the Lord in large numbers are thrilling. He is faithful!

Fish to Fishing
Chulhee Choi
South Korea, 2009

C hulhee is a spy sent from the Korean sending base!"
Really, I was a fifty-eight-year-old former CEO of a major fish company in Korea, trying to adapt along with my wife to a new and strange environment: the WEC center in the USA. We had come to undertake English language study and candidate orientation, and although God encouraged us through His Word, we were shaken many times by the challenges of learning a new language and a new international mission culture at our ages!

My English tutor's teasing comment reflected my intense interest in how the American sending base worked. Early in our language program, the annual American staff conference took place. We were allowed to join in, and I was there, missing not a single hour of meetings. Of course, I couldn't entirely understand the discussions and lectures, and I sometimes felt like an alien, but the Lord spoke to me: "Chulhee, I have something I want to reveal to you here. Look carefully at the American sending base and draw for the future of the Korean sending base with a ten-year time frame."

Though I was stunned by this strong voice of the Lord to me and wondered what it meant for the future, I began to observe and think carefully about how the sending base operated.

During our candidate orientation course, we participated in Open Air Campaigners (OAC) street evangelism on a weekly basis in the city center of Philadelphia.

On our last day with OAC, we stopped by a poor residential area. We called neighborhood children together so we could present the gospel through illustrations on a big board.

The day was bitterly cold and windy. One candidate, a Korean lady, began to draw and share the gospel. The wind blew hard and shook the wooden board. Our OAC leader asked me to quickly go behind and hold the board for her. For quite a while, standing there holding the board with both my hands freezing, I regretted forgetting to bring my gloves. My hands went numb. I couldn't see anything because of the board right in front of my eyes.

I muttered to myself, "Who would dare to ask me to do this kind of thing if I were in Korea?"

At that moment I heard the voice of the Lord again: "Chulhee, this is your role and your job for the future."

I was so astonished that my hands and heart quivered. The Lord was confirming my calling, which my wife and I had accepted back in Korea when I resigned from my position as CEO. I had first become acquainted with WEC eight years earlier and been caught by the vision of C.T. Studd, the founder of WEC, and of Byung Kook, the Korean sending base director. I thought some day in the future I might retire from my job and help WEC full-time. But God's plan was different from mine. My life began to shake like a ship lurching through big waves.

Although I was a prudent person, always looking before leaping, my wife and I agreed that God was asking me to resign from my company and calling us to support the workers on the field from the Korean sending base. In Philadelphia the Lord showed me again that I should quietly support the Korean missionaries behind the scenes, so that they would be able to work well as they served Him.

I am not a person who majored in theology, nor a worker with years of experience overseas. I am well aware that I lack many things. But I am thankful to God that He uses me as a vessel for Him and now has asked me to help the Korean sending base. Thirteen years have passed since I was captured by and became bound to WEC. Many people say to me that they can't understand my decision to leave a respected CEO position and become a missionary living by faith.

I can only say how blessed I am to spend the rest of my life being able to walk with the Lord serving in WEC!

Korean dancers

From Cow Shed to Conference Center

By Gerhard Bargen
Queensland, Australia, 1960s

very WEC property represents a miracle. Tell us about this one," requested Charlton Smith, who had just arrived from England.

Tamborine Conference Center in Australia does represent a miracle—from cow shed to comparative mansion, from nothing to comfortable well-equipped conference center. All in three months! "What is impossible with man is possible with God!"

The Keswick Convention had acquired a fifty-acre property at Tamborine Mountain. We were allowed to host a conference on the property and make use of the existing buildings on the site. To make room for seventy participants, we had to utilize every available building, even the cow shed, which became the men's dormitory. No one objected, and it was quite a novelty to pioneer this way. We went in with shovels and brooms and much laughter. The cows had gone. We cleaned the place as well as we could. An old garage was transformed into a kitchen, and we were ready to start. For two years we enjoyed holding our conferences there.

Then in 1965 the Lord disturbed our little nest! Friends approached me with gifts, believing we should purchase a block of the land from the Keswick Convention where we could erect suitable buildings and conduct our conferences. This came as a surprise, as we had not so much as thought of such an idea! We were fully occupied, we thought, with our regular outreach from the WEC base in Brisbane. Nevertheless, the conviction that the Lord was speaking became clear, and we knew we must obey. We took a WEC plunge of faith

Youth camp at Tamborine Conference Center

into the deep and were amazed that as soon as we took the step, the Lord went before us.

Buildings came to hand cheaply. The Lord provided labor to demolish, move and erect them. We held many "working bees," with no leisure moments. Why many came to help, and then came back again, is still a puzzle to me! In fact, people who simply heard of the venture asked if they could join us to help. Some lost weight, as well as perspiration, but one thing was certain: all slept soundly as soon as their heads touched the pillow.

We went ahead with plans, and money came in as it was required. A dear brother, who accomplished a colossal job carting materials up the mountain, passed on a gift of $200 on completion of the job. Others gave freely of materials, time and advice. The center grew like a mushroom.

Bill and Ena Pethybridge, WEC youth leaders from Britain, were our guests at the first "camp" at our new center. Much was still unfinished, but we experienced the true blessing of the Lord, raising our hearts in praise and gratitude for the site and for the grace given to "step out." I am convinced that we, as individuals and the church, are impoverished because of our reluctance to launch out into the deep. In our unbelief we linger in cow sheds when the Lord would lead us into "mansions" if only we believed. "According to your faith will it be done to you" (Matt. 9:29).

Taken from WEC Australian Magazine, 1960

Gerhard Bargen, originally from Russia, then Canada, joined WEC in 1940 for service in India. He sailed via Australia and finally took a ship from there to India in the company of Audrey who was to be his wife. Their ship was sunk, and they consequently spent three and a half years as prisoners of war in Japan. Eventually returning to Australia, they got married and became WEC representatives in Queensland for thirty years.

Holding Class on the Run
Gill Bryant
Senegal, 2009

We knew we had to leave as the sound of gunshots and mortar shells drew closer and closer. In 1997 Senegal's political unrest was boiling over into the village where our school for missionary kids was located. We evacuated the school that summer, leaving behind everything familiar to the students, teachers and staff as we moved with uncertainty into the future.

Bourofaye Christian School (BCS) dates back to 1959, when WEC missionaries' children were first taught in a school in the south of Senegal. Twenty years later the school opened on a larger, more rural site in the village of Bourofaye. This spacious location had been an agricultural Bible school. The campus was beautiful, with many different trees and plants, a sports field and a running track, and amazing wildlife. Those who taught and looked after the children were aware of the huge trust placed in them by the parents, and BCS was known for its family atmosphere. The staff also sought to build good relationships with the neighboring villages and employed a number of local people. All this changed during the summer of 1997.

Immediately after evacuating, we began to wrestle with the question of where to host the students when they returned in the fall. The team prayed hard and, just in time, the school was offered the site of a former Bible college on the edge of the city of Dakar. This answer to prayer came just as students were scheduled to return.

The next weeks were chaotic, filled with getting the new site ready for the students. With only a two-week delay, BCS started its fall semester in a new place with new uncertainties. How long would we be there?

As Christmas 1997 approached, the question of the school's future loomed bigger in our minds. It was becoming obvious that an early return to our previous campus was not an option, and that months might become years.

We wanted to go back as soon as possible. We could not contemplate abandoning a school site that had seen so much investment of lives, energy and money over the years. Regular prayer days were held, with some of the older children volunteering to fast alongside the adults. On one occasion a whole class wrote a letter to the adults, exhorting them to trust God for all that was needed for the future. However, as years of intense prayer, soul searching and disquiet passed at the new Dakar site, God changed our hearts.

We received life-giving words of Scripture from other WEC missionaries who were praying for us during this time: "Enlarge the place of your tent, stretch your tent curtains wide, do not hold back: lengthen your cords, strengthen your stakes. For you will spread out to the right and the left" (Isa. 54:2–3).

In 2001 everyone had come to a realization that taking the school back to its old home would not be possible. This was hard for many; nevertheless, there was a God-given unity.

We applied the exhortation to "enlarge the place of your tent." We had built on and improved the Dakar site, so when we handed it back to the Assemblies of God in 2002, it was in a good state of repair, with many additional assets.

However, we had not finished "lengthening our cords." Further faith challenges were to come as we contemplated the need to leave Dakar at the end of our lease. Where would we go? How, and with what, would we rebuild? How would we cope with running a school, constructing buildings and moving at the same time?

Some staff drove hundreds of miles to look at possible sites, while prayer continued. By now money was coming in toward the building of a new school. We began to look at a piece of land close to the sea, only seventy-five kilometers from Dakar, in a rural setting. How could we have confirmation that it was God's will for us to move to Kiniabour?

We needed to see all the paperwork in place quickly. We got the building permit in a record time of five months. On October 21, 2001 the whole school worshiped on the open field site at Kiniabour and dedicated the land to God. We looked out at nothing but bushes and one tree. God was going to have to work wonders if we were to have a school ready for September 2002.

Building the new school was a story in itself—one of perseverance, faith and the practical support of hundreds of people. Both staff and children saw their prayers answered in many ways: the provision of finances, the completion of paperwork for the land, the resolution of construction hurdles like the well and the electricity supply. God provided many teams and individuals who came to build, paint and do all kinds of work to help us get ready.

The move itself was overwhelming and exhausting. One staff member commented years later, "I remember thinking to myself during one of those classic long-exhausting-moving-shifting-painting days, *one day this whole year will become a sentence . . . the year we moved BCS to Kiniabour.* And so it has!"

Today BCS at Kiniabour has more than seventy students of seventeen nationalities and serves the education needs of a number of mission agencies working in several West African countries. God's faithfulness was shown every step of the journey of this school.

Librarian Gill Bryant and her teacher husband Steve worked at the Bourofaye Christian School from the late 1980s. Since returning to the UK, they have served as international consultants for missionary children's education.

The Brook Dried Up

Beryl Shannon
Congo, 1990s

I was sitting on the couch reading WEC's *Worldwide* magazine when a small picture ambushed my heart. The year was 1994; the place was Isiro, in the Democratic Republic of Congo; the photo was of Margaret Coleman, a former member of the Congo field.

The caption stated her desire to retire as editor of UPESI, the Swahili Good News paper and asked, would anyone like to take on the job? My heart immediately leaped and responded, "YES!! That's for me!" My head said, "Don't be ridiculous, you can't edit UPESI from Africa. Besides, you are far too busy training Sunday school teachers to take on another ministry." End of story. The thought went onto the back burner of my heart.

Fast forward to 1998. Margaret Coleman once again featured in my life when she made a short visit to the Congo. I didn't see her. but the memory of her request pounded in my heart. This had to be from God. I knew it was time to move on from twenty-five years of work in Africa to editing UPESI. But how was I going to leave the Congo to begin this new ministry on another continent?

On August 2nd war broke out. We WECers were gathering in Isiro for our annual conference, but while we were still assembling, the Isiro airport closed. Truckloads of soldiers disappeared behind shops and homes all along the main street, preparing for action. Then word came that Wycliffe Bible Translators team members were going to evacuate the country. WEC decided to go with them. How? When? Where? By then Missionary Aviation Fellowship had pulled out over the border. Would we drive north to the Central African Republic? No, it was too dangerous and would take too much precious fuel for the fifteen adults and four children from three missions to go that way. We decided to travel by road the seventy kilometers to Nebobongo as possibly mission planes could come from outside the country to pick us up using the grass airstrip there. Tentative arrangements were made for planes to come on Sunday, August 16.

Government officials did not want us to leave. Would they prevent us by force? The rebels were coming up from the south. When would they reach Nebobongo? Then the unthinkable happened. The church didn't want us to flee either, believing our departure would endanger the church leaders. Would they prevent the planes from landing on the airstrip? Several of the expatriates were also against evacuating. The trauma of that final week pulled us in every direction. Church/mission relationships were strained. Friendships were stretched to the breaking point. One of our colleagues went into severe shock. All of us prayed, some as they walked the length of the airstrip over and over. We prayed, individually trying to work out what God's will was in this terrible crisis. Each person seemed to have his/her own idea about what God was saying.

God began speaking to us through His Word. Several of the missionaries received the same Scripture verses from the Lord: "He reached down from on high and took hold of me; he drew me out of deep waters. He rescued me from my powerful enemy, from my foes, who were too strong for me" (Ps. 18:16–17).

The Lord spoke to me along different lines, however. I plainly heard Him speaking through another verse: "Some time later the brook dried up" (1 Kings 17:7). I had spent twenty-five years in the Congo, and now my brook was drying up. It was my time to move on to another land, to another ministry.

Finally Sunday arrived, but the question raged on: would we leave the Congo or would we stay? Early that morning we stood in a circle under a large tree and each stated whether he/she would go or stay. The majority ruled, and the planes were called. We trooped down to the airstrip for our noon appointment with two small planes. No one knew if soldiers or rebels were standing in the bushes waiting to attack or take us hostage once we had boarded. We didn't know if perhaps the local children would run onto the airstrip to prevent the planes from landing. We did know this was God's plan.

The sign agreed upon with the pilots was that we would lay down two white sheets if everything looked alright. This we did, but suddenly two young men we had never seen before jumped over the hedge, grabbed the sheets and, after a tussle, ran off with our sheets. By this time the planes were circling. When they saw the sheets disappear, the first pilot started to pull away east.

What were we to do? Suddenly someone noticed that Maud Kells was wearing a white cotton jacket and yelled for her to throw it on the ground immediately! She did, and both the pilots received the message and landed. Within seven minutes we were all safely in the air heading for Nairobi.

We learned later that soldiers were on the way to stop the planes, but their tires went flat. They spent the whole day trying to repair them without success The following day the rebels appeared from the south. God had taken us out of a dangerous situation. My heart was glad. My question, "How would I leave the Congo?" was answered. God released me from the

Congo, and I was on the way to England to join SOON Ministries and begin editing UPESI, a ministry my twenty-five years of Sunday school work in Swahili had prepared me for.

Canadian Beryl Shannon worked in the Congo from the early 1970s until the events in the article. Since then she has continued to edit the Upesi Swahili broadsheet in England.

My Journey with a "Faith Mission"
Byung Kook Yoo
South Korea, 2004

*I*n April 2004 we were preparing to hold WEC leadership meetings in Seoul. I felt a little nervous since this was the first international conference the Korean sending base had organized and fifty participants were expected.

Though it was the custom for participants to come at their own expense, I could not ask them to pay for meals and accommodation as we hoped to show "true Korean hospitality" and welcome our guests wholeheartedly.

When we estimated expenses, the total exceeded 50,000,000 Won, or about $50,000. This was an issue because the balance of our finances was less than 100,000 Won, or $1,000. As we have always done, we made up our minds to follow our faith mission practice of trusting the Lord to provide all of our needs without making appeals.

Before we looked to the people and churches around us to provide, we decided to have a period of fasting and prayer. News of our situation must have gotten around, for one day we had a call from someone who knew the pastor of a large church in Seoul. The pastor had once visited WEC International's main office and left with a good impression. This man went on to say he had mentioned to the pastor that we were fasting and praying for provision for the conference. When the pastor heard this, he replied that it would not be difficult to help such an honorable organization with an important conference coming up. We were advised to write an official letter to the church which would give us an immediate donation to cover the entire costs.

As we faced the reality of our huge financial need, we quickly sent an official letter to the church without giving it much thought. What was the matter with the offer? After all, the church could help us right away. Less than a week had passed when we got a message from the missions department of the church inviting us to come and share our story in detail. I went over to the church and met with the staff. They were already aware of our conference and stated the final step would be to send an official description of all the expenses and the funds would soon follow.

As everything went so quickly and simply, I felt as if a heavy burden had been lifted off me. We wouldn't need to continue our difficult fasting and prayer commitment! I wanted to boast to everybody in the office that our biggest financial problem had just been solved.

Suddenly I thought of my many colleagues who had been sent out across the world. Then I was struck by the image of our Lord Jesus looking worried. I couldn't understand why I felt troubled when I was supposed to feel cheerful. Eventually I realized it had to do with the principle of faith. Hadn't I always emphasized the importance of keeping the principle of faith, one of the four pillars of WEC? When I saw workers struggle with weak financial support and delaying their departure, this is the one thing I would emphasize. I taught them not to ask people for financial support. I was the one who taught them over and over again, until they were sick of hearing it, that it is the Lord who has called us and he will send us out.

Now I, a leader in a faith mission, was tempted to abandon our faith principle in the face of this urgent need. If I took the church's money, how could I tell the other workers to never be anxious about finances but present all their requests to the Lord, who would meet every need? I felt ashamed of myself. Did $50,000 really seem so big? Did I not trust the Lord, the provider of all our needs?

I wrote a polite e-mail to the person responsible for the mission department of the church, asking him to forget our request and explaining that it went against our principle of trusting the Lord alone for provision. Soon after, this person replied saying he had never encountered this before. He said he could not understand why an organization would reject financial support from a willing church without any special reason. But he was amazed and refreshed by the fact that an organization with such a principle existed.

The support from the church didn't work out, but our Lord is always faithful. Unexpectedly, we were offered the use of a nice meeting place for the conference, which saved a significant amount of money. The fifty leaders came, held a successful meeting in a good environment and left Korea having received a warm welcome and excellent hospitality.

Even though we don't know where all the finances came from (and there was no single large donation), by the end of the conference, our finance office was left with extra funds! As always, the Lord is in the midst of us. He does perform miracles such as feeding thousands with five loaves of bread and two fish, proving that He is with us forever. Because of His mighty resources and great promises, He can be trusted to meet all our needs without us asking any human being for help.

Byung Kook and Bo in Yoo joined WEC in 1986 and served in Gambia, West Africa for ten years until they were asked to commence the WEC base in South Korea. After pioneering this work for eleven years and seeing many Koreans join WEC, they became its directors for international mobilization. They have three daughters.

10

Love in Action

To go forward, we must go deeper.

Dieter Kuhl

When love is a factor, the difficult is do-able. God's grace makes all things possible though it doesn't make things easier.

Tom Harvey

I have made you known to them, and will continue to make you known in order that the love you have for me may be in them and that I myself may be in them.

John 17:26

Love Builds Bridges in Kashmir
Daphne Jacobs
Kashmir, India, 1950s

One afternoon Betsy, a new worker on our team, asked my husband, "Anything special at the clinic this morning, Steve?"

"Well, yes. The old Balti woman came to ask my wife to go and see her little grandson. He's very sick, but Daphne isn't well enough to go see him."

"Maybe I could go. Surely there's something I could do."

"Thank you, Betsy, but what can you do? You don't speak the language, and it's a long hike."

"I'll go!" Betsy moved quickly, assuring us she could examine the woman's grandson and give him some medicine.

After a time of prayer together, Betsy left with a posy in one hand and a bulging bag over her shoulder, winding her way down into the valley.

By tea time she was home, radiant and praising the Lord for His help. "It was a worthwhile visit," she said. "I have told Granny to come back to the clinic when the medicine is finished."

Four days later Granny returned.

"How is your grandson?"

"Oh, very much better. Miss Sahib's visit did us all good. She read such sweet words from *Iinjil-i-muqquddas* (the Gospel). Indeed it was sweet. She said you would all pray, and God has answered your prayers. Our little boy will live. Please come again to our home!"

"But Granny, what did you understand? Miss Sahib does not yet speak your language!"

"True. But she speaks the one language we all know, and the whole world understands."

"What is that?"

"The sweet language of love. We felt her love and knew she cared. The fruit and flowers made our little boy happy. Miss Sahib sang so sweetly about Jesus and read from the Gospel. She gave us her time. Please let her come again."

So hearts and homes were opened in villages nestling in the Himalayan foothills of North India.

Love builds bridges.

Taken from WEC Australian Magazine

Steve and Daphne Jacobs served in India from 1942, followed by outreach among migrants in the UK and Australia.

A Living Bible Translation (Isa Arthur, 1924–2010)

Nicky King
Guinea-Bissau, 2010

If you didn't know, you would find putting an age to Isa difficult. At first sight I suspect the impression would be of an old lady, back bent with arthritis and small, the sort of person you would not notice when you passed by in the street. But if you ever had the honor of getting to know her, the impression of an insignificant old lady would quickly be replaced by one of a gleeful school girl lurking inside her wizened frame. Isa was one of those people who don't fit into a common mold. Who could stand against her silent, all-conquering grace, her spiritedly disarming, dry humor? External appearances were deceiving. On the outside she was almost ninety years old, but on the inside, age didn't count in Isa's way of thinking.

For most of her ninety years she had lived and worked in the little West African country of Guinea-Bissau. Originally she had gone out from Scotland as a trained nurse to help those unable to help themselves. Then, as she gained a command of the local Portuguese Creole language, she had turned her energies to translating the Bible into the local dialect so the people could read about her Lord and Savior for themselves.

Although I'd studied the intricacies of Bible translation at college, I had never appreciated the subtle but vital nuances of language. How do you translate a phrase such as "Though your sins are like scarlet, they shall be as white as snow" (Isa. 1:18) when the people you are writing for have never seen

Isa Arthur and church member

snow in their lives? How do you express things to come if the language you are using has no future tense? How do you describe the good shepherd parables of Jesus if people have never seen a sheep, let alone a shepherd? All these things Isa wrestled with over many years so her translation of the Word of God would be presented fairly and accurately to the people of Guinea-Bissau.

Linguistic difficulties were not Isa's only problem. In the early days her translation work was done with pen and paper. Fairly easy for those of us with filing cabinets, a regular supply of dry paper and working pens. Easy for those of us living in politically stable lands with a reliable supply of food and water. But for someone living in a land where humidity and mildew creep insidiously into paper, where dust and heat destroy pens, where incessant work to secure food and water claims most of your time, where civil war, famine and flood mean abandoning the last two years' work in order to save your life—the situation is much different.

In later years when laptop computers and floppy disks became the means of translation work, you would think things would be easier. But for someone living in a remote part of the world, how do you learn to use modern technology on your own? How do you protect a sensitive laptop from the ravages of dust-laden winds, circuit shortening humidity and the vagaries of solar-powered electricity?

For those of us who have grown up in stable western democracies with pure water coming from a kitchen tap, a profusion of food at the corner shop, and support engineers and software educators at hand, such tasks would still be daunting. For an aging woman alone in a West African country with few luxuries and little technology, this would seem almost impossible—but not for Isa.

Despite constant interruptions and demands on her time ("Miss Isa, Miss Isa, come quickly; my son has broken his leg"), Isa doggedly continued her God-given task.

Why did Isa do this? Why did she sacrifice her life to such a work? Isa was a trained nurse, a recently appointed ward sister in a prestigious Scottish hospital when she had the call to go to Africa. Why? She could have stayed in Scotland. She could have risen in the nursing profession. She could have had a comfortable home, a car, holidays in luxurious resorts. She could have had wealth, security, status. She could have had a husband, a family and grandchildren to bounce on her knee.

But to do so would have meant turning a deaf ear to the call of God in those early years. Not that for one fleeting instant did the thought of resentment or regret enter her mind. The call to Guinea-Bissau was a call from God, and where God called, God would enable. Isa's call was not to things seen but to unseen things; not to earthly rewards but to heavenly rewards. Not for her own benefit but for the benefit of others—and of her God.

Written communication with Isa was difficult when she was in Guinea-Bissau—fragile air-mail letters at the mercy of wind and rain, and of any passing person who fancied the colorful stamps on the envelope. Only during her home leave periods did we have the opportunity to enjoy her company. Every five or six years she would return to Scotland to embark on a tour visiting friends and supporters and giving talks to churches and interested groups up and down the country.

I don't know how she stood the pace, being whisked here and there by car, ferry and train, with an afternoon ladies' meeting in one church and an evening talk at a church fifty miles away—with a hurried tea in between and an unfamiliar bed at night. Then the following morning began with an early start and a drive to another location.

I don't know how she remembered all the people she met on those tours. To me they would all have become a sea of faces merging into an easily forgettable mediocrity. But not for Isa. She loved people. Not just groups of people: Isa remembered not only names and faces, but relatives, jobs, histories and hopes and fears associated with each name and face. Isa seemed always to be writing letters to people. Whenever we took her somewhere, she would meet us clutching a handful of envelopes and a request to pass by a postal box on the way.

We learned from Isa during her home visits. Being away for five or six years enabled her to discern the changes that had taken place since her last visit, changes that we, because we were constantly immersed in our culture, could not see. She was never critical or condemning; she just made passing comments and dispassionate casual remarks that made you examine yourself and your culture and question where we were going. Were there more of those game show programs on the TV? People seemed much fatter since her last visit. Why were there fewer children playing in the streets?

Although she never criticized her native Scottish culture, you could tell it had become alien to her and Guinea-Bissau was where she felt at home. She never said so, but you could sense that she was dismayed by the materialism, selfishness and emptiness that gripped the Scottish people.

On the day we booked plane tickets for her return to Guinea-Bissau, you could see a perceptible change in her expression. A few tension wrinkles that had crept over her face during her home leave melted away instantly at the confirmation that on a certain date at a certain time she would be on her way back to Guinea-Bissau. Back to civil war perhaps, back to a military dictatorship, back to lack of water and electricity, to mud and dust and termites. Back to what had become her home, surrounded by people who had come to love her and value her as their own.

At the age of eighty, Isa decided to retire back to her home in Guinea-Bissau. Retire is perhaps the wrong word, for she had a Bible concordance already started and enthusiastic plans for other translation projects. For many months she visited friends and supporters to say her final farewells; she would not return to Scotland.

Isa will never have her name engraved in bronze on some statue in a city square or museum. She will never be mentioned in the yearly reports of a multinational company, never see her genes passed on through grandchildren. Her last will and testament will not bequeath house or fortune to those left behind. All Isa owns on earth can be carried in her handbag. Instead, her name will be held in the hearts of the uncountable number of people on whom she has showered graciousness and unselfish love. Her reward will be with the saints, to whom the God of this world and the next will say, "Well done, good and faithful servant."

Isa spent most of her life translating the Bible into Portuguese Creole. In a way she didn't need to do this. Her life has been the translation of the Bible into Portuguese Creole. For the people of Guinea-Bissau, Isa was the walking embodiment of the Word of God. Isa's life was a living sermon.

Nicky King and his wife Jane knew Isa Arthur for well over thirty years and had the privilege of taking her back to Guinea Bissau for the last time. Working through the Kingserve Trust in Scotland, they were able to assist Isa in her vocation and continue working with missionaries in Africa and other parts of the world.

Love without Words
Eva
Middle East, 2009

The huge earthquake that hit precisely at the center of a large town in the strictly Islamic country where we work only lasted for eleven seconds.

In those seconds the lives and possessions of multiple thousands of people were destroyed. The destruction was devastating to see. Even a traditional bomb could not create such havoc and take so many lives! Walking through the ruins of what just days before had been a beautiful and welcoming area, all we could do was think of possible ways in which we could help.

Thank God, within a short time our organization received a large amount of money, as people all over Europe were donating from what they had for those who had lost everything but their lives.

During the first weeks, together with many other aid agencies, we helped distribute all kinds of emergency relief items: tents, blankets, food, hygiene packs and so on. Then other organizations left, but the situation for the people was still extremely difficult. Many victims started to show signs of deep depression as the first shock wore off.

So we stayed on and continued to reach out, with activities which would have a longer-lasting effect on the beneficiaries, enabling them to pick up their lives again. One day a man whose family had been especially hard hit by the disaster came to us. Seventeen of his relatives had died. "Why are you doing this?" he asked. "Our own government is not really helping us, and our spiritual leaders are also nowhere to be seen! You have come from a faraway country to help us. Why are you doing this?"

Not knowing how much we could say, as "government observers" seemed to be present everywhere, my husband replied, "Why don't you yourself think about that?"

A few days later we returned to the same place to continue with our activities. The same man came up to us. "I have thought about your question," he said.

"And what is your conclusion?"

"I think that it must be the love of Jesus Christ in your hearts that makes you do all these things for us."

Wow! What could we answer but, "You are completely right. That is exactly the reason why we wholeheartedly do this."

At times as Christians, we feel we have no message when we cannot talk about our faith. Yet clearly the reality of Jesus Christ within us shines through in who we are! I wonder why unbelievers discern this so much more readily than we do. One of our colleagues used to say, "We are always proclaiming the gospel, but very rarely we use words."

Love Your Enemy
Anonymous
Pakistan, 2006

On July 16, 1985 at half past nine in the evening, I left home for Karachi airport to meet a colleague. I arrived ten minutes early, so I walked up and down outside the airport buildings.

As I was passing the departure lounge, a man tapped me on the shoulder and asked if I knew a man he pointed at. I looked at the man, who looked like a Pakistani, and said I did not. I turned to walk on, but my questioner insisted that the other man was my friend. I repeated that I did not know him and had to go and meet someone at "Arrivals."

He asked me to go with him to the security control office. I was protesting again when ten to fifteen security men surrounded me with their guns drawn. I decided to go with them! I sat in the office thinking this would all be cleared up in the next few minutes, but I was sadly mistaken. My wife only found out what had happened the next morning after waiting up all night for my return.

As the full story came out, the Pakistani-looking man was in fact a Dutch national with Indian heritage, who had been caught trying to leave the country with two hundred and forty grams of heroin in a lady's purse in his inside jacket pocket. He claimed that a white man with a beard had given him the purse to take into the departure lounge. He was asked to point out the man who gave him the purse. I was the first white man with a beard to pass by—so he incriminated me! I was placed in the customs lock-up, a heavily guarded room holding ten other prisoners, for two weeks. In the almost bare room, I had to share a sleeping mat with my accuser.

As we had come into the prison together, the other prisoners asked, "Is he your friend?" "No," I replied, "He is my enemy." I did not want them to think we were in this together.

Each day my wife brought me food and drinking water. What a boost to my morale to spend two or three minutes speaking to her.

There in prison God challenged me with, "Love your enemy." I read in Romans 12:20, "If your enemy is hungry, feed him." I had preached on that chapter many times, but now to put it into action was hard. Finally I gave my accuser some of my food. He turned around and said that he knew I was innocent and he would tell the customs men.

Seven days later we stood before the judge. "Is this the man who gave you the purse?" "I stood straight, thinking that it would now all be over.

"Yes," came the reply.

Oh, no, I thought. *No more food for you, mate.*

But then God spoke to me: "I did not say give food to your enemy only if he tells the truth."

Okay, Lord.

Being in prison was a good opportunity to share my faith. One American who was on a drug charge rededicated his life to Christ. A Muslim who wanted to know why I did not curse God later accepted a Bible.

After two weeks I was taken out of prison to court. I will never forget turning the corner to see fourteen people from various Christian groups and nationalities waiting there with my wife. Later I learned they had been at the court for three days. They represented thousands who have since stood by us and identified with us. I was granted bail of £7,000. Many hearings followed.

Looking back I can see that God used my experience in prison to speak to people. I still do not know why it took ten months for the case to be dropped, though possibly it was to focus prayer on the needy city of Karachi. Keep praying for those who are still held in Satan's grip.

A Life Strengthened by Grace
Maria Röbbelen
Liberia and Gambia, 2010

In 1957 I set out on a cargo ship from Hamburg, heading for the unknown in Liberia. In those days we had no idea what lay ahead. There wasn't the instant access to information that we have today. We could only find out about a country by reading or hearing from someone who had visited.

Traveling with a companion was a great comfort. Hanna Förster was also going for the first time. Our courage came from the assurance that we were called and sent by Jesus and that He was going with us. We expected to be away from home, family and friends for four years. Traveling by sea had its blessings as we had time to recover from all the rushing around before leaving and to prepare for the busy life ahead. The voyage also helped us gradually adjust to the extreme change in climate.

At first we had no telephone in Liberia, and the mail took months to arrive (Christmas parcels reached us at Easter). Roads were extremely muddy; the village of River Cess was in the middle of the jungle and consisted of a few huts. Water was carried from the river and had to be boiled. Our diet was that of the local people—rice every day, for every meal. We had meat only if a hunter had been successful.

As a nurse, I worked on the medical side, helped for the first four weeks by my predecessor. She then set out "on trek," leaving me alone in the work with no knowledge of the language. I had to deliver babies under the watchful eyes of the old village midwives, without any previous experience and relying very much on prayer.

One particular incident (1963) comes to mind. We were in the midst of the rainy season. Time and again I was awakened at night by the mass of water pouring down. One night the rains roused me, and I suddenly heard a knock on the door. I was called to see a woman with a severe hemorrhage. I soon saw that she must be taken to the mission center, as I could not give her the help she needed in her hut. With two hours till daybreak, there was neither a hammock nor any men to carry the woman—they had to be called from the next village.

I returned home, and very early in the morning went back again to the hut. It was still pouring rain. When I came to the river, the water had risen and almost reached the bridge. Would it still be there when I returned? There was no time to waste. Meanwhile, enough men and a hammock had been found, but there was no branch on which to fix the hammock so it could be carried more easily. The woman's condition had worsened.

Eventually we were on our way, but the river had become a lake. The bridge was not to be seen, and the water reached far over our knees.

The four men carrying the hammock followed slowly. Although invisible the bridge was still in its place. Full of gratitude I

Maria Röbbelen with Liberian mothers

An earlier photo of Maria

stood on it until the four men reached the bridge. Shortly afterward it was carried away by the floods. I could not change my wet clothes until midday, for now the priority was on saving the woman's life. She fully recovered.

Originally, Hanna and I were headed for Gambia and expected to stay in Liberia for a short time to gain experience; to start with we didn't even unpack all our things. Seven years passed before the opportunity came to start work in the country of our calling. When independence was granted to Gambia in 1965, we found an open door for medical work and were able to obtain visas. We and another colleague, Ruth Dieterich, arrived in August 1966. Ninety-five per cent of the people were Muslim, but we were given complete freedom to preach the gospel. The men who gave us official permission probably thought three women were harmless!

Once we moved to Gambia, we needed to find out how and where to start and the best way to get close to the people. While traveling through the country, we came to Sibanor where we came across a man who had met Christian workers in the past. He welcomed us and became our friend and advocate, giving us a piece of land where we were able to build our first clinic. My first priority was to learn the language, but on our second day almost a hundred people waited on our doorstep to be treated, so we had to start our medical ministry immediately.

We soon made friends and on Sundays went into the surrounding villages to share the gospel. We were made very welcome, and many people showed an interest but only a few took the step to follow Jesus. Family bonds were too strong; and those who wanted to take that step were threatened.

I enjoyed the work, thought it was grueling; most of the time I was on my own. The three of us had different temperaments, and our life was not always easy, but the Lord led us together in prayer, and He laid down the rules of the work. One of the lessons I learned (and which I passed on to new workers) is to go with the knowledge that God has sent you, but not to have ready-made answers for everything. God will have many good and surprising experiences in store.

The best way to describe my years of service, as I see it, is "Grace and nothing but grace." They are summed up in the words of a song: "You have made my life so rich."

Over the years the work has developed immensely. Not only did a medical work come into being, but agricultural projects, translation work, several training opportunities for income-creating jobs and, more recently, a center for nutrition on the north bank of the Gambia River.

Maria Röbbelen was one of the first overseas workers sent out by WEC Germany. Together with Hanna Förster, she went to Liberia in 1957 and with Ruth Dieterich to Gambia in 1966. Maria remained there until 1991.

Brothers

Judy Raymo
Congo, 2010

Background note: WEC founder C.T. Studd first went to Congo in 1913. He began a work in the northeast that by 2010 included a network of churches led by national pastors with an estimated attendance of two hundred and fifty thousand; a medical ministry with hundreds of rural clinics and four hospitals operated by Congolese and international staff; educational institutions, including six Bible schools, three high schools and numerous primary schools; and practical development projects. Much remains to be done. As a 2008 book, Blood River—A Journey to Africa's Broken Heart, *vividly describes,*

> Congo stands as a totem for the failed continent of Africa. It has more potential than any other African nation, more diamonds, more gold, more navigable rivers, more fellable timber, more rich agricultural land. But it is exactly this sense of what might be that makes the Congo's failure all the more acute. . . . Much of its territory has long been abandoned to a feral state of lawlessness and brutality. With a colonial past bloodier than anywhere in Africa . . . People remember flickers from its past—the brutality of the early colonials, the post-independence chaos of elected leaders beaten to death, corrupt dictators whittling away the nation's wealth, mercenaries running amok in wars too complex for the outside world to bother with, rebels who rely on cannibalism and fetishism.[10]

When the Belgian government gave independence to Congo in 1960, the ensuing struggle for control led to a bloody civil war. By 1964 "Simbas," followers of the assassinated rebel leader Patrice Lumumba, violently took over

Bill McChesney

territory in northeast Congo, the area where C.T. Studd first worked in the "Heart of Africa." In spite of the troubles, life had been relatively normal for many months. By the time warning was received by radio on August 22 that the American consul advised evacuation, roads were already sealed off by checkpoints and rebel posts, and some workers had already been living in occupied territory for weeks. Beyond any law or restraint, the Simbas reverted to magic, cannibalism and mindless cruelty toward those from "colonial" or Western countries. The hated "whites," including children and Roman Catholic priests and nuns, suffered threats, ridicule, beatings, barefoot forced marches over gravel roads, mock trials, aborted executions and torturous deaths over the next four months. Jim Rodger and Bill McChesney were among those from WEC. Jim and Bill couldn't have been more different.

Bill, twenty-eight years old, handsome, full of humor, was a practical fellow from hot, sunny Phoenix, Arizona, USA. He'd done well at Bible school and WEC candidate orientation, and arrived in Congo in 1960. His jobs on the field included maintaining and repairing all the mission vehicles at Ibambi, the headquarters for the area. Africans and fellow workers appreciated his humble spirit and his disinterest in earthly possessions or success.

Jim, aged forty-five, came from cool, gray Dundee, Scotland and was a

Jim Rodger

schoolteacher. As Len Moules, WEC's UK sending base leader at the time, explained:

> It's a miracle that Jim ever got to the mission field. He came to our WEC headquarters as a candidate three times, and three times he was turned down. Academically he was brilliant. He had a Master of Arts degree with Honors in Languages; from many aspects we couldn't have had a better candidate.
>
> But what do you do with a man who gets on a bus and then forgets where he's going? He has to get off to collect his senses as to why he's there and where he is going. On three occasions that happened. Well, this isn't missionary material, really, is it? Although he had a deep love for Africans and was an accomplished, certified school teacher with an honors degree—well, that's all very well, but these other things are very real indeed.
>
> I didn't think we could send a man out to the heart of Africa who had lapses of memory as drastic as this. And so the third time we said, "Jim, we're afraid not. You just look to the Lord to find some appointment at home."
>
> Jim came back the third time and said, "I know God has called me. God's called me to Congo and I'm going." And the WEC staff said, "We're sorry, but we think it would be far better if you stayed at home." Well, the missionaries in Congo heard this and said, "We want this man and we'll take every responsibility."
>
> I wrote back, "All right, it's on your heads. If he's not satisfactory or anything like that, you've got only yourselves to blame. We warned you. When he gets there he may wonder why he's out there. He has lapses of memory."
>
> Well, Jim went out. And Jim loved the Africans and the Africans loved him from the day he arrived. If ever a home staff were wrong, we were wrong over Jim Rodger.

By October 1964 European mercenaries had begun to turn the tide battling against the Simbas. In retaliation, and as pressure on the government to recall the mercenaries, the rebels turned their full wrath upon foreigners, especially Belgians and Americans. Along with others, Bill was arrested, then returned to Ibambi several times. Due to severe beatings, he became weak and was quite ill at times.

On November 14 both Jim and Bill were arrested again and kept in Wamba. For ten days the two men were allowed to spend much of their time walking slowly together, talking of the Lord and forming a firm bond of fellowship. When Bill was sick, Jim cared for him day and night. On their last day, as paratroopers began to rout the Simbas and rescue hostages in the capital, the infuriated Simbas beat Bill so badly he could no longer stand. Jim carried him. Bill's clothing had been ripped to shreds, and some Roman Catholic priests gave him their clothes to keep him warm that night.

On November 25 Jim, Bill and all other white males in Wamba were marched into a courtyard and ordered to declare their nationalities. Bill acknowledged that he was an American, and Jim answered that he was British.

Sentence was pronounced: "All Americans and Belgians are to die. All others will be spared."

The Simbas ordered Bill to step forward, but he was weak and unable to move. A priest, who survived, heard Jim say to Bill, "If you have to die, I'll die with you." Jim helped Bill to the position where Americans and Belgians were being lined up.

One of the Belgian priests, about to die himself, called out to a Simba who seemed to be in charge, "That man is British—he is not an American!" Someone else kindly reminded Jim that he should report his nationality, and he would be safe. He and Bill were again asked their nationalities, but Jim did not answer. Their hands were tied behind their backs to their ankles, and they were thrown to the ground.

The Simbas executed twenty-nine men at Wamba that day.

Catholic nuns were forced to watch the slaughter. *Time* magazine reported:

> According to survivors, the Simbas raced around screeching, "Kill, kill, kill them all!" The Belgians were shot, clubbed to death, or tied up and hurled alive into the Wamba River. But that was killing with kindness compared to the fate of American Protestant missionary William McChesney. They performed a mad war dance on his prostrate body until internal bleeding from ruptured organs ended his agony. Then the Simbas plucked out his eyes and threw his corpse into the river.[11]

A priest who survived reported that after Bill was knocked to the ground, a Simba jumped on his neck, visibly breaking it, so the frenzy of the rebels seems to have been taken out on only a human casket, while his spirit was already with the Lord he loved and for whom he lived and died.

The Simbas also trampled Jim to death.

In 1971 Len Moules visited Congo.

> Eventually I arrived at Wamba. Oh, what a welcome! The crowds were waiting for us; they ran beside the Land Rover. We went in under the garlanded arch, and very soon we were unpacking our kit outside a little rest house. It seemed as if it had seen better days, and the missionary in charge said, "C.T. Studd built this." I could believe it! But the next words sobered me: "Bill and Jim spent their last night in this room."
>
> I put up the camp bed. I lay on my back on that bed in that room. "Bill and Jim spent their last night here." If only walls could speak. If only they could tell me what went through the men's minds. Just outside on that little veranda there had been a Simba guard, daubed from head to foot with mud mixed with the blood of animals. He was hideous in appearance, standing outside with a spear, waiting for any op-

portunity or excuse to impale them. And inside were Bill and Jim, possibly knowing it was their last night on earth. What could these walls tell me?

Bill McChesney was an American, Jim Rodger a Scotsman. The American was almost under the sentence of death already, but not the Scotsman. The nationals were against the Belgians and Americans at that time, but those of different nationalities were given a few days' reprieve. Bill must have known that this was his last night on earth. And Jim? Jim had promised Bill, who wasn't too well, "Bill, I'll never leave you. I'll be at your side right through to the end."

I was sleeping that night in a room where they had spent their last night. I can't help but feel that these words were in Jim's mind: "Now my heart is troubled, and what shall I say? 'Father, save me from this hour'? No, it was for this very reason I came to this hour. Father, glorify your name!" (John 12:27–28).

The next morning I went down to the local prison. The prison officer opened it up. I walked into the yard. There was the spot where the line of prisoners had stood that day. Jim and Bill were in that line. It was on this very spot, as I stood in the middle of that prison yard, that the command was given, "Belgians and Americans, one step forward." Jim Rodger, the Scot, stepped forward side by side with Bill, whom he would never leave. One of the Roman Catholic priests there said, "But he is a . . ."

The words weren't heard in the Simbas' cries as they fell on Jim and Bill. They were knocked to the ground and, where I was standing, they were trodden on until they were dead.

Later that afternoon I stood on the bridge and was told, "The bodies were thrown down there." I am a man, and sometimes we feel that tears should be foreign to a man, but my eyes were wet that day.

I lay in that room. I stood in that prison square. I went to the bridge. And I followed the footsteps of a man who said,

"Father, save me from this hour? No, for this purpose I have come to this hour."

Jim and Judy Raymo (USA), with their seven children, served in mission in UK and then worked with WEC in Tasmania, Australia and Canada, as well as in candidate orientation and national leadership in the USA.

11

Protected

The Lord is good, a refuge in times of trouble. . . . He cares for those who trust in him.

Nahum 1:7

It is not faith to believe that Jesus is in heaven. Faith is to believe that Jesus is right here in my very presence, that He is within me, and that I am in Him, that He will never fail or forsake me, and that what He has promised He is well able to perform.

C.T. Studd

I am glad that God is strong-willed. When He says "I will," He will.

Linda Nagel

Witchcraft

Betty Nowland
Touba, Ivory Coast, 1960

Does God speak through dreams?

Before Hazel, my Canadian co-worker, and I went to pioneer a new ministry in the northern Ivory Coast village of Touba, we heard the area was renowned for witchcraft. The population was predominately Muslim, but there was also a small tribe of animists. Other tribes were afraid to set foot in the Touba district. We went out full of enthusiasm, not really knowing what was ahead, but trusting in Jesus. "I can do all things through the strength of the One who lives within me" (Phil. 4:13, PHILLIPS).

While I studied the local language, two veterans of Muslim work, Adeline and Helen, went to Touba for six months to "spearhead" the way for us two younger missionaries. They contacted government officials and the tribal chief. And they rented a mud hut for us, which was to be our home for fifteen months.

African village

Adeline and Helen began to travel out into the bush to find villages where they could share the Good News.

When we arrived, we continued to trek extensively over the area. The *prefect* (government official) told us there were over four hundred villages in the district. What a thrill to be the very first to tell them about Jesus! We visited in both animist and Muslim villages.

All was going well until I began to have severe pain in my right leg. As both of us were nurses, we did all we could to relieve the pain. Nothing seemed to help, so we journeyed to the nearest doctor, 119 kilometers away. He couldn't help either, so we were completely cast on the Lord. We spent much time in prayer, and one night Hazel had a dream.

In her dream she saw a fetish hidden in the straw roof of our house, above the doorway. Then she heard a voice say, "This is what is troubling Betty." When she woke, she pulled up a chair and began searching in the straw.

"Whatever are you doing in the middle of the night?" I asked.

She didn't answer but kept on searching until she found the fetish, a miniature African broom, a bundle of twigs tied together with red string. She looked shaken as she sat on my bed and told me her dream. I quickly responded, "If one part of the dream is true, the second part is true also." We both knelt down and thanked God for revealing this to us. We claimed the covering of the blood and committed it all to the Lord. The severe pain left my body!

The next morning we showed the fetish to the local evangelist, Jean Paul. He turned grey and explained that this was the strongest witchcraft of the area. The meaning of the broom was to kill us both—to sweep us out of the village. We lit a fire and rejoiced together as we saw the little broom consumed in the flames! Truly the Lord is faithful to His promise in Mark 16, where Jesus tells us to go into all the world and preach the good news—and nothing shall by any means harm us!

In spite of many health obstacles, Betty Nowland from Australia served God in a church-planting ministry in Ivory Coast for eighteen years.

No, Never Alone

Janny Riemersma
Kalimantan, Indonesia, 1981

After several colleagues left Merakai, Indonesia, I was alone at this village, five to six days' river travel, or a one-hour flight, from the coast. Other groups of workers lived seven to ten hours away by boat. I eagerly awaited the return of another colleague so we could serve together in this strategic location with six hundred inhabitants.

One night I woke up and heard a choir singing, "No, never alone, no never alone, He'll never leave or forsake me, He'll never leave me alone."

Initially I thought I had left the tape player on, but soon realized I didn't have a tape of this song. God let me hear it for a purpose, to forewarn me and ask me to trust Him.

The next day my field leader arrived to tell me my colleague wasn't coming back. I was to be alone as a foreign worker in Merakai from 1981 to 1983. The God who forewarned me in song that I would never be alone had prepared my heart and assured me He was always with me.

Lena, a seventeen-year-old village girl, became a spiritual friend. Though much younger than I, she was a companion who loved the Lord and ministry in the church. After two years I moved to the Bible school to help with administration and teaching, and Lena went too. She completed Bible training there and met her husband. They now minister together to area churches.

In 2007 I visited Lena and Ayung and their two sons, who call me "Granny."

God never left me alone, and He gave me spiritual children and grandchildren as well!

Janny Riemersma lived in the interior of West Kalimantan, Indonesia for seventeen years prior to her return to Holland as trainer of new workers.

A Table in the Wilderness
Graham Bee
Ghana, 1982

*L*iving and working in Ghana in the early 1980s was a challenge! Numerous military coups, even where junior officers overthrew senior officers, had caused disruption. J.J. Rawlings and his revolutionary new government tried to control rampant inflation by forcing government-controlled prices on shop owners. Rather than sell at a loss, shopkeepers buried their goods in the bush and sold them on the black market. Cocoa, the main export, was being smuggled across the border and sold for much higher prices in Ivory Coast; consequently there was less export revenue coming in.

The country struggled to meet payments for overseas goods and services. A Ghana Airways passenger jet was stranded in London because there was no money to buy fuel for its return journey. Food imports dropped, and the black market flourished.

Fuel was in short supply. Once I spent two and a half days in a queue in the tropical sun with my vehicle to obtain a mere six gallons of fuel—enough to enable me to travel back up north. I was number 166 in the line! One of the mission vehicles was stolen overnight, despite being parked bumper to bumper with other cars in the line-up.

Those of us who changed our foreign currency at the official bank rate could not afford to purchase much at the inflated local prices. As missionaries, our only options were to purchase limited items at the foreign currency shop in the capital or to travel over the border and shop in neighboring countries.

Shopping in neighboring countries was not simple either. In the days before credit cards, we had to plan well in advance and have money sent to a bank in the country where we planned to shop so we could access their local currency. Then we needed an exit visa, a re-entry visa, a visa for the country we were going to, an international driver's license, an international vehicle permit and international car insurance!

We lived four hundred kilometers from the capital where all these things had to be organized, so we could only go every three or four months and would purchase goods for others on our team too. On home leave trying to purchase clothes in various sizes for our children for the next four years, the lady at the checkout asked my wife, "How many children do you have?"

When sharing about these things on home leave, people would often ask, "How can you live there and put up with this?" We replied that every problem was an opportunity for God to show His greatness. We asked them what buying bread from their local bakery did for their faith. "Little," they replied. Shopping was merely a matter of choosing what kind to buy.

We told them about an afternoon when we were gathered together to pray for WECers worldwide and told the team we had come to the end of our flour supply. Bread was not sold in the town, and since we did not have the necessary permits, we could not go elsewhere to buy flour. Together we encouraged ourselves in God and reminded Him of His promises to provide for our needs. We knew He could do for us what He did for the psalmist and "provide a table in the wilderness"; together we prayed that He would.

The next morning on our two-way radio, SIL workers, who shared the same frequency, called and asked if anyone in WEC

Lady feeding child

needed flour. They had received an allocation, had distributed the flour to their workers and still had one large sack remaining.

You can imagine how we rejoiced in God's loving provision that day! As far as we know, this had never happened before and has never happened since—only on the morning after we prayed that God would literally provide our daily bread. Rather than being a problem, running out of flour became another opportunity for God to demonstrate how faithful He is.

Graham Bee with his wife Marj, from South Australia, joined WEC in 1969 and served in Ghana and then in leadership roles in Australia. He continues in an advisory and teaching role.

Safety
Judy Raymo
Lebanon, early 1990s

S irens wailing in the middle of the night. Guiding drowsy little boys, carrying the smallest down dark stairways. Sitting in the bomb shelter as rockets screamed overhead and burst with ground-shaking explosions. Helping the boys recite Bible verses about God's care and protection. Singing and praying."

Our twenty-year-old daughter was describing her experiences in Lebanon.

One thing I've always appreciated about C.T. Studd, the founder of WEC, is that he never sat in a comfortable office in London directing the mission. He went off to Africa at the age of fifty-two, in poor health, and poured himself into evangelism, translation and church leadership in uncomfortable and even dangerous surroundings until his death. He never asked those who followed him into WEC to do what he was not already doing.

As leaders of the WEC USA sending base, we were often contacted by parents who were believers but worried about their children heading for mission work abroad. Questions like "How are you going to guarantee her safety?" "Why does he have to go to a dangerous place like . . . ?" "There is so much need here, why should my child go overseas where who knows what could happen?" were common.

We would try to patiently explain that their (adult) children were answering the call of God for their lives, that there is no place in this world where safety can be guaranteed and that truly the safest place for anyone to be is where God wants him or her in His plan. While reassuring them that every reasonable health and safety precaution would be taken, we explained that working as a cross-cultural worker does involve risks a person might avoid by staying home. Their children, aware of this, had still chosen to obey God's call.

This was all well and good until the day *our* daughter, Melanie, a university student, announced that she wanted to join WEC short-term to serve for a year in a boys' orphanage in Beirut, Lebanon. To our generation of Americans, Beirut is a synonym for chaos, based on news images of piles of rubble and figures waving automatic weapons at stopped vehicles. In fact, we had sometimes told Melanie to clean up her room, saying, "It looks like Beirut in here." At the time, Lebanon was hit regularly by Israeli rockets, and Syrian soldiers with machine guns patrolled the street.

Reassuring reluctant parents about their child's decision is one thing; seeing your own daughter choose to work in a war zone is quite another. I remembered years earlier talking to my own mother about the privilege God was giving her when both my sister and I, with my husband and small children, headed overseas. Thinking about how the Lord holds us to our words,

Soldiers in Beirut

I had to remind myself that the same faithful God, who called and led us, was calling and leading Melanie—and giving us the privilege of releasing our child for His service.

Jim had an even tougher time than I, partly because Melanie is the only daughter among our seven children and also because he had experienced war firsthand and could not only imagine rocket attacks but could remember what they were like. We gained new understanding and patience toward the parents who expressed their misgivings and fears to us.

In the end we knew God was leading Melanie to Beirut, and we knew that, like C.T. Studd, we must do what we encouraged others to do. Jim was able to visit Melanie in Lebanon, and though he found the constant presence of armed soldiers a bit disconcerting, he was encouraged by what God was doing in the lives of the boys at the orphanage and in Melanie's life. He saw that even nights spent in a bomb shelter were being used as God's tools to bring them closer to Him.

Melanie experienced life as it is lived by so many people, including our fellow Christians, in insecure areas throughout the world. She learned that even as rockets exploded, God was faithful and present and speaking to her of His love and care. Her walk with Him took on new depth. She forged friendships that continue despite distance, separation and cultural differences. And her parents were reminded again: the "safest" and best place for any of us is not determined by geography or governmental stability but by God's plan.

Jim and Judy Raymo (USA), with their seven children, served in mission in the UK and then worked with WEC in Tasmania, Australia and Canada, as well as in candidate orientation and national leadership in the USA.

Trapped by Giants and Liberated by God

Patty Toland
Venezuela, 1999

It's one of those things you know you'll experience many times in life to varying degrees, so you sort of brace yourself for it. But eventually you forget and get really busy putting all your eggs into one basket. At least that's what I did. Then the bottom fell out of my basket!

It was in 1981 that God clearly called me into missions. As a result, I terminated my classes at a secular university and began studying Bible and missions. I was sure God was leading me to work in Africa among a tribe that had no church and worshiped evil spirits. Twelve years later, my dreams became real as I stepped off the plane into hot, humid, lush, green West Africa. The anticipation and joy were almost insuppressible. I could almost taste these emotions as they welled up and tried to burst out.

Little did I know that seven months later I'd fly out of the country for medical treatment and be told I probably could never return due to poor health. When this happened, all I had been living for suddenly swirled around and settled upon my shoulders, leaving me in questioning darkness. "God, where are You? Why can't You overcome it? Why did You lead so clearly, then pull the carpet from under my feet? How can I go on when all my hopes and dreams have been dashed?"

My journey through these internal battles began with darkness and confusion; gradually I became trapped by unbelief, anger and bitterness. The first step into unbelief came as I began to wonder why God had brought me all the way to Africa just to abandon me there. I neither felt, saw nor sensed His presence. I searched for Him, longing for a word, a verse or some small feeling of assurance, yet I heard nothing. I had a kitten and a co-worker who comforted me, but He didn't. He remained silent. I was incensed at His apparent inability to be a true Father as the Bible portrayed.

Not until a whole year later did I slowly (I emphasize slowly) begin to recognize that He had manifested His presence to me through my co-worker and even the kitten. I was so focused on trying to experience something supernatural from Him that I missed His presence in the natural surroundings. He was physically with me through them! I wanted Him in a supernatural way and missed Him in the ordinary.

At one point while lying in a hospital room, I read the Bible out of sheer boredom and loneliness. Psalm 50 said to offer up a sacrifice of thanksgiving to God and that He would be glorified. Feeling my bitterness of spirit rise up and giving in to what I knew wasn't the truth, I chose to declare audibly to God, "I have nothing to be thankful for." I waited for lightning to strike me dead (which I would have welcomed as the most merciful thing He could have done) and instead heard a gentle voice, "That's why it's a sacrifice." It had never occurred to me the cost of whispering thanks in my bitterness and anger was worth more to Him than years of thanks during the easy times.

As time went on and improvement in my health was not apparent, all that I believed about God and the Bible was shaken to the core. I realized my faith was shallower than the depth of my circumstances. Capitalizing on that was the Enemy, seeking of course to finish off the last morsel! I knew this was a battle for my mind.

The only way to give God a fair chance was to at least read the Bible again from beginning to end, allowing it to seep into the sparse cracks in my thinking that were still slightly open to Him. To read the whole Bible in a bitter, angry state of mind is quite a challenge as there are no givens. My theology was revamped as I saw how much the Bible spoke of suffering and testing rather than how much He wants to bless us and make us happy. Even Job looked to the north, south, east and west and couldn't find Him, but was still convinced that God knew where he was and that when God was done testing him, he would come forth as gold (Job 23:8–10). I wasn't that convinced but was intrigued that even Job couldn't sense God's presence.

My last and perhaps greatest internal battle during the journey through the traps was to slowly peel my fingers off of my own ambitions. I honestly didn't know I had them. I thought they were God's, but when I wasn't willing to relinquish them, I came to the conclusion they were mine.

The entire health battle lasted nine years, and I realized that the physical struggle had stripped only part of my being. There was much more to be gotten rid of, which seemed to surface only through suffering—and in my case, it's only then that I am willing to let go, for survival's sake.

There is a deeper spiritual well which brings true abundant life in Him; the drops I've tasted are sweet, and I wouldn't trade them for anything. I wasn't able to say that during the deepest part of my trial, but as He healed my spirit and I looked for His will above mine, a whole new freedom was released. The best part has been getting beyond myself in a new way and being ready to consider things I was previously closed to. As a result, I have been brought into a whole new life—a deeper one in God and His fullness than I otherwise would have known.

My passion is working directly with the unreached. But since I left Africa, God has set me to working in mobilization and training in Latin America. Though this is not my passion, I can see how God uses it. I'm convinced my passion for the unreached fills and gives life to my teaching. I am involved in training and mobilizing out of obedience, because God had me lay down my personal agenda and exchange it for His when the bottom fell out of my basket. If I am honest, I really believe that God by His wonderful grace is using me more through training and mobilizing than if I had gone directly to the unreached. That thought is humbling and proves to me that He knows better where I fit in His kingdom than I do. Just knowing this fills my soul with joy.

Patty Toland (USA) has worked with WEC since 1990 in Ivory Coast, Venezuela and El Salvador.

Presence of the Father
Karina Macleod
Brazil, 2010

After ten years in Brazil, I took stock of my time at WEC's Missionary Training College: varied, stretching, fulfilling, eventful. And the Latin students? Gregarious, enthusiastic, friendly—a lovely sense of community at our residential college, with plenty of dynamic team interaction.

Then, out of the blue, I spent six weeks largely on my own, weak and ill with an unexplained tropical fever. Instead of being surrounded by lively Brazilian students in a world religions class or hosting a meal for my tutor group, I was alone in my bedroom on the college campus, hearing the daily bustle of students and staff but separate from it.

In that hard time of enforced stillness, God ministered in a way both simple and profound, using images that encouraged me during the next seven years in Brazil and continue to speak to me today in my home ministry.

I had a lot of time to think during that illness: about childhood experiences in Scotland, my conversion and call to mission as a teenager, taking part in a WEC prayer group in my hometown, short-term mission in Africa and long-term work in Brazil.

I recalled with gratefulness the Christian home I grew up in. One day two pictures came clearly to my mind—my final two memories of my father who died suddenly when I was ten. In these images I saw wonderful analogies of how the Lord cares for us as our perfect heavenly Father and how He had walked with me in experiences at home and in cross-cultural missions.

In the first of my two memories, we are on a family outing, climbing a hill. I am holding my dad's hand, I am imitating him by wearing his sunglasses and hat, and both of us are carrying picnic baskets. I don't know the way to the top. It's a new experience, but I'm fine because my father knows the path and the challenges ahead. How precious it is to walk in the presence of the Father, holding on to Him, imitating Him, going up with provisions.

Holding onto my Father and rejoicing in seeing others holding on—this made me think of Eliane, diagnosed in the middle of her college course with a debilitating disease, but resolutely persevering. Adelio, our blind student, was always an inspiration. Luis and Tina were such good examples in the learning curves of cross-cultural marriage.

Then there was Nina, willing to endure freezing Scottish winters in her desire to use her native enthusiasm and warmth in discipling others, and many graduates holding on as they obeyed the call to leave a land where churches are growing to serve in places deeply inhospitable to the gospel.

Imitating the Father means accepting people with their differences—students and staff of many nationalities, denominations, generations and personality types. The challenge of contextualization in cross-cultural ministry is inspired by Jesus' example of identifying with us. Just as my dad didn't laugh at my feeble efforts to copy him, my heavenly Father honors my fumbling attempts to walk in His footsteps. He always builds up; He never humiliates.

Going up and facing different challenges on the climb: for expatriate college staff, this means mastering Portuguese so as to communicate well in the people's heart language. For all the team, it means investing faithfully in the growth—spiritual, emotional and intellectual—of our students. For my roommate, Billie May, it means setting up "Love in Action," a ministry with street children. There are always so many challenges, both costly and rewarding.

With provision: how often as we prayed together as a body of His people we saw God supply when students were unable to pay their fees. At other times, when resources (personnel or finance or other) were scarce, the Father gave wisdom and grace. He gave grace too in sad, hard times: when a student drowned in a river on the college property; when the newly-elected leader for WEC Brazil suffered a fatal heart attack; for me, personally, when news came of my brother's death in Europe.

In my second memory, I see myself on my father's knee, enjoying his embrace and listening as he chats with a visitor. I keep fairly quiet, content to be near my father, to hear what he has to say.

In His presence there is comfort, care and closeness, confidence and communication. When, for example, as a staff we didn't know what to do, we sought to listen. Although tempted to come up with answers ourselves or to preempt a careful work God was doing in a student's life, we longed to be still, to be sensitive to His voice.

These simple but profound truths about our Father transform our journey. We can always delight in His company and care. Wherever obeying the Great Commission takes us, we can rest in the presence of our Father God who is all-knowing, all-wise, and perfectly good.

Karina MacLeod from Scotland served on the teaching staff of WEC's training college in Brazil for seventeen years.

Joevelina's Story
Joevelina
Central Asia, 2010

I'm from Brazil and have been part of WEC since 1996. My husband and I work in Central Asia. Here are two of our faith stories.

We were in Brazil waiting for support to go to England to learn English and then to Central Asia. We were visiting and speaking in many churches. It's easy to feel down when we can see many Christian people without vision and passion to reach the lost. Although we had visited more than one hundred and forty places, we got only promises, nothing else.

One night we were exhausted as we visited another church. I needed to preach, but I felt dry inside. The Lord started speaking to me during the worship time; He told me that support wasn't the real reason I was going from one church to the other, but to connect with people to pray for us and the country where we would work. He even said He could use anybody to provide support, even non-believers, but for prayer He depends on His church. The Lord filled us with confidence that day.

Our church denominational leaders gave us three months. If in those three months the Lord didn't open the doors for us to go to England, they were going to send us somewhere else. We knew the Lord wanted us in Central Asia. Although at that moment it looked impossible for us to go, we decided to believe. We started telling people and churches that we were going to England in three months.

At one church in my home state, the pastor asked us, "You said you're going to England in three months; how much money do you have toward your expenses?"

I looked at my husband and replied, "We don't have any money."

The pastor couldn't believe it. He asked again, "How do you tell the church you are leaving in three months if you don't have any money?"

I said, "We are going by faith."

I'm pretty sure that dear pastor thought we were crazy, but he didn't say any more because he didn't want to hurt us.

And this pastor didn't know the full extent of our problems. We owed WEC Brazil $1,000 (US) for our accommodation and living costs. We hadn't received much support for a year while preparing to leave, and we saw that debt growing bigger each month.

Our work in that church finished on Sunday evening, and on Monday we left to go to my mom's house in another city. The pastor's questions and many others occupied my mind. When I got to my mom's, I called the WEC office and asked the treasurer the total of our debt. She took a few moments to answer, and I wondered why. Then she said, "You don't have any debt; in fact, you have $2,000 (US) in your account!"

I nearly started dancing; how could it be? That was the amount we needed for plane tickets and the first month of living in England. We never found out how that money got into our account, but we were assured that our Lord is faithful and fulfills His promises.

Three months later we flew to England. We left our country with the support we needed and went to live with an English family who really blessed us and continues to bless us today. We studied in an immigrants' school free of charge. Every time we had a need we could trust the Lord because we knew what He had done before and would do again. He is the one who met all our needs. Praise His name!

Another story comes from our first home leave. We had just finished our team's conference when we received a call from Brazil saying my husband's dad had died. We wanted to return to Brazil, but we didn't have money for the plane tickets. Our leader came to us and said that he thought we should go, that our family needed us and we could begin our home leave. He even said the field would lend us money for the tickets, and we could give it back when we returned. We accepted because we saw this as God's answer to our prayers. In a week we packed everything and jumped on a plane to go home. But when we got to Brazil and saw how much we needed to spend to help our family, the field debt was a heavy burden on us. We couldn't see how we could pay back so much money. Except for our pastor and a close friend, we didn't tell people at home how much we owed the team because the amount was too many zeros for Brazilian minds!

When we arrived at my mother's house, we saw we had another problem: some months before, a big storm with high winds had ruined the roof of her house. (Half the house is mine from my father's inheritance.) We felt we couldn't go back to the field and leave my mom, an elderly lady living by herself, in such a house. It would not have been a good witness to the people in my hometown who know I'm a believer.

I went to the bank and found I had about a thousand dollars. Repairing the damage to the house would cost us four times as much. We decided to start rebuilding by faith. As soon as we started, the Lord sent enough to cover every bill. We don't know how it happened; it was just the Lord. But we still had to pay the field for the money they had lent us for tickets.

One month before we left for the field, the treasurer wrote to us and asked, "Have you received an unexpected gift? If you did, please don't use it for anything else, because it's for your ticket expenses."

We didn't understand; we hadn't received anything, so we told him that. He wrote again and explained that team members had put money in to help with our tickets and somebody else had asked how much we still needed. That person had sent the money to our account. When we got to our place of service and went to the bank, the money was all there to give back to our team. The Lord had once again showed His faithfulness to us. We can trust Him—He doesn't forget our needs.

Warned and Protected
Jutta Weinheimer
Guinea-Bissau, 1999

Thursday, May 6, 1999: The big washbasins were filled with water and standing ready in the bathroom of our apartment in Bissau. Our four little children, aged six months to six years, were about to wash off the daily dust and sweat when we heard shelling.

It was 100 percent clear what that meant. Two days prior, a faithful Christian and church worker named Tiago told one of our colleagues, "When the first shots ring out, you'll have ten minutes to leave."

We all knew we had to flee as soon as possible. Tiago showed up a few minutes later, urging us to go.

"Just take the suitcase and the box of food and put them into the car. They're all packed and ready to go," I said to my husband Thomas. As Thomas and our two colleagues packed the two available cars, more and more people poured into our place at the mission headquarters, hoping for a ride.

I quickly washed the children and tried to keep everyone calm even as people were running around frantically. Listening to the shooting outside, my six-year-old started crying. "The Lord Jesus will protect us," I said as I tried to comfort her—and that's what I believed.

We had only been back in Bissau for three weeks, after living in Senegal as refugees since the start of the Guinea-Bissau civil war in June, 1998. Guinean pastors and friends had felt it was safe enough for us to come back—even with small children. As the acting field leaders, we believed our return was a positive signal for others in our team to prepare for a return to the field as well. We felt it was God's time.

When all the missionaries—both those returning and those who had stayed all along—met for the first day of prayer "after

Travel in Guinea-Bissau

the war" in April 1999, I wrote in my diary: "Meta spoke about peace. I am not sure about that. But I have the assurance that this is the place where God wants us to be. If there is going to be another evacuation, it will be in God's hand. I'm not scared."

Three days later I wrote: "There is strong political tension and I am reflecting on the possibility of another evacuation."

I spent the following three weeks mostly cleaning and unpacking, but we continued to see signs that the peace might not be permanent. Thomas and I started discussing the possibility of a "third war," but we decided not to pack anything. After all, I had just finished unpacking!

I picked up the Bible and turned to Jeremiah 11:20, which said, ". . . to you I have committed my cause." Reading the context, we found that Jeremiah had been in a life-threatening situation without knowing it. Were we in a dangerous situation without realizing it? The second verse in that day's scheduled reading was First Peter 5:7: "Cast all your anxiety on him because he cares for you." That night I wrote in my diary that God would show us when we'd have to leave.

The following Tuesday, Thomas met two German biologists downtown. They told him they could tell that fighting would start again within two or three weeks. Was that God warning us—again? I wrote in my diary that I felt I needed to hurry up and pack an emergency bag.

And that's exactly what I did on Wednesday, May 5.

The next day the shelling and shooting started around six-thirty in the evening. We left the city along with thousands of people who didn't have the comfort of a car but had to flee on foot. How much these people had suffered already! I cried, and my daughter was distressed that we were not able to take more people in our car—especially when she saw an old man carrying his wife on his back.

When the war started, we had hoped and prayed for a quick end. This hadn't happened in the past. Listening to the shelling during the night, I wondered how long it would be this time. We had brought quite a lot of food and clothing, and were prepared for a long wait.

Early the next morning, the radio news announced that all foreigners were advised to leave Bissau and go into the interior. Since we knew of a house in the interior ready for our use, we wanted to head off immediately. But some locals convinced us it wasn't advisable to return to the capital even if we were only passing through on the way inland. So we stayed on.

As we waited, we were able to provide a meal to some refugees. And while we sat there, cars passed us containing the dead and injured. I praised God that the children were unaware of this. We also saw many people covered in mud because they hadn't been allowed to use the road and had to flee through the waist-deep mud of the rice fields. We were shocked to hear that fifty people had been killed at a Catholic center in Bissau where they had taken refuge.

By early afternoon the radio reported that fighting was coming to an end. Less than twenty-four hours after we had left, we were back in Bissau, and the war was finished for good.

I was and am so grateful that God prepared us for this situation. I have no idea how I would have reacted had we not been prepared.

Jutta Weinheimer, with husband Thomas and their four children, spent eleven years in Guinea-Bissau before returning to take up WEC leadership in Germany.

12

Directed

We must make a conscious decision to trust Him and to refuse all doubt.

Traugott Boeker

There is going to be heat and drought but He is going to be adequate.

Shirley Strong

The Lord will guide you always; he will satisfy your needs in a sun-scorched land and will strengthen your frame.

Isaiah 58:11

Remarkable Meeting
Eva
Norway, 2010

*I*t was six in the morning when the phone rang insistently. Knowing this would have to be an emergency, I picked it up in a hurry.

"Who did you say I am talking to? Yazib . . . ? You mean the Yazib from . . . ? Yes, yes. . . . You have fled the country and now you are here in Norway? I see. . . . You would like to come here to talk about what to do next? Yes, of course you can! . . . OK, we will see you in about an hour, then."

Completely amazed, I put down the phone. Yazib had actually fled his country and was now here in Norway! I could hardly believe it.

My thoughts went back to the time when we first met his family, while we were living in a Middle Eastern country.

That day, as usual, traffic in the capital of that country was hectic and slow. This was partly due to the only freedom enjoyed there: the freedom to do whatever you like behind the wheel. Traffic rules are considered guidelines, interpreted in the way most beneficial to any driver at any given time. My husband John, out on business, was glad to be heading home after a tiring morning. A taxi, without any official signboard, stopped for him. When the driver proposed a reasonable fare, John agreed and leaned back in his seat at the back trying to relax.

The driver, however, was one who really enjoyed talking to foreigners.

"Which country do you come from?" he started.

"I am from Norway," John replied warily.

"Hey! That is wonderful," the driver replied in perfect Norwegian.

Taken completely by surprise, John asked, "How on earth do you know my language?"

"I lived in Norway for seven years as a refugee!"

"Really? So are you back here because you did not manage to gain residential status in Norway?"

"No, unfortunately. After seven years we were sent back home, and we had to pick up our lives here again from scratch."

"Where in Norway did you stay?"

"We were in a big center for asylum seekers near Oslo."

"Hmm, I know that one. You would not happen to know Mr. Sven Johansson, would you?"

"What! Do you also know Mr. Sven? He is one of our best friends over there! He visited us ever so many times and in the end took us to his church. We have become followers of Jesus as a result of everything he told us. My wife and I were both baptized, and we are still ever so happy that we got to know the Lord in Norway. Even if that was our only purpose for being in your country under such unpleasant circumstances, we are happy because we gained status in God's kingdom—for eternity! Apart from that we finally found peace for our souls."

Tears came to his eyes when he realized afresh the difference the love of Jesus had made in his life and those of his wife and their only son, Yazib.

Although John was aware the driver could easily be deceiving him, trying to find out if John's real reason for being in the country was the so-called "spreading of foreign religions," this seemed unlikely. Besides, he sensed in his spirit that the man was completely sincere.

"How unbelievable that in a city where millions of people live, we meet up in a taxi like this!" he said. When they reached our house, John insisted that the driver, whose name was Amal, come in with him to drink a cup of tea and meet me as well.

That was the beginning of a long and deep relationship between Amal's family and us. We appreciated their courage in secretly attending church services, even though concerned for their safety. In this country it is life-threatening to turn your back on Islam and become a follower of Jesus. Nevertheless, Amal and his wife Pasha both felt that it was essential to help them grow spiritually. They told us many people had turned to Christ and needed Bibles. The only thing we could do was distribute God's Word in their own language to as many as possible of these new believers and pray that God would keep them all safe. Later we moved back to Norway.

When Yazib arrived at our house one hour after the early phone call, he told us the full story. He and a friend had been distributing CDs containing testimonies of converted Muslims. His friend was caught and immediately put in prison while Yazib managed to escape. With help from a church, he was able to leave the country, and now he was in Norway! Finally he was able to phone his parents on their mobile phone, to say he was safe and was at our place. Amal and Pasha shed tears of relief and praised the Lord for His care for their son!

What Yazib did not know was that at the same time we met in Norway, Amal and Pasha had been visited by the secret police. They came in the middle of the night and entered the house by force. They intended to get Yazib while he slept at home. Although his parents could honestly say they had no idea where their son was, they were seriously beaten up.

Afterward neighbors in their apartment block took them to the nearest hospital. They didn't think Amal would survive, as he was unconscious and barely breathing. He had three broken ribs, a broken nose and many internal bruises. Pasha had her leg broken.

The police also confiscated the ownership documents of their house, stating that Amal and Pasha would get them back as soon as they informed the police of the whereabouts of their son. From then on they were homeless. Amal also lost his employment, and they became dependent on their respective families.

While Yazib endured a year of uncertainty concerning his future, his parents also went through a very difficult time. However, whenever we talked to them, they would always emphasize that God was faithful and that He was enabling them to endure. Their only prayer was for their son to be safe and to receive official status in any European country. When this prayer was answered in a positive way, they became much more relaxed themselves. By that time Yazib was twenty-one years old, and according to the law, his parents could no longer be held responsible for his actions. Thanks to money raised by our home church, Amal and Pasha were able to go to a Christian lawyer, who emphasized this fact in court, and the ownership documents of their house were returned to them. After over a year of extreme stress, they were able to move back into their home. Their testimony stands strong. They continue to share about God's faithfulness to every individual who loves Him.

Are Amal and Pasha secure and safe now? Will they be all right? According to our earthly standards, absolutely not! But they are safe and secure in God's love and care. That is why they will be all right, no matter what may happen. Let's continue to pray for all the others under similar pressures.

Pressing On
Yosina and Veronika
Indonesia, 2009

*T*his has not been easy," Yosina thought as she packed suitcases for her family of four's first journey home to Indonesia
from Central Asia. Many times they had gone the second mile
to serve the Lord as part of the international WEC family. They
were new workers in their team, their support was low and they
spoke little English. Adjusting to the culture of a predominantly
western organization had been difficult.

Putting another pair of trousers in the suitcase, Yosina's mind
went back to earlier times. Her husband Mex was a quiet man
from the island of Timor, where people were generally outgoing. He had received a clear call to serve God in Central Asia
while studying at Bible college. Although loyal to her husband
and ready to follow him, Yosina took more time to become convinced of God's call on her own life.

Once they were both certain of God's call, the next step was
to find an organization to join. Some of their lecturers at Bible
college were WEC workers, but when Mex and Yosina testified
to their call, the response was not encouraging. Mex was not an
outgoing person, they were already in their forties, and they did
not speak English well. However, they continued to believe God
had called them and would equip and provide for them, so they
applied to WEC, moving to Surabaya where the mission's office
was located.

In Surabaya Mex and Yosina felt nobody believed in their
call. Some people thought they wanted to join in order to go
abroad. Most Indonesian churches thought they were joining
an international organization to receive a salary. Their relatives

wondered why they wanted to leave their present ministry to take on such a tough life. But Mex and Yosina decided to follow God's call no matter what.

Before leaving for candidate orientation in Britain, they needed to find support from Indonesian churches, but few were willing to invite them to speak. One day they received an invitation from a church in Malang. They went along as a team with the WEC Indonesian sending base leader. They found the pastor quite enthusiastic. As they were leaving, they were handed an envelope containing 1,000,000 rupiahs (US$400 at the time). But it was specifically designated for another family who worked with a different organization in Central Asia. It was difficult for Mex to hand over that money when it was the amount they needed themselves, but they continued to wait on the Lord, rich in God and filled with joy.

By now the whole team in Surabaya was trusting God along with Mex and Yosina for 1,000,000 rupiahs as a sign He wanted them to go to Central Asia. A few weeks later, a gift for this exact amount arrived in another envelope; this time it was for Mex and Yosina. Then a stranger came to the door and handed them an envelope containing US$500. In the midst of the biggest economic crisis Indonesia had ever seen, God provided all the money needed for them to go.

Finally Mex and Yosina were able to travel to England for candidate orientation. Mex's poor English limited his communication, and he was even quieter than in Indonesia. He also had a medical problem with one of his ears. When acceptance time came, they were turned down. The candidate committee felt they hadn't adjusted to the organization well enough, and their English must improve.

Mex was sent to Whitby in the north of England for a few months to complete more English courses, while Yosina and their two children remained at the UK WEC center in the south. During this time they cried out to the Lord to heal Mex's ear. Eventually the family was given permission to move on to Central Asia.

Once there, they faced adjusting to the cold weather, fitting into the international team and learning yet another language. Again they were ready to go the second mile and prove that God had called them and enabled them for their ministry. During these difficult times the Lord showed that He had called them by providing for all their needs, opening doors for ministry and helping them to persevere.

It has been tough, but God has carried us through every difficulty. Isn't He amazing? Yosina thought as she locked the last case. "Thank you, Father, for all Your help and loving care! It has all been more than worth it." They had seen God touch lives in Central Asia, make them active members of the team and teach the whole family precious lessons of faith and obedience. Mex's favorite song had become, "The Lord's my Shepherd, I'll not want . . . And I will trust in You alone!"

Faith takes Action!

Jonathan Chamberlain
Netherlands, 2009

"Faith without works is dead," says James in the Bible. C.T. Studd believed it and lived it! He was a man of action whose faith led him to go forward when all the evidence said this was disastrous. WEC, the mission he founded, became infused with the same DNA. Consider the following examples:

1931: C.T. Studd died in Congo, and people say the mission he started will die with him. But those left behind know the work is from God, not just a human personality. "God enabling us, we go on!" they say.

As an act of faith, they ask God for ten new workers to join the mission by the first anniversary of C.T.'s death. God honors their faith. The next year they pray for fifteen more workers. In those two years God provides twenty-five people and the money to send them out, despite the economic depression at the time.

2009: Millions of people have yet to hear the Good News about Jesus Christ. Mission agencies everywhere still call for new workers. But the church in Europe is in serious decline, and world mission is slipping off their "radar screens."

Cornerstone, a WEC Bible college for training mission workers, began as an act of faith twenty years ago in the Netherlands. A former convent and primary school WEC had purchased by faith proved a great facility for a residential college, accommodating forty students plus staff and volunteers. In 2009 a full complement of staff was living by faith because they knew God had led them there to serve His global mission purposes. Cornerstone "exists to train Christ's servants from all nations to take his gospel and plant churches among all nations" (the college's mission statement). But what happens when those "servants of Christ" stop knocking on the door for training?

By April only two students are accepted for the new Cornerstone year starting in August. The economic recession is biting hard. The college budget is based on an intake of twenty new students. The staff begins to wonder how to adapt to the reality that there will not be a first-year class this time. But God says, "What is impossible with men is possible with God." Staff and students set aside time every Wednesday to pray. A faith target of "25" is written on the board. The weeks pass. The group holds on in faith.

The previous year not one new single man had applied, but men are needed more than ever in missions. So the men in the prayer meeting go to the single men's living quarters and pray for those rooms to be filled, sensing that God has heard and will answer.

Suddenly, breakthrough! New applications begin streaming in. By August twenty-three new students join the existing student body coming not only from the Netherlands, Germany and Switzerland but also from Romania, Poland, Italy, France, Kenya and South Africa. The men's corridor is full!

God still honors the prayer of faith. Faith can take action just as it did when WEC started!

Roasting marshmallows

Jonathan and Linda Chamberlain worked in Indonesia and Singapore for several years before joining the staff of the International Office in 1999. Later they were in leadership at WEC's training center in Holland before moving to a mobile leadership training role.

God's Well
Neil Rowe
Guinea-Bissau, 2008

The field leader in Guinea-Bissau took me to the largest of a group of islands, fifty miles offshore, where a colleague was developing an agricultural program for the people, some of whom had become believers. But the team had hit a snag. Changing weather patterns associated with the southward advance of the Sahara Desert had led to decreased rainfall. Now the island's wells were drying up, and the believers were preparing to sink a deeper well on their land.

They were not the only ones looking for water. A team of Russians was also on the island, "invited" by the pro-Communist government. Officially, they were building a hospital, plus a long, straight road across the island for local traffic! However, since the only local traffic on the island was a tractor and two other vehicles, a road was definitely not a top priority. Clearly they were creating a military base and an airstrip. But like us, they desperately needed water. They had been drilling all over the island with sophisticated equipment for two or three years but to no avail.

When I arrived, the Christians asked my advice about where to put their well—as if I could see below the ground! All the equipment needed for the well, including the huge, two-meter-wide concrete lining rings, was sitting there waiting for the word to start.

I professed my total ignorance but wandered the four-acre plot until I reached the lowest spot and suggested starting there. We stood together, arms round each other's shoulders in a symbol of solidarity, and asked God for water—just as simple as that. We didn't know precisely how low the water level was, and our faith level may have been quite low too. But the men started the laborious job of digging with their primitive tools.

Before long we heard unexpected news. The men had struck a layer of solid rock. Rock which should not have been there! The island was unusual in that it had no rock anywhere: it was composed of sand and cockleshells. Hundreds, probably thousands, of tons of shells were gathered in huge deposits, well above sea level.

Hitting rock was particularly depressing because our laborers had only excavated a few meters and would have to dig much deeper to reach the water table. They did not have the equipment to penetrate rock, and all we could suggest was trying to see how thick the rock was by chipping away at it with a hammer and chisel.

The next news was startling. Water was gushing out of the rock at the rate of twenty thousand gallons a day! When the Russians heard about it, they left their sophisticated equipment to take a look. We feared that they would commandeer the well, such was their desperation for water, but they settled for piping away half the flow! Maybe they were influenced by

the miraculous event. People across the islands called the well "God's Well" or the "Miracle Well."[12]

Neil Rowe served in various leadership roles at the UK WEC center as well as adviser to the African fields in the 1970s and 1980s; later he and his wife had responsibility for fields in the Middle East.

His Way is Best
Ilse-Marie Neuroth
Germany, 2010

When Chrissie and David met for the first time during an operatic production in Scotland in 1934, neither of them knew God was leading them to perform an outstanding duet for Christ with their lives. David had just finished his banking apprenticeship. Chrissie, a lover of music, accomplished singer and pianist, was working for a hat-making business. Soon they were planning their future: engagement, a banking appointment for David in Trinidad, marriage after four years and then life as a couple somewhere in the West Indies.

But in Trinidad David met a man to whom Jesus Christ was a living reality and came to faith in Jesus in 1937. Once God had spoken to him, David gave up his appointment and sailed back to Britain—where Chrissie had found Christ as well. Both of them started training at the Glasgow Bible Institute to prepare for ministry with the China Inland Mission.

When Chrissie was turned down for service overseas due to a heart condition caused by severe flu, both were shocked. "We had been so confident that this was the right way, His way for us! But no amount of wishing could alter the facts," David writes in his memoirs.

Their interest was caught when they found out WEC had work in a number of semi-tropical areas more suitable for Chrissie's health. At one stage they thought this would lead them to serve in Bulgaria, but God had different plans. With World War II at its height, they were asked to become involved in the WEC regional center in Manchester, England. God was pointing them to a ministry of mission mobilization. In 1947 David moved to Switzerland, leaving Chrissie and their son in Britain since no residential permits were granted for the family. They were separated for over a year while David was learning German, making contacts and preparing to launch a mission magazine. Fourteen

David and Chrissie Batchelor

months after his arrival there, he founded WEC Switzerland. A month later the first issue of *Weltweit* magazine was published.

Gradually the idea of work in Germany came to the forefront. David continued to travel to make the challenge of missions known, not only in Switzerland but also in Scandinavia and Western Europe. "In the first ten years on the Continent six to eight months on average each year were spent on the road," David wrote. He was separated from his family for long periods of time. Finally, in December 1950, they were able to move to a small village in Alsace, although the traveling did not end. Chrissie backed her husband's ministry wholeheartedly and contributed much by releasing David.

After several years the Batchelors moved to Mulhouse, France. In the winter of 1956–57, three German lady candidates spent the first three months of their candidate orientation with them. Events pointed toward another change to help prepare German candidates in Germany.

"When we finally recognized this as God's leading," David wrote, "we found ourselves facing a possibility that had never even crossed our minds up to then: going to Germany on our own and placing the boys in a Christian boarding school in Britain. Christopher was seven years old and Fred twelve. Even now, as I write about it twenty-two years later, I can almost feel again the cold shivers that ran down my back at the thought. . . . Yet we would testify that God has blessed us as a family, despite the separations."

The first "base" in Germany was an all-purpose room plus kitchenette. The Batchelors followed no strategy other than "being open to His leading in providing German full-time workers and vowing to the Lord never to stand in the way of any change in leadership he would indicate sooner or later." God gave them a special relationship with two churches, one in Lübeck, in northern Germany, the other in Mannheim, more in the south. In the following years fourteen members of the Lübeck church were led to join WEC, including two sons of the pastor.

Another move followed to northern Germany, where WEC had been registered in 1959. The Batchelors started praying urgently for a larger and more central German location. They were pointed to a former children's home in the Taunus district, which they visited in November 1963.

"Our first glimpse of the house was under the worst possible conditions, at dusk and at the end of a tiring journey," David wrote. "Unoccupied for nine months, it looked from the outside eerie and forlorn. The catches of some cellar windows had obviously been forced and many panes were broken. In the grounds the grass was knee-high and rotting fruit lay everywhere. . . . It looked quite different by daylight. . . . There was no doubt about it, for our purpose the place had real possibilities."

The last payment for the house was made in April 1967. David noted, "In the course of these years God taught us many lessons. . . . Throughout the period in which these payments were being made, we continued to accept and send out new workers to the fields and saw His hand open to us in corresponding increases in the monies sent in for their support and for the work generally. But this did not happen automatically. . . . It is part of the testimony that, despite our mistakes and failures, we never turned to Him in vain."

Looking back in 1966 David summarized: "After our modest beginnings in 1950, we look around this lovely well-furnished place with its delightful garden, the garage housing two mission cars, the kitchen with its modern facilities, the household cupboards with linen, crocks, cutlery and equipment . . . and we just have to praise the Lord, who has made it possible! . . . Chrissie had a warning from the local doctor about her heart. . . . When

I think that it was this weakness which kept her, and us, from going to the field in 1940, and then turn my mind to all that the Lord has enabled her to do in the years since . . . I can only praise Him for His faithfulness."

Ilse-Marie Neuroth has been part of WEC Germany's administrative and editorial staff since 1990.

The SOON Story

Pauline Lewis
England, UK, 2010

The other day I was sitting at the desk in my office looking at my computer, minding my own business, as one does, when up on the screen came an article by Evan Davies, a member of WEC International. What caught my attention was a picture at the end of his article: the photo of a building, which I had not set eyes on for nearly fifty years.

In front of the building was a road where my friends and I had skipped with a large rope; a pavement where I had played hopscotch, made slides on ice and roller skated with metal skates. An old car was parked by the pavement, which reminded me

of my dad's old Morris Minor, the first car he and his other colleagues in WEC owned.

Each window of that building spoke to me of my family and the rooms we had lived in for the first sixteen years of my life. I had walked out of that front door every day to go to school, Paxton Primary and Kingsdale Comprehensive. We crossed that road every day at lunch time to have our main meal in "the hostel" opposite. It was the main building of the former WEC base in Upper Norwood, southeast London. We lived at number 34 Highland Road from 1946 to 1962.

Seeing that picture challenged me to write. That building holds so many memories of my childhood years. What a privilege to be brought up there! My father, John Lewis, was the mobilization coordinator for the mission and served alongside the British WEC leader Norman Grubb. My mother was involved with the mission candidates, and my grandparents were there too working in the kitchens of "the hostel." WEC staff lived by faith, trusting God to supply all they required without making their needs known. As children, my brother and I never had any sense of need. There was always food on the table and clothes to wear. Our childhood was a happy one.

During my early teens my parents started a new literature outreach called *SOON*, based on a similar ministry in French called *BIENTOT*, founded by Fred and Lois Chapman. Six months after *SOON* was founded, disaster struck when my father suffered a major heart attack. WEC staff prayed with him, and God gave the word "This sickness will not end in death. No, it is for God's glory" (John 11:4). Standing on this promise, my parents continued to lay the foundations for the new *SOON* ministry.

In 1963, a year after my father's illness, we moved away from the WEC base. God provided a building which became the main *SOON* center in the small Sussex village of Bolney. The

Street distribution

work grew, reaching nearly every country of the world by means of easy-English, evangelistic news sheets, named *SOON* from the phrase in Revelation 1:1, "what must *soon* take place." Bible correspondence courses and readers' clubs were developed to follow up the papers. During this period I started nursing training, and my brother married.

After eleven years another move was necessary, and God provided a new base in Willington, Derbyshire. The property was called Vere Lodge, and here *SOON* continued to grow. Since the year 2000, workers for four other language papers in French, Swahili and Fula have joined the team at Willington, forming *SOON Ministries*. A large evangelistic website has also developed. Every three months 1.5 million of these various language papers are sent throughout the world by several thousand volunteers, who wrap and post the papers from their homes. Each day responses come back from readers by letter and e-mail. Here is what one said:

Sorting room

I was born in a remote village among Hindu families. I worshiped idols in order to gain success in life. According to the

Hindu faith there are 330,000,000 gods and goddesses. I worshiped them daily, but idols could not change my life. I lost peace, hope, money, everything. One day I saw an advertisement inside a daily newspaper. I wrote to them. They sent me a course about the way to a meaningful life. After completion of the course they sent me a New Testament and suggested I attend a church. I went to the church and attended every service. I gave my life to Christ and was baptized.

My parents rejected me seeing that I had become a Christian. They stopped supporting me. It was a hard and difficult time, because I had no means of feeding my children and wife. I keep walking with Christ because I have hope in him. I want to study theology. My wife is now in Christ and our children go to church to worship the true and living God. We are planning to start a new church in our area and I am praying for our families and relatives. We want to see them in Christ for the best and true life.

Mr. M. Sharma, Nepal

Following nursing training, I went to Bible College and joined the *SOON* team in 1977. I have been a full-time team member for thirty-three years. During this time God has provided for all my needs and, since my childhood in number 34 Highland Road, has provided three different homes that have each been part of WEC.

John and Pauline Lewis

To the Land of Goshen
HyeSook Choi
Canada, 2011

KyungHo and HyunOk Yoon are from different religious backgrounds. KyungHo grew up in a very traditional and strict Confucian family. He wandered through shadows without knowing God until he accepted Jesus Christ as his Savior at the age of twenty-five and in three years was called to ministry for God. On the other hand, HyunOk was brought up by gracious Christian parents.

KyungHo and HyunOk met each other through Campus Crusade for Christ and married while working together on the same campus. Having the same vision for the world, they devoted themselves to ministry in Korea and the Philippines. As they saw many new workers arriving in the Philippines, they sensed encouragement from God to move where there was greater need. God guided KyungHo and HyunOk to serve in a restricted country in Asia with WEC International.

After language study they moved to a city where people were hardened to the gospel and took over a house church others had worked with for twelve years. The church was composed of twenty people, mostly women. They wisely divided the people into five groups, held evangelistic meetings targeted at the husbands, and saw much fruit and spiritual renewal.

Then they received an unexpected e-mail from the boarding school in Thailand where their son was studying:

> We are very sorry to inform you that your son was suspended from school because we found out that he and some other friends were drinking and doing drugs in a bar on New Year's

Eve. We suggest that you stay with him for six months so that you can help him and enable him complete his diploma.

KyungHo and HyunOk were shocked and confused. Without fully understanding God's plan, they left behind their entire ministry because of their son and went off to Thailand, depending on God's goodness and faithfulness alone.

The six months together with their son was a dark time and the lowest point of their lives. Instead of the change they expected, their son's behavior continued to be rude and without any sign of humility. Hope was gone, their faith shaken. Day after day they cried out to God.

At one point the Holy Spirit spoke to them from the story of David and Absalom. They came to understand David's heart cry. Then the Holy Spirit helped them to see the heavenly Father's heart toward His rebellious children and the love that made Him come to earth to die for sinners. KyungHo and HyunOk were convicted about their Pharisee-like attitude in their service for God and their lack of the real heart of God the Father. They realized they had not sought the glory of God but had become merely "professional" missionaries.

They took more than a week to cry and repent of their sins. God renewed them, giving them a new passion for the lost. Although outwardly they seemed to achieve nothing in those six months, they were able to go back to their place of service after laying down all their burdens for their son.

In spite of their increased boldness in witness, they were discouraged by little response. One day they read, "Throw your net on the right side of the boat and you will find some" (John 21:6). They asked the Lord, "Where is the right side of our boat? We also want to catch a large number of fish."

One morning they saw a man with a blackened face sitting on a chair and learned he had been burned by an electric fire

Land of Goshen farm, Canada.

as he was working as a builder. They bought some Aloe plant, which is good for skin burn, and applied it on the burnt areas twice a day, praying in the name of Jesus. The man was healed within two weeks. He professed faith in Jesus, and his friends also came to the Lord. KyungHo and HyunOk learned through Matthew 25:31–40 that the right side of the boat for them signified people in need:

> Then the King will say to those on his right, "Come . . . take your inheritance . . . for I was hungry and you gave me something to eat, I was thirsty and you gave me something to drink, I was a stranger and you invited me in, I needed clothes and you clothed me, I was sick and you looked after me, I was in prison . . . and you came to visit me."

As time went by, they realized they were under scrutiny by the security services. They prayed, "What should we do?" God answered them as they were meditating on Genesis 46–47. "Jacob! Jacob! Don't be afraid to go down to Egypt. . . . I will go down to Egypt with you" (Gen. 46:1-3). They left that country in 2007 with a promise from God in Genesis 47:27: "Now the Israelites settled in Egypt in the region of Goshen."

When they returned to Korea, they kept asking God, "Where is the 'land of Goshen' for us?"

One day they received an e-mail that two leaders from Betel India wanted to visit the WEC Korea sending base on their way home from Mongolia. As they exchanged e-mails, they were strongly burdened to pray for this visit to Korea, especially in relation to the promise of Goshen, and decided to pray for forty days, meditating on the book of Exodus. They heard God's call to broken people through Exodus 3:7–10: "I have indeed seen the misery of my people in Egypt. . . . So I have come down to rescue them . . . and to bring them . . . into a good and spacious land, a land flowing with milk and honey."

As they meditated on these verses, three pictures came to their minds: the suffering of God's people in Egypt under Pharaoh; the time of pain with their son in Thailand, and the drug addicts and their parents' pain.

Kyung Ho and Hyun Ok could not avoid the cries of the broken and knew God was leading them to broken people like drug addicts even before the Betel leaders arrived. A suggestion was made that they move to Betel India to reach the addicts. When they set off, they were already gray-haired, middle-aged and experienced. But the new ministry in India plunged them into a situation where they had to live with the addicts and learn to deal with their deeply rooted self-righteousness and pride.

At the end of a year when their visa was to expire, they began earnestly praying about their next step. During prayer, they felt a strong burden to rebuild relationships with their children whom they had seen only a few times in nine years. They told the Betel leaders about this burden and the need to move to North America to be near their children. God led them to the WEC Canadian center, since their son was studying at the University of Toronto. Again they obeyed the Lord and moved to Canada in June 2009.

Soon after, they wrote their story:

We are so glad and thrilled to tell you about the amazing way the Lord has worked. During the WEC Canada conference, we were able to share how God had led us into the Betel ministry. . . . After the conference, two WECers arranged a meal for us to meet a Korean business couple who owned a big farm. . . . We had an historic meeting with them and shared with them the origins of Betel and how we were now involved. At their request, we traveled together to their farm, which was twenty-eight kilometers away.

When we were entering the farm, the first thing that caught our eyes was a sign in four-foot-high, green letters, "The Land of Goshen Farm." We got out of the car and broke down in worship and tears. We were overwhelmed. Startled, the owners of the farm asked why we were crying and we told them our story.

Then we heard the other side of the story:

In 1993, the business couple had been guided by God to buy property to be used for a Christian community in the future. For the last ten years they had maintained it with much difficulty, but the Lord had not told them what to do with it. So they started praying and felt that they would only have it for

ten years. In the coming October it was going to be the full ten years so they were getting nervous. When they heard our Goshen promise and remembered their prayer, they sensed that it was from God and finally decided to donate it to WEC for broken people. . . . We felt as if we smelled the fragrance of the alabaster jar of perfume broken by Mary at Jesus' feet.

Henry Bell of WEC Canada continued the story:

Before accepting the farm we all committed to a month of prayer to confirm the Lord's will. At the end of that time we knew the farm was to be a place where the poor and broken could hear of the love of Jesus and be restored by him. On October 18, 2009, a number of us gathered on the Land of Goshen Farm to pray and dedicate the property to the Lord. In April 2010 I signed the contract to obtain ownership of the property for the Mission.

KyungHo and HyunOk were able to move into the house on the Land of Goshen Farm on October 5, exactly ten years after God had first prepared it for them. The house was fully equipped with all the necessary furniture and facilities, donated by friends of the donors. KyungHo and HyunOk felt as if they were entering a holy temple.

As a footnote to the story, KyungHo and HyunOk added:

> Whenever we meet our son, there is excitement and joy. What he does for us doesn't matter. It is just a joy to be close together, being his parents is a joy and happiness on its own. What our heavenly Father really wants from us is not works but a loving relationship. We learned it in depth through this relationship with our son. . . . Recently he came to stay with us for a week and we lived together as if we had never had a problem. He doesn't say anything about what has been going on in his mind, but his eyes tell us that spring has come in his heart.

> The story of the land of Goshen continues . . . Hallelujah!

The author, Hye Sook Choi, and her husband Chul Hee moved from business management in 2006 to Christian work with WEC. They were asked to take on the acting leadership of the South Korean WEC base and give direction to this rapidly developing mobilization ministry.

Our God Is an Awesome God!
Jill McKinnon
Chad, 2009

Oh yes, I believe it, sing it and even try to live it. Funny sometimes, words go round and round in my head. There was a week when "awesome" kept on popping out at me. Then on Sunday during my devotions, the first line reminded me that "our God is truly awesome." I'd decided to set aside a morning to read and pray, because I was conscious that a lot of challenges were coming my way in the very near future.

As I finished my prayer time, I went through to the back of the building, past a door which I would normally have taken the time to prop open, as it has a tendency to slam and get stuck. I was sure one day someone would be locked in. As I went through, there wasn't a breath of wind, but sure enough the door slammed, leaving me locked on the wrong side, on a Sunday. My eyes went to the high, smooth walls surrounding me . . . . No, no Lord, it would be much simpler if You just opened the door. I argued on that I knew quite well that I didn't have the strength to pull myself up over the walls. My awesome God wasn't going to move the mountain; He was asking me to pull.

But Lord, there is an easier way.

Jill McKinnon

OK, so I pulled, and a few seconds later I was sitting on the wall. I laughed and sang back my praise to the awesome God who had helped me to pull myself up.

It amazes me that the all-powerful, sovereign Lord should choose me to pull with Him to accomplish His work! That same awesome God has called me to reach nomads. This isn't going to happen in my strength, probably not even the way I imagine it. I've spent the best part of ten years getting out into the bush, walking trails, sleeping on the ground and traveling on some rickety vehicles so I could rub shoulders with the nomads and share my faith with them. Many listen, some ask questions. There have been glimmers of interest, but no one has made any claim to believe.

Yet God has done some awesome things. In a male-dominated society I've been given freedom to sit and read with the men, often with the religious teachers. God protected me from more than one close encounter with a snake. But that same awesome God allowed an aggressive cancer into my life—which took me "out" of ministry for almost eight months. Looking back at that period, I can see how God used it to achieve things which wouldn't have happened otherwise, at least not for a long time. So I continue to sing praise and to walk those miles in the hot sun—sometimes hungry, sometimes thirsty, but all the time looking to share God's love with the people He has called me to.

One of the first challenges after my wall-top encounter was a trip to the capital city, a diversion thousands of miles from the people I'm called to reach. This time I stayed in a new neighborhood, where I knew no one, so I decided to go for a walk. Fifteen minutes later someone called my name! I turned to find a nomad I've known for years. He was living one hundred fifty meters from my friend's house.

Through him I met another nomad, a young man with a real

hunger for the truth. "Barry" was well prepared and had clearly read a lot, being one of the few nomad boys who had been sent off to school. He wanted a Bible, but he didn't want anyone to know he had it. We had only a short time, but we read together, and I explained as clearly as I could about God's promise of salvation for all who believe in the death and resurrection of the Lord Jesus. He asked what he had to do to become a Christian, if there were special words he needed to say, and the words he would need to say when he prayed, and if he now had to go to church.

As the sun set, our time drew to a close; we read one more psalm together. Seeing the light in his face as he exclaimed that they were "beautiful words" was truly awesome. Then he was gone, a nomad on his path, hopefully following a new and good shepherd.

I'm currently splitting my life between a nomad camp and team responsibilities in town. Some days I feel I have too many balls up in the air, and any second they are going to come crashing down. God is still awesome. He could transform the lives

Jill teaching

around me without my intervention, but He has asked me to pull with Him. He hasn't asked me to do everything, and at times I say no, but gradually He is encouraging me not to be overawed by the high cement wall, to lift my hand in the expectation that He will pull me up.

"I lift my eyes up to the hills—where does my help come from? My help comes from the LORD, the Maker of heaven and earth."

Scottish worker Jill McKinnon joined the Chad team in 1996 with a burden for nomadic people. She spends periods of time living and traveling with nomads, building relationships and trust with both men and women.

13

The Church Grows

He took a motley crew and molded them into a construction unit and a fighting force.

Shord van Donge

Our work is to evangelize, and I know of no work that so keeps the heart hot and the soul on fire and in tune as the preaching of the gospel.

C.T. Studd

All over the world this gospel is bearing fruit and growing, just as it has been doing among you since the day you heard it and understood God's grace in all its truth.

Colossians 1:6

From Buddhism to Christ

Nina Drew
Kashmir, India, 1968

orje came from a princely family. His ancestors had held firm control over the people of the mountainous province of Ladakh in the days when it was an autonomous state, but by 1968 it was the most eastern province of the Jammu and Kashmir State.

The inhabitants of this high, mountainous area are different from those over the pass in the plateau of Kashmir. The people of Ladakh are related to the Tibetans—hardy, cheerful little folk, following the form of Buddhism known as Lamaism. Although Dorje and his family no longer had any actual power in the state, they were highly respected by all. Those of lower social standing would bow three times with foreheads touching the floor as they entered his audience chamber.

The respect Dorje received as a member of a princely family was further enhanced when he entered the lamasery as a novice. He had proved his devotion to Buddha by giving up worldly prospects for the religious life. He was intelligent, and within a few years he became well-versed in the Tibetan religious classics.

A Kashmiri

Ideals Unattainable

Dorje had not entered the lamasery to impress the local population. He entered it with a hungry heart. He had high ideals, but he knew he was not attaining them. For hours he sat in the Buddha position, meditating. He must learn to control his thoughts. Why was it that he could not attain to his ideals? The more he meditated on humility, the more conceited he became; as he meditated on purity, evil thoughts flooded his mind; he knew the ethics but not the power.

Life was frustrating. Dorje wanted to escape the constant round of births and deaths to that state of annihilation called Nirvana. How could it be accomplished?

A day came when Dorje met a Christian from his own country. This man was the son of a high official from Lhasa and had previously been a Buddhist. In true Tibetan fashion the two men sat facing each other over steaming cups of salted, buttered tea, discussing the meaning of life.

Life Attained

First, Dorje expounded his Buddhist faith. Then his friend told of the riches he had found in Christ. The hunger in Dorje's soul intensified as he recognized the very things he was seeking were all here in Christ—forgiveness for past sins, power to overcome, escape from the round of births and deaths into a place called "heaven" and the constant presence of the One who not only shows the way but said, "I am the way." Dorje became a Christian.

He gave up his career in the lamasery and took up a secular position. Eventually his ability was rewarded, and he was made a high official in the town. He worked conscientiously but soon found that spiritual powers could stir up opposition. The Buddhists resented a Christian being promoted to a high

Tibetan dancing

position, and they held riots and processions. Imagine Dorje's feelings when his enemies' malice reached the peak of escorting him through the town in manacles to face a false charge of theft!

Peace in Jail

As he sat in jail awaiting trial, the promises of God's Word came to him with fresh reality. Christ, who also had suffered trial on false charges, said, "I am with you always" (Matt. 28:20). His peace flooded Dorje's troubled heart.

The Lord caused the case to be tried in a nearby town away from his tormentors, instead of in the local court. It was obvious that his enemies had no case against him, and he was completely cleared. The magistrate told him he had the right to sue his persecutors for defamation of character. Dorje's answer revealed his Master's spirit: "Because I am a Christian, I forgive them."

God was leading Dorje into a new career. Since his conversion many years ago, he had been meeting with a little group of Ladakhi Christians. From his experience of God, he often shared the Bible with them, and he became their pastor. His understanding of Buddhism made him an excellent evangelist.

Yet this was not God's full purpose for Dorje. His study of the Tibetan classics through many years had been God's preparation for his greatest task. For several years Dorje was engaged in producing an entirely new translation of the Bible in Tibetan. The work

Trekking in the Himalayas

needed to be as near perfect as possible, acceptable not only to the people of Ladakh but to Tibetans from all parts of Tibet.

Christ had revealed Himself to Dorje's seeking soul after years of searching. He found the true meaning of life in Christ who said, "I am the way, the truth and the life" (John 14:6). Dorje not only drank of the truth himself but has enjoyed the privilege of leading others to know Christ.

Taken from WEC Australian Magazine, 1968

Nina Drew from New Zealand embraced the vision for working in Kashmir with WEC in 1959 and served in that mountainous area for many years.

The Power of Redeeming Grace
Elaine Crane
Assam, India, 1950

A certain well-known Nepali woman, striking in her figure, gaudy attire and golden jewelry, used to disturb the peace of the town from time to time in a drunken state. Singing ribald songs and shouting out rude and quarrelsome remarks, she would stagger unsteadily down the busy road through the bazaar. More than once the police had called at her home and taken her into custody for producing potent homemade liquor. She was notorious for her looseness of character. Her husband, who was in the army during those days, was hard and cruel.

One evening, squatting by the smoky fire, she portioned out her son's rice for the evening meal; she then served herself. She was ready to eat, but her son, a small, delicate child of ten, stopped her and said, "Mother, our teacher says we must give thanks to God for our food. Let us close our eyes, and I will pray as he has taught us."

The woman was amazed. What was this her son had learned at the Christian school? Hadn't her friends said he would be ruined if she sent him there? But above all else she wanted him to have the chance of an education, as she never had. So she shut her eyes as the boy prayed for the first time.

The father would sometimes come home on leave. There was an idol in one corner before which he worshiped, and from time to time he made offerings of food. In his own corner the boy folded his hands and prayed to the living and true God for those who did not understand.

Then the woman decided to go to a Sunday service with her son. He had told her all he knew, every word he had taken in at the small Christian school. Her husband would be angry, she knew, for he could not bear to hear anything of the religion his son learned in school. But the woman liked the service, so she kept going. When she was seriously ill, the teacher's wife came to her house and prayed for her. She recovered almost immediately. Her recovery caused her to lose all faith in idols, and she began to think of becoming a Christian.

When the father found out, he was furious. He said he would kill the woman if she ever went near the Christian school again. He threatened her and dragged her outside, along the open road to the jungle. He carried a murderous-looking kukri (Nepali knife) in his hand. But she was by no means docile under such treatment. She fought and spat, kicked and screamed. Somehow she broke free from his grip and escaped. After this they both got drunk again!

In their midst was always their one small, frightened child, who believed in the Lord Jesus. Whenever the father was away, the boy would plead with his mother to go to services. Often she went, but afterward she went back to her sin and shame.

Infuriated because his son believed and fearing the mother would follow the boy, the father came home drunk and in a rage, intending to kill them both. The bare blade of the kukri glistened in his hand. But someone had warned the woman and child that he was coming. With a few moments to spare, they began to run away. The raging father followed till he lost track of them. No one knows what happened, but the next day his body was found down a well. He had chosen his way . . . and the end was death.

Such a death brought fear of her husband's spirit and of demons upon the woman. She had to make a living for herself and the boy, and for a time they disappeared.

We were about to hold a vacation Bible school for the children, so we gave out invitations for any and all to come. We

Nepali peasant girl and child

found the boy, Rajber, playing by the roadside. He had left school and in idleness was wandering about, with temptation on every hand. His mother had been falsely accused and thrown into jail for stealing. We invited Rajber to come to the Bible classes. He did. The thirst after God was still in his face.

At the end of the Bible school, Rajber's mother came to the final meeting. She began to come near again, and eventually asked for teaching and baptism. During some Nepali holidays her brother came especially to be with their old mother, and naturally she would partake in all the feasting. They came to her house to eat with her the food offered to idols. But with the boy, she had fled to the jungle, where she stayed till the celebrations were over. Even then, her relatives came and pleaded with her again. But she had turned her heart toward the Lord. Suddenly old things passed away, and all things were new. She was a different woman from that time onward.

Easter Sunday was a special day, for Rajber was to be baptized. A woman in white came down to the front of the congregation to give her testimony. Today was not only her son's baptismal day but hers also! How the hard face had changed! Now it was clear and shining. "From today I shall no more be numbered with the Hindus," she said, giving her confession before the crowd, "for I have found the heavenly treasure, the heavenly life, and the heaven-given salvation. From now on I shall follow only Him." In the stillness of the forest, she stepped down into the crystal-clear pool to receive the ordinance that symbolizes death to the old life of wickedness and sin, and of resurrection into the newness of life in Christ.

The sound of a drunken woman's song has long since passed away. A child's faith and prayers led his mother to Christ. Surely angels in heaven have rejoiced over one sinner who has repented.

Sometime later in an outlying Nepali village, the crowd listened intently to the gospel; yet something more is needed: a word from one of their own. "I was a great sinner, but my son brought me to the Lord," she tells this wild crowd of the marvel of redeeming grace. "I was once like you," she continues in compassion. Once like them? Could it ever be? This woman—so clean and tidy, with the smiling face—like them? So dirty, wild, resentful, quarrelsome, and obviously heavy drinkers—like them? Could it ever be? The gospel of Christ is still the power of salvation to everyone who believes!

Taken from WEC Australian Magazine, 1950

For many years Elaine Crane lived and shared her love for Jesus with the Nepalese who were based in Northeastern India. On her retiring to Australia, she encouraged Christians there to pray for Nepal and for those who served her Lord around the world.

"We See Such a Change in Our Husbands"

Maria Röbbelen
Gambia, 1975

For several years we had been going almost every Sunday to the village of Kampant where a few adults and children would gather together under a tree. We sang with them and preached the gospel. Often there was a hustle and bustle; we became tired and hot, and asked ourselves, "Should we keep going there? Are they really serious? Isn't it becoming too much?" But we kept going.

Our colleague Len Harvey had been gathering with some of the men in the evening. One time twenty men were present. Len was astonished and asked, "Why have you come?"

They answered, "Do you think we would skip our evening meal if we weren't really interested?" We realized that here were people who really wanted to know.

While Len was away on a short holiday, an urgent message reached us from Kampant that some men wanted to burn their jujus (charms or fetishes—objects that are kept to give protection from evil spirits). At first we were

Gambian women

a bit skeptical. We didn't want to rush things, so we said, "Mr. Harvey is away. Let us postpone this till he is back."

But they insisted it was impossible to wait. Len must interrupt his holiday and go to Kampant. On his way he decided he would first talk to the people and ask why they wanted to do this. When he arrived, the fire was burning. The men started throwing their jujus into the fire. Not long after some women came and said, "We see such a change in our husbands. We too want to walk this way. We also want to burn our jujus!"

It was a beginning. Similar things happened in Kamamodu, another village. Sometimes we had gone there with a sigh because it was so far away, and there were so many villages closer to us. But we had made it a rule to wait till people asked us to come and to go there regularly only if they showed a desire. In Kamamodu the men also burned their jujus. After that the women came and wanted to walk the same path. The church in Gambia was growing.

Taken from WEC German Magazine, 1975

Maria Röbbelen was one of the first overseas workers sent out by WEC Germany. Together with Hanna Förster she went to Liberia in 1957 and with Ruth Dieterich to Gambia in 1966. Maria worked there until 1991.

Struggle of Faith
Elaine Kitamura
Japan, 2010

The only place open for you to go is Kinomoto!"
"Oh no!"

This was my reaction to a directive from the Japanese church leadership in 1996. Tears flowed. The pronouncement came at the end of a particularly difficult period in the ministry of my husband Shuichi and me. We were both exhausted. Shuichi and I had been encouraged to think about outreach in a new housing area, where there were possibilities for growth. But out of the blue we were directed to Kinomoto, which one worker had called "the missionaries' graveyard."

In spite of freedom to preach the gospel in Japan, and large numbers of missionaries here, vast areas remain basically untouched by the gospel. Over the years many rural towns and villages have been left in the "too hard" basket. They are heavily populated and follow closely one upon another. The people are hard-working, kindly, community conscious and totally committed to their religious traditions.

The area centering on Kinomoto, with a population of nearly thirty thousand in four small towns and eighty-five villages, is one of these hard places—it is difficult even by rural standards! Kinomoto has 213 Buddhist temples and 119 Shinto temples. Each family home has its own Buddhist altar for ancestor worship. Every child born is offered up to the Shinto spirits, and each home takes its turn of responsibility for the Shinto temple. WEC has had work here since 1952, and although there has been the occasional conversion, most have moved out or gone back into the world.

Back in 1996, the Lord in His compassion saw my tears, heard my cry and spoke to my heart as clearly as an audible voice: "Will you go there for Me?" In the years since then, I have been grateful for this word.

We came here knowing that everything had been tried and had failed. We had no strategies; we could only wait on the Lord and see what He would do. God's word to me the very first morning was the same as His command to the trembling Gidion: "Go in the strength you have and save Israel out of Midian's hand. Am I not sending you?" (Judg. 6:14). His word to Shuichi was, "The Lord is . . . not willing that any should perish, but that all should come to repentance" (2 Pet. 3:9, KJV). In other words, no matter how hard things appear to be, God's desire for these people is salvation.

One key happening was an opening into the educational world. In Japan, particularly in the countryside, it is impossible to do anything without "trust," that is, a personal introduction. In addition the educational world plays a major part in country life, and teachers are held in high esteem. Shuichi found that our arrival coincided with a good friend becoming vice-principal of one of the local schools. This led to an opening for one of our missionaries to give a lecture to parents and teachers. One thing led to another, and this work began to bloom. With more of Shuichi's university friends becoming principals and vice-principals of the twenty-four primary and high schools in the

Kitamuras teaching English.

area, there was an ever-open door for Shuichi into their offices to introduce church-sponsored activities and literature.

Over the years more than forty invitations for public talks, visits to school classes and other similar activities have come our way. In addition I have taught English part-time in four different schools, building valuable relationships with staff and making our name known in the homes of the children. Bit by bit, to a slowly increasing number, Christianity has become no longer an alien concept, but rather an integral part of the community, its existence taken for granted.

Every year the Lord sent people to encourage and help us in our isolation—with gospel concerts, special English programs, Bible distribution, literature provision and distribution, and so on. Many of these were things we hadn't planned, presented by people we hadn't invited! We sensed God was saying, "I've got My plans. You just need to cooperate!"

Many have heard the accounts of Japanese soldiers who hid in the jungles of the Philippines for years after World War II finished. The one who lasted the longest was Mr. Onoda. He hid on Lubang Island for twenty-nine long years and refused to surrender because he had given his body and soul to serve the Emperor. Only one young man succeeded in reaching him, and only after going into the jungle and pitching a tent, living there quietly till Mr. Onoda trusted him enough to show himself.

But there things stopped. Mr. Onoda could not be convinced it was alright to come out. "If my superior officer comes here in his uniform, and in the name of the Emperor declares the war over, and commands me to come out, I will. But not otherwise!"

This story gripped Shuichi's thinking as a parable of what we were to do. The Japanese people are hidden away in the jungle of idolatry and sin, and are suspicious of any attempt to lead them out. They dread the social consequences of trusting in Christ. First, we had to be totally committed to reach them. Next, we had to pitch our tent. Now we are patiently building up friendships and developing trust to win a hearing, continually using these bridges to present the gospel in non-threatening ways. In the name of our heavenly Emperor, we declare the spiritual war for the hearts of mankind to be over. But His command to come out still needs to penetrate their hearts. The truth must be grasped and believed in order to set them free. The trickle will not become a flood without a great work of the Holy Spirit— and the key to this is intercession.

When we arrived in Kinomoto, there were ten church members on the roll, but this soon went down to five. Later there were further losses, with three deaths, one by suicide. Replacement has been so difficult! There have been four baptisms in fourteen years, people who really love the Lord, but two of these have moved out of the district. Currently, in addition to the three local members, we are blessed and encouraged by the attendance of an international group of five Christians (Chinese, Filipino, American and Canadian) plus two Japanese ladies who retain their membership elsewhere. But where are the local converts?

Pastor Kitamura and Elaine outside their church

Despite numerous setbacks, seemingly insurmountable difficulties, spiritual attacks and pressure to close the work, God has kept us from discouragement. This is due to the support of faithful prayer partners, and the door to the community has continued to remain open.

Our hope is, first of all, in the absolute authority of our Lord, who has declared He will build His church and that the gates of Hades will not prevail; second, it is in the steadfast love of the One who is not willing that any should perish.

Elaine left Australia for Japan in 1969. Today she and her husband Shuichi Kitamura, lead Kinomoto Church, which is located in the least Christian part of the least Christian state.

An Open Door
David Smith
Guinea-Bissau, 2009

Linda and I arrived in Guinea-Bissau in January 1976, less than two years after the country gained independence from Portugal. Our particular vision was to share about Christ in the eastern half of the country, which was predominantly Muslim.

WEC was the only Protestant group in Guinea-Bissau, starting with the entry of Bessie (née Fricker) Brierley in 1940. In the subsequent years about fifty churches, many preaching points and a Bible college were established in the predominantly animistic western half of the country. Most of the churches had local pastors.

No Christian worker had been allowed by the Portuguese to move into the east, though various exploratory trips had been made. After independence the emergence of a Marxist government seemed to make such a move even less likely. However, the Muslims began to threaten resistance and even secession if the government enforced atheism. The official response was "freedom of religion."

Gene McBride, our field leader, approached the government with the proposal that they convince the Muslims of their sincerity by allowing us to move into the Muslim half of the country. They agreed on the condition that the Muslim governor of the city and region of Bafata approve. Gene and I traveled to Bafata with our request.

Four of us were seated in the governor's office. The governor was behind his desk. Gene and I were seated in chairs facing him about ten feet away. To our left, along the wall about halfway between us and the governor, was another man who was introduced to us as the mayor of the city of Bafata. The governor seemed quite cordial, but the mayor was positively cold.

As Gene and the governor exchanged greetings and some small talk, including identifying us as Americans rather than Russians (Marxists), the governor became warmer while the mayor remained nearly frozen. I stayed silent unless spoken to. I was quietly praying.

The governor had one question for me: did I believe in God? I assured him I did. He answered that we were welcome to move east. He wanted anyone who believed in God to help counter the teaching of atheism.

In September 1976 we moved with our daughter Becky to Bafata. Due to the Portuguese influence, any official action required substantial paperwork. Our official documentation stated we were free to travel to any town or village and share the gospel as official representatives of the mission and church in the regions of Bafata and Gabu—essentially the entire eastern half of the country.

As a result, we had tremendous freedom to work. Wherever we went, we were given permission to share the gospel and then listened to an even longer presentation of Islam. When the people found we were not Catholics but evangelicals, we were invited to make return visits.

Both the governor and the mayor were Muslims. The governor was definitely more moderate and saw us as potential allies against atheism. The mayor was a staunch Muslim who did not want any non-Islamic influence in the area. A few months later the governor was removed from his position and the mayor became governor, but by that time Linda and I were already established in the community. The official policy concerning us was that as long as we did not attack either the political or religious order, we could stay. This really did not hinder our ministry. We simply taught the Bible without mentioning Islam, atheism, Catholicism or animism. When there were obvious contradictions, we simply stated, "The Word of God says . . ." The listeners then drew their own conclusions and made their own choices.

When people asked us questions about supporting the government, we encouraged them to respect their leaders and give them time to learn in the job. Even though we discovered that one of the "seekers" was a plant put there by the authorities, we found that our answers more than satisfied the chief of police, and before long we were good friends.

Our plan for the first year was to share the good news in Bafata (fifteen thousand people) as much as possible and make definite approaches to the two next largest towns, Gabu (the other regional capital) and Bambadinka. Benjamin Constant and his wife had lived in Gabu many years. He was a professing evangelical, converted in Cape Verde. He invited us to begin regular meetings in his home.

Unknown to us, Antonio and Guiterria Gomes lived in Bambadinka. Antonio had been captain of the small WEC boat previously used for evangelism in the Bijagos Islands of Guinea-Bissau. He now worked for the government at the river port of Bambadinka. On my first visit to his town, I bumped into him in the street. He immediately asked us to begin meetings in their home. God had prepared the way, and within the first year we had informal fellowships in our home in Bafata, as well as in Gabu and in Bambadinka. When we returned to America three years later, the evangelical church had a good foothold. Other Christian workers (both foreign and local), and later other fellowships, moved into the area. The door remains open.

David and Linda Smith spent four years in Guinea-Bissau and subsequently served at the USA sending base in mobilization and English teaching. They have two children.

Introducing Mr. Wong
Maurice Charman
Taiwan, 1973

I met Mr. Wong in a rubber factory. No doubt you are thinking this is a strange place—even stranger if I told you that on Sundays this factory becomes a church for the fifty employees. Mr. Wong, a mountain aboriginal from Taiwan's east coast, had moved to the city of Taipei for Bible training. He needed part-time employment to supplement his income, hence the rubber factory and later the small church.

At our first meeting, amongst the machinery and furnaces, the Lord seemed to be telling Mr. Wong that I could help him in his Bible studies. For several months Mr. Wong was a regular twice-a-week visitor for Bible study. I found out later that the notes he was taking so copiously were the basis of sermons and studies he was giving to the tribal villages each weekend. This in itself was a tremendous challenge to me, as all I taught was being taken so far so fast. I realized that Mr. Wong's natural simplicity could easily be marred by a "complicated" approach to the Scriptures.

His theological understanding was minimal—in fact, in some areas non-existent—but his favorite expression was, "It's here in the Word, so I did it!" Did what? Rebuked and cast out evil spirits in the name of Jesus, prayed for the sick with amazing results, etc., etc. Do you wonder at my concern that this child-like faith be kept intact?

One weekend in particular stands out clearly. During the week Mr. Wong had expressed his concern for one of the villages and felt strongly that he should pay the people a visit. On the way he stopped to see his sister, and he was urged to stay there and forget the village. As this thought was beginning to take root in his mind, Mr. Wong saw a clear vision of the village he planned to visit, with the devil himself blocking the way. This was all the incentive he needed. He must go to this village! As he took a short "siesta" before leaving, another experience confronted him. While lying on his bed, a presence came into the room and began choking him. Never having experienced anything like this before, Mr. Wong was not sure of the reasons for such an attack. But he was able to call out the name of Jesus and obtain instant relief. On the road he was again confronted by a demonic presence that further hindered his progress. What to do? A cry to the Lord, and an angel appeared and handed him a sword. Mr. Wong had no idea how to use the sword, but he swung wildly and was delighted to find his way cleared once more.

Later there were further more intense challenges. A cry to the Lord brought the presence of another angel, who simply wrapped his arms around Mr. Wong and urged him to press forward. As the two advanced, all opposition retreated, and so they reached the village.

With all this vividly in his mind, Mr. Wong was assured that he must proceed. These hindrances were not of the Lord. What a tremendous weekend he had in that village! Hearts were prepared by the Lord for the Bible study. Sick people were prayed for and healed—truly a victory for Jesus.

Taken from WEC Australian Magazine, 1973

Called by God to Christian service at the age of nineteen, Maurice Charman trained in Australia, served in Taiwan for seven years, with his wife Ruth ran an Asian student hostel in his native New Zealand, pastored a Chinese church in Melbourne, started the WEC sending base in Singapore, lectured in Tasmania and led the WEC NZ base.

I Believe I've Found My Timothy

Keith Stevenson
Arabia (Middle East), 1935

I believe I've found my "Timothy." He came up to me near the house. He was interested and knew John 3:16 by heart. Apparently he was in Mr. Upcher's party on his trips around the Bedouin here. This morning he came early for the service. I invited him to get down to pray, and he did and afterward began to pray for himself, taking the Lord into his heart. He then told me his purpose was to serve Jesus without any other thought or care.

Ten months ago he dreamed of one with a cross on his breast coming to him on a horse, inviting him to follow Jesus. He said his people thought he was mad when he spoke of God leading him and said they'd kill him if he became a Christian. But he's really got hold of Jesus and is ready to go with me anywhere.

On Monday I walked for a breather with Abdullah over to the tents of some of the Amoor Arabs pitched around the north end of the town.

The Lord was leading wonderfully, for we found Kharsir in a tent; after fraternal kissing, first on the right cheek then the left and then down to the shoulder, he cer-emoniously received us on to the bedding spread in the front.

Just then up came Khaleel (the "Timothy" I wrote about). He'd been

Arab tents

cutting stones in the hill. I got them to talk and declare their spiritual experience in Jesus to each other. Then Kharsir began his coffee-making, clanging and pounding. Up came Sheikh Mowadif, of all people. There were my three key contacts in one shot. The neighbors gathered around and we shared with them all about God's work through Jesus the Son. Khaleel is staunch and gave a definite clear witness. Then as Kharsir was about to complete the coffee-making, I said we were going to speak our thanks to Jesus, all of us who were ready to, and got on my knees and uncovered my head. Kharsir came right across from his fire and got down with us there. Old Mowadif could see this witness of us four, if he can't always hear. We told our hearts' love for Jesus before them all.

Taken from WEC UK Magazine, 1935

In 1933 Jack Wilson had a fruitful ministry among the Saleib tribe in Syria and Lebanon, seeing many of them come to Christ. A dozen churches were planted from Jordan to Lebanon between 1927 and 1938. In 1934 Jack Wilson and his Australian colleague Keith Stevenson met up in Beirut and trekked into the desert. Jack lived and ministered in Palmyra at the time, so it is likely that this story took place in the deserts of Syria.

Pants into Pews!

Jim Mitchell
Thailand, 1970s

*T*he mud was ankle deep, but Mr. Eem didn't mind. He wore old tattered trousers—his only trousers of any use, if the truth be told. As he splashed through the mire, slipping and sliding to keep upright, he rejoiced in the Lord Jesus. Today he was going to buy new trousers at the Bantak market. He could see himself in them already, fine cloth, smartly pressed, and new for the meeting next Sunday. He grasped the money for them tightly in his hand: 300 Baht (about $10).

He slithered down the river bank into the "long-tailed" motor boat ferry, hardly two feet wide and a foot deep. Half a dozen other passengers squatted on boards that served as seats. The owner wound the rope around the starter wheel and yanked hard. The engine howled into life, deafening all the passengers. The boat slid into the mainstream and roared towards Bantak market.

On landing Mr. Eem scrambled out of the ferry and went to visit "Aunty Ray," the oldest church member. Church meetings were usually held in her house.

Thai builders

"Hello Aunty, how are you today?"

"I'm fine, but I'm so excited about getting the church built. The wood is ordered, and the men are bringing it any day now. But we're still short of money to buy slates for the roofing."

"We're excited about building the church too. We're praying every day for the Lord to help get it done. We still need quite a bit of money though, don't we? And most of us Christians are pretty poor anyway. Where will we get it?"

"Oh the Lord will supply it all if we keep trusting Him."

Just then Mr. Eem saw the bundle of used clothing lying in Aunty's little tailor shop.

"What's in the bundle, Aunty?"

"Oh, just some used clothing someone gave me. Hey! There's a pair of trousers in there that might fit you."

She opened the bundle and hauled them out. He tried them on, and she laughed at the sight. They were wide enough to go around him twice; long enough to cover his toes and then some.

An idea came: "Say, Aunty, can you alter them to fit me?"

She got out her tape measure and a mouthful of pins, measuring here, pinning there.

Thai church

"I think I could do it easily."

Snip! Snip! Snip! Whee-ee-ee went the treadle sewing machine.

"There you are, try them on!"

Mr. Eem tried on the used trousers, almost a perfect fit.

"That's wonderful. How much for altering them?"

"I'm not charging another Christian for used trousers."

"Would 300 Baht be enough?" There was just a hint of a twinkle in his eyes.

Aunty gasped.

"You must be daft today, Mr. Eem! You know you can buy new trousers in the market for 200 Baht. What are you talking about?"

"I came to market today with 300 Baht specifically to buy new trousers. Now the Lord has given me these lovely trousers. Do you know what I'm going to do? I want to give this 300 Baht toward building our church here."

Matching deeds to words, he handed over his money, rejoicing. "Cheerful givers are the ones God prizes" (2 Cor. 9:7, TLB).

Taken from WEC Australian Magazine

Jim Mitchell and his wife Emma worked in Thailand from the early 1960s; later they served as managers at WEC's UK center before their retirement.

Long-Range Planting
Traugott Boeker
Sumatra, Indonesia, 1964

In the mid-1960s Colin and Janet Harrington from New Zealand followed God's call to take the gospel to the unreached people groups on the vast island of Sumatra. They felt led by God to a port on the southwest coast. Soon their little van inscribed with the bold letters Persekutuan Injil Internasional (International Gospel Fellowship—the Indonesian version of WEC) became a popular sight on the streets of Bengkulu and beyond.

A man of the Serawai people group further south, who came into Bengkulu for business, noticed the van. That word "Injil" (gospel) stuck in his mind. As a devout Muslim, he knew that the Koran encourages followers of Mohammed who experience religious doubt to "ask those who have been reading the book [Injil] from before thee . . ." (Surah Ten, Yunus, verse 94).

Sumatran plate dance

Not long after the Serawai man returned home, the post office in Bengkulu received a letter addressed "To the Gospel in Bengkulu." The postal service quickly concluded this must be for the person who had been driving that "gospel car." The letter contained an invitation to visit the Serawai area.

The Harringtons felt their Indonesian friend and co-worker Frederic Tobing would be the best person to respond to the invitation. Tobing's wife came from that area, and for a long time they had prayed for the salvation of the Serawai people. On the day when Frederic Tobing arrived, the men of the village came together—they were keen to hear the gospel. After hearing the story and discussing it among themselves, more than 300 people asked to be baptized.

That such a large number of people from an Islamic people group in Indonesia would collectively turn to Christ is unique to this day. A living church continues among the Serawai people of South Sumatra.

But this is not the whole story. A hundred years earlier, in the mid-1800s, German missionaries working with a Dutch mission board began to share the gospel among the Pasemah people of South Sumatra, who live right next to the Serawai people. They labored for years in this difficult area. Friends and churches back home prayed fervently for these people in the south of Sumatra, but there was no apparent fruit.

Then one of the Germans became so seriously ill that he was taken to Bengkulu and placed on a ship to take him back to Germany. Before the ship could leave the harbor, he died. His body was laid to rest in Bengkulu, side by side with colleagues who had lost their lives in the struggle to take the gospel to that part of Sumatra. In view of many difficulties, the mission abandoned the work among the Pasemah and moved to another Indonesian people group that was more responsive.[13]

However, the intense, unceasing prayer of many was not in vain. One hundred years later God's time had come, and WEC team members, together with their Indonesian colleagues, were privileged to harvest where they had not sown.

Traugott Boeker served in Indonesia for many years in theological education before taking on WEC leadership in Germany with his wife Hanni prior to joining WEC's international office.

A Waving Forest of Arms
Jack Harrison
Congo, 1934

This Conference in 1934, held only three years after C.T. Studd's death, was the biggest thing we have ever seen in these parts of Congo. The ground was black with people. Yet in spite of the tremendous numbers, they were not at all out of hand. Dead silence and perfect reverence during prayer, and attentiveness and responsiveness to the messages, all showed that God was with us in power.

It is all so beyond description—the crowds, the beaming faces, the eagerness, the singing, the roars of Hallelujahs. One could only stand before them amazed and awed.

A government agent who lives near us at Ibambi came to one of the meetings with his wife. He had seen all the preparations and had asked about the local people who were coming. It was explained that ten thousand people of some eight distinct tribes would be present for four days or so. He could not take it in and suggested there would certainly be trouble and fighting

Early Congo church conference

through having such a mixture of people on the place. We tried to explain about the love of God in the hearts of men breaking down tribal barriers, but the point was lost on him.

At the meeting he attended, he saw it all for himself. The different tribes were asked to stand in turn to show him how many there were. First, the Baramboz, then Bazandes, Medjes, Balikas, Babaris, Bayogos, Babudus, Balumbis, and all so obviously happy! Somebody stood up at the commencement of the meeting and handed up a woman's stool that had been lost, another handed up a small knife and asked that inquiries be made for the owner. Then came different things: colored beads, a tax-medal, piece of pencil, native plaited hat, etc. All these had been lost and found and handed up to the platform to be returned to the owners.

It was unbelievable to the agent. To many in the public service, all the locals are liars, thieves and deceivers because they do not understand God's working in men's hearts. But we who know the glorious liberating power of the gospel saw that these people in front of us were thoroughly changed.

To see the multitudes dispersing after each meeting was something to be long remembered. Perfect stillness during the benediction, followed by another brief pause, and then the thousands stood to their feet. In local style they carried their small stools and chairs above their heads as they left, and to us on the platform it looked like a great waving forest of arms.

At night time the sleeping places were worth seeing. Inside, every available inch was packed tight with human beings: outside, hundreds of little fires peeped out of the dark, with groups of people around each one. More often than not they would be singing and praying right into the night. Those in one shed would be singing a hymn quite different to the people in the next shed, and so on—it was impossible at a distance to tell what they were singing with so many tunes going at once. Day and night the whole center was vibrating with prayers and praises.

Taken from WEC UK Magazine, 1934

Jack Harrison joined C.T. Studd in the Congo in 1922 and eventually succeeded him in leadership of the field for fifteen years until his death in 1947. He married Mary in 1924, and they had a son.

A Touch of Revival
Betty Nowland
Zuenoula, Ivory Coast, early 1960s

I would travel all over the world to see what you have seen!" a man I didn't know exclaimed after hearing my story and seeing my slides of the moving of the Spirit I was privileged to witness in the 1960s.

One morning my co-worker, Hazel, and I received a telegram from our field leader: "Come to Zuenoula—special meetings." We quickly packed our small car and set out on the long, hot, dusty trip to Zuenoula, headquarters of the WEC work in Ivory Coast. Arriving at dusk, we drove into the mission center and felt excitement in the air. We were warmly welcomed. While giving us refreshments, people began to tell us what had happened that day.

Frank and Winnie Chapman had been speaking to the church about the recent revival in Equatorial Guinea, where they worked. Apparently while they were on furlough in England, Norman Grubb suggested that on their return to West Africa, they should visit all the WEC fields in the area to tell their story.

Feeling weary, Hazel and I retired early, but we heard a rumble of prayer from all over the compound. The three tribes represented in the Zuenoula church, Gouro, Mossi and Baoule, had each gathered to pray all night. This wasn't unusual for them, as they regularly held special nights of prayer for revival.

In the morning the church was crowded with most of the missionary personnel and African Christians. Missionaries spoke about their experiences of being touched by the Holy Spirit. At noon we all went off for dinner. But two young pastors, Jeremie and David, went into the bush to pray.

We had just finished the first course of our meal when David burst into the dining room. His face radiant with joy, he was jumping up and down, shouting excitedly, "We have seen the Lord, and He is so bright, shining white and beautiful! Come down into the church, He wants to bless us!"

Jeremie was shouting the same message out to the Africans, who were sitting around in the shade waiting for their meal to be cooked. The women left their pots on the fire, and all began running down to the church. We quickly finished our meal. By the time we arrived in the church, Jeremie and David were standing in front on the platform speaking to the people.

As Hazel and I were not Gouro speakers, we didn't really understand what was being said. We just looked around in amazement at what we were witnessing.

A spirit of repentance had fallen on the people, and they were sinking to their knees, begging the Lord for mercy and forgiveness. After a time they would jump up, their faces filled with joy, and begin praising the Lord with all their might. Another missionary came over, stood behind us and said, "Do you know what you are seeing? Jeremie is speaking in tongues, and David is interpreting!" She then translated some of what the two men were saying. The theme of the message was that there is no such thing as a small or large sin in God's sight; all are heinous to Him. Repent, ask forgiveness, and the Lord will bless you.

The church was full of noise and action. The leader of the Mossi women was standing beside us. She was looking around, as bewildered as we were. Suddenly she fell to the floor in repentance. I grabbed the baby off her back, fearing it would be hurt! She behaved the same as the rest. When she arose praising the Lord, we asked her what had happened. She spoke our language, Dioula, so we could communicate with her. I will never forget her words, "I was looking around, thinking to myself that this can't be of God as there is too much noise. Then I was struck down and had to confess unbelief."

Things like this went on all afternoon. At one point a good number of people rushed down to the front of the church, and many were healed, although no special call had been given to come down for healing. One man ran outside, calling that he was not going to confess his sins. He ran only as far as the first mango tree, where he was struck down in similar manner to all the others. At the top of his voice, he confessed his sins and was forgiven.

A young girl about ten years of age gave a prophecy that she saw a fire and then lots of little fires springing up all around. Later many of the folk from the village next to the mission grounds rushed over saying there was fire all over the rooftops of the houses and the church!

Suddenly the noise ceased as quickly as it had begun. The Christians began to tell what had happened to them. They confessed to us how the Spirit had convicted them of their sins. We were surprised to hear that some had committed adultery, returned to witchcraft, were stealing, etc. I remember smiling when one man said he had hated his mother-in-law! As the young pastors had said earlier, all sin was heinous in God's sight.

In the weeks that followed, teams went out into the villages to spread the good news. Many were saved, healed, and even raised from the dead. One Mossi elder had prayed for years for his father's salvation. He led a team to preach in his village and had the joy of leading his dad to the Lord.

Six weeks later, the Spirit moved in a similar way among the young women in the Girls' Bible School at Vavoua. The head girl, Dorcas, had witnessed the moving of the Spirit at Zuenoula and wanted to see the same in the Bible school. One day she went into the bush to pray and saw a vision of the Lord. She remarked on the brightness of His garments. He told her He wanted to bless them at Vavoua as He had done at Zuenoula, but couldn't because there was too much sin in their midst. Coming home with a radiant face, Dorcas told her fellow students what the Lord had said.

As the girls began to repent and receive forgiveness, they began to praise the Lord and say they could see a bright light in the sky. None of the missionaries could see it. A missionary from Burkina Faso was on holiday at Vavoua and was so amazed at how the girls were acting; he took lots of slides of all he saw. When his mother had these photos developed in England, one

showed a light coming down on the faces of the girls. The camera had picked up the light the girls were saying they could see.

Many people have examined this slide and say it could only have been a bright light in front of the girls. This was the slide I was showing in a meeting in Adelaide when the man remarked, "I would travel all over the world to see what you have seen!"

Trained as a nurse in Queensland, Australia, Betty Nowland worked for eighteen years in Ivory Coast in church planting outreach.

"Harry, Can You Help Us?"
Joann Young
UK, 1990

*H*arry, can you help us?"

Coming out of the bank, Harry had run into two Asian brothers, clearly upset and anxious. "Yesterday the leaders of the Asian Assembly in Handsworth announced they are leaving, and the meeting is closing down."

WEC members had been instrumental in this thriving church plant. The church had grown and prospered and finally become independent of WEC, appointing its own leadership. This sudden disruption left a group of church-goers bereft.

My husband Harry and I were part of the WEC's UK Immigrant Team, but our background was the Middle East, our work among Arabs and our acquired language, Arabic. Most of the rest of the team had worked in India and spoke Hindi,

Urdu or Punjabi. We had been with the team seventeen years and had our own responsibilities. When Harry said to me, "We'll have to be at the Asian Assembly on Sunday morning," I had no idea what was in store for us. Harry felt continuity was paramount.

On Sunday we faced an eager congregation, biblically well-taught, but no one had held church office or been involved in teaching. Only then did we realize the enormity of the task we had taken on. It became a full-time job. Harry chose men to train for elders, while I took on the women's work and the Sunday school.

A mother of five came to us and said, "I have always wanted to serve the Lord, what can I do?" We made her superintendent of the Sunday school. She may not have had the "training" thought necessary, but she was a spiritual woman and knew the Scriptures; she also knew how to keep order. We conscripted young people from the Birmingham Bible Institute and the Birmingham City Mission to help with the girls' meetings and the boys' club. Some who spent their internship with us stayed on for further service.

Although we felt our own work was being put on hold, we loved being in the Asian community. The opportunities seemed endless: hundreds attended weddings and funerals; home and hospital visits, birthdays, anniversaries—every occasion was an open door to give a message and meet people. Whole families, neighbors and friends turned out for baptismal services. After three years we felt the church was on its feet, and it was time for us to move on. But something happened to keep us fastened to the spot: two extraordinary conversions.

Wives were often converted before husbands. Some suffered badly because of their stand for Christ. Nurinder, a Hindu, had been converted for seventeen years. She couldn't attend church on Sundays but would come to the midweek prayer meeting, if her husband was working, or to the ladies' meeting in the afternoon. She would go home and teach her children what she had learned.

One evening her husband, Mohinder, went to a local shop. In a back room idol worship was being practiced. What was going on greatly frightened him, and he rushed home. He told his wife he wanted to listen to her tape of Indian preacher Jordan Khan. Now she was frightened and thought he was setting a trap for her. She ran to the bathroom and prayed, and felt she should do as he hadasked. He played the tape through twice and then went to his room. As he knelt before God, he said it was as if a large sheet of paper hung before him with a list of sins. As he read it, he kept saying, "Yes, Lord, that's what I've done." He confessed and repented.

You can imagine the great amazement when this whole family walked into church on Sunday, and it was an even greater wonder when Mohinder stood to his feet and prayed a prayer of confession and thanksgiving.

Shingara's wife had been a Christian for eight years. As a Sikh, he was tolerant. Though he had no interest in Christianity, he allowed his wife and children to attend church. She was bright in her faith and witnessed to her friends. In fact, on the very night in which she was later rushed to the hospital to give birth to her fourth child, she had been standing at the window of a friend's car talking to her about Jesus.

The trip to the hospital that night was catastrophic. Shingara's wife was rushed inside with convulsions, and when her husband next saw her, she was on a life support machine, having delivered a healthy baby girl. The church prayed and fasted for her, and we visited the hospital almost daily.

One day Harry was in the hospital corridor praying with Shingara and his brother-in-law when Shingara felt a hand on his shoulder. He opened his eyes; no one was there, but he sensed the presence of the Lord. Soon after that he opened his heart to the Lord Jesus and was able to tell his wife he had become a Christian. Though she died shortly afterward, Shingara's wife lived long enough to rejoice over this news.

At the same time the Wolverhampton Asian Church was flourishing, having seen the conversion of a number of young men. Juge Ram, a government housing officer, was one of them. His wife, Geetha, had been a WEC team member. As Juge grew in his Christian faith, he sensed a call to something else and began a theological correspondence course with a Bible college in Wales. As they looked to the future, the church in Handsworth made an approach to see if Juge and Geetha might join the work. In our fifth year there, Juge and Geetha started coming, attending all the meetings and working alongside us, while Juge continued his secular job.

A year later, Harry was conducting a men's Bible study when he had a heart attack; he fell over onto Juge's shoulder and died. They knew the time had come for full-time service. As converted Hindus brought up in Western culture, he and Geetha were the ideal couple to step into leadership.

Fourteen years later, the church continues to thrive. The congregation serves all age ranges, with new people coming in regularly. They have an active witness on the streets in an almost totally immigrant area; other ministries include TESOL classes and an energetic children's work. Juge has never wanted a purely Asian church. Though the services are still bilingual, with singing and praying in both Punjabi and English, the congregation is a mix of nationalities. God has really helped us.

Joann Young is from the USA; she and her Irish husband Harry served many years in the Middle East before moving to the UK, where they joined a team working among immigrants. The team later changed its name to Neighbors Worldwide, reflecting the changes in the status of the local population.

Epilogue

A century ago WEC's founder, C.T. Studd, said,

> I have no ambition to start another waterlogged craft in the huge stream of Central Africa, but to evangelize the world and have Christ back. . . . I am persuaded that when we see our duty as it is written plainly over the New Testament, and go in to perform it, we shall have a chance to glorify God. But if not, I am equally convinced that we shall be just one more humdrum mission society, and had better never have started out thus upon God.

At the century mark WEC continues its voyage on course toward the goal. Rather than becoming a stagnant institution bogged down by set budgets and self-preservation, the mission still seeks to move at God's command, to be ready to embrace new strategies and to attempt to bring Jesus to the least-reached peoples of the world.

The stories in this book have given you a glimpse of who we are: people who, whether their stories have been told or untold, have over the years faithfully kept the ship afloat and on course—people of fifty different nationalities who share one passion and consider each other family.

As Louis mentioned in his foreword, WEC's story is still being told. Our task is not complete, and we trust that God's people will continue to obey His call to join us in making Him known to the nations. As you have seen from our stories, and as C.T. Studd explained,

The "romance" of a missionary is often made up of monotony and drudgery; there often is no glamour in it; it doesn't stir a man's spirit or blood. So don't come out to be a missionary as an experiment; it is useless and dangerous. There are many trials and hardships. Disappointments are numerous and the time of learning the language is especially trying. Don't come if you want to make a great name or want to live long. Come if you feel there is no greater honor, after living for Christ, than to die for Him.[14]

Judy Raymo

WEC International

WEC International includes more than eighteen hundred workers drawn from fifty countries serving in multicultural teams among nearly ninety unreached people groups throughout the world. Evangelical and interdenominational, WEC's ethos is based on its commission:

Our Commission

- To bring the gospel of our Lord Jesus Christ to the remaining unevangelized peoples of the world with the utmost urgency
- To demonstrate the compassion of Christ to a needy world
- To plant churches and lead them to spiritual maturity
- To inspire, mobilize and train believers for cross-cultural mission

WEC has sending bases in sixteen countries which recruit, screen, send and help support field workers, as well as six training centers to prepare people for cross cultural ministry.

Workers are involved in many types of outreach and support ministries, including:

- producing the prayer handbook *Operation World*,
- establishing churches,
- providing medical and educational services,
- caring for children in crisis,

- drug rehabilitation,
- encouraging national missionary-sending agencies.

Our Lifestyle

- We fervently desire to see Christ formed in us so that we live holy lives.
- In dependence on the Holy Spirit, we determine to obey our Lord whatever the cost.
- We trust God completely to meet every need and challenge we face in His service.
- We are committed to oneness, fellowship and the care of our whole missionary family.

Our Convictions

- We are convinced that prayer is a priority.
- We uphold biblical truth and standards.
- We affirm our love for Christ's church and endeavor to work in fellowship with local and national churches and other Christian agencies.
- We accept each other irrespective of gender, ethnic background or church affiliation.
- We desire to work in multi-national teams, and we are committed to effective international cooperation.
- We believe in full participation and oneness in decision-making.
- We value servant leaders who wait on God for vision and direction.
- We promote local and innovative strategies through decentralized decision-making.
- We make no appeals for funds.

For further information contact: www.wec-int.org

Endnotes

1. From reports in *The Guardian* (UK), February 7, 2009.

2. Ibid. Source for some fire facts: Bushfires Royal Commission, 02/12/09, 12524.

3. Justin Tan, tribute of March 10, 2009.

4. Ibid.

5. Ibid.

6. Roger Steer, *George Mueller: Delighted in God* (Singapore: OMF, 1985), 221.

7. Anita L. Waring, "In Heavenly Love Abiding" (hymn), public domain.

8. *Full Steam Ahead to the Heart of the Amazon!* (London: WEC, 1923).

9. David Grann, *The Lost City of Z* (New York: Doubleday, 2005, 2009), 4.

10. Tim Butcher, *Blood River—A Journey to Africa's Broken Heart* (New York: Grove Press, 2008), 7–8. Other information sources used for this story were: www.wec-int.org/cms/fields/congo; Leonard C.J. Moules, ed., *This is No Accident* (London: WEC, 1965); Pat Wright, *On to the Summit: the Len Moules Story* (Eastbourne, UK: Kingsway, 1981); Dave Cornell, "Love's Summit Reached," Worldwide (Australia/New Zealand edition), March, 1965.

11. *Time*, January 8, 1965.

12. Taken from Neil Rowe, *Trusting Not Trying* (Gerrards Cross: WEC, 2008). Used by permission.

13. From S.W. Frickenschmidt, *Unter den Palmen von Pulu Tello* (Bückeburg: n.p., 1929).

14. C.T. Studd (origin of quote unknown).

This book was produced by CLC Publications. We hope it has been life-changing and has given you a fresh experience of God through the work of the Holy Spirit. CLC Publications is an outreach of CLC Ministries International, a global literature mission with work in over fifty countries. If you would like to know more about us or are interested in opportunities to serve with a faith mission, we invite you to contact us at:

CLC Ministries International
PO Box 1449
Fort Washington, PA 19034

Phone: 215-542-1242
E-mail: orders@clcpublications.com
Website: www.clcpubli cations.com

- - - - - - - - - - - - - - - - - - -

DO YOU LOVE GOOD CHRISTIAN BOOKS?
Do you have a heart for worldwide missions?

You can receive a FREE subscription to
CLC's newsletter on global literature missions
Order by e-mail at:

clcworld@clcusa.org
Or fill in the coupon below and mail to:

**PO Box 1449
Fort Washington, PA 19034**

FREE *CLC WORLD* SUBSCRIPTION!

Name: _____

Address:_____

_____

Phone: _____ **E-mail:**_____